CENSORING SCIENCE

ALSO BY MARK BOWEN

Thin Ice: Unlocking the Secrets of Climate in the World's Highest Mountains

CENSORING SCIENCE

Inside the Political Attack on Dr. James Hansen and the Truth of Global Warming

MARK BOWEN

DUTTON

DUTTON
Published by Penguin Group (USA) Inc.
375 Hudson Street, New York, New York 10014, U.S.A.
Penguin Group (Canada), 90 Eglinton Avenue East, Suite 700, Toronto, Ontario M4P 2Y3, Canada (a division of
Pearson Penguin Canada Inc.); Penguin Books Ltd, 80 Strand, London WC2R 0RL, England; Penguin Ireland,
25 St Stephen's Green, Dublin 2, Ireland (a division of Penguin Books Ltd); Penguin Group (Australia), 250
Camberwell Road, Camberwell, Victoria 3124, Australia (a division of Pearson Australia Group Pty Ltd); Penguin
Books India Pvt Ltd, 11 Community Centre, Panchsheel Park, New Delhi—110 017, India; Penguin Group (NZ),
67 Apollo Drive, Rosedale, North Shore 0632, New Zealand (a division of Pearson New Zealand Ltd); Penguin
Books (South Africa) (Pty) Ltd, 24 Sturdee Avenue, Rosebank, Johannesburg 2196, South Africa

Penguin Books Ltd, Registered Offices: 80 Strand, London WC2R 0RL, England

Published by Dutton, a member of Penguin Group (USA) Inc.

First printing, January 2008
1 3 5 7 9 10 8 6 4 2

REGISTERED TRADEMARK—MARCA REGISTRADA

LIBRARY OF CONGRESS CATALOGING-IN-PUBLICATION DATA HAS BEEN APPLIED FOR.

ISBN 978-0-525-95014-1

Printed in the United States of America
Set in Granjon, display set in Fairfield LH 55 Medium
Designed by Leonard Telesca

*for Jack and Leigh
and Wendy*

Contents

I left Earth three times, and found no other place to go.
Please take care of Spaceship Earth.
—Wally Schirra

We need to develop a generation of habitual truth-tellers.
—Paul O'Neill

Chapter 1

The Cardinal Rule

ONE SWELTERING JUNE AFTERNOON IN 1988, an understated Iowan named James Hansen turned global warming into an international issue with one sentence. He told a group of reporters in a hearing room, just after testifying to a Senate committee, "It's time to stop waffling . . . and say that the greenhouse effect is here and is affecting our climate now."

At first, it seemed that our policy makers got the message. Two months after the hearing, the senior atmospheric scientist for the Environmental Defense Fund, Michael Oppenheimer, told *The New York Times,* "I've never seen an environmental issue mature so quickly, shifting from science to the policy realm almost overnight." By the end of the year, thirty-two climate-related bills had been introduced in Congress. More than a decade after that, however, in April 2001, Oppenheimer conceded that he had been wrong. None of the bills had gone anywhere, and the prospects for an effective policy response were looking increasingly dim. After less than two months in office, the new president, George W. Bush, had announced that he would abandon a campaign promise to regulate carbon dioxide from coal-burning power plants, our greatest contributors to the greenhouse effect, and then swiftly pulled out of the Kyoto Protocol, the first binding international agreement to limit greenhouse gas emissions. As Christine Todd Whitman, then the administrator of the Environmental Protection Agency, later put it, this "was the equivalent to 'flipping the bird,' frankly, to the rest of the world."

In late 2004, after four more years of inactivity and concerted foot-dragging by the federal government—as well as suppression, twisting, and censorship of climate science on a breathtaking scale—Jim Hansen decided it was time to make another statement. It took about a year for the right venue to present itself, the fall meeting of the American Geophysical Union (AGU), in December 2005 in San Francisco. His speech took place on Tuesday afternoon, the sixth.

This is the story of the six or so months during which the dangerous human-made warming of our planet finally did shift from science to the policy realm. Perhaps. It is still too early to tell. The battle to effect true change has been long and so far unsuccessful. Jim didn't shift public opinion quite as single-handedly this time around; however, as before, he provided the spark.

The AGU's fall meeting always takes place in San Francisco, and it is a large event. More than 12,000 scientists, students, teachers, and so on attend. The press is well represented, so headlines often result. The majority of the people who present papers at the meeting petition for the opportunity by submitting an abstract, while a select few are invited to speak. Jim had been invited to give a lecture in memory of Charles David Keeling, the legendary greenhouse pioneer who had shown that the atmospheric level of carbon dioxide has been rising steadily since 1958, when he first began monitoring the gas with an instrument on the summit of Hawaii's Mauna Loa volcano. Keeling had died about six months before the meeting. His son Ralph, a distinguished climate scientist in his own right, had extended this invitation to Jim.

Jim wanted to use this opportunity to, in his words, "connect the dots." He wanted to tell everything he knew about global warming, from the science, to the disastrous possibilities, to the solutions . . . and maybe to the special interests who have blocked solutions; he wasn't yet sure about that. And he wanted to make it crystal clear. "I felt that I had to write this down," he says, "not just give a talk, because the communication process is always distorted by repetition or the interpretations people place on what you say—newspapermen especially. They have to write their stories very quickly, and they don't have time to send it back to let you check the accuracy."

AGU is a huge operation. You're supposed to get the computer file with your slides into their system at least twenty-four hours before your talk. Jim typically works about eighty hours a week, and to maximize efficiency he often waits until the last minute to focus on a project. He had nowhere near finished his talk by Sunday afternoon, as he and his wife, Anniek, prepared to drive to Kennedy Airport from their apartment on Manhattan's Upper West Side. He worked on it in the terminal building and on the flight west. By the time his deadline arrived on Monday afternoon, he had still not completed the wording on some of his slides, so when he handed in his presentation, he got permission to replace it the next morning. After going out to dinner with Anniek that night, he continued to work on the slides as well as the text from which he intended to read.

He awoke before dawn and worked as quietly as possible in their hotel room. (About a year later, upon accepting the Duke of Edinburgh Conservation Medal at St. James Palace, London, Jim would acknowledge the debt he owes to Anniek, "who generously tolerates my inordinate obsessions.") Taking advantage of the time difference, he retrieved some new graphics electronically from his research assistant, Darnell Cain, back in New York. As he handed in the flash drive with his presentation—just in time—the AGU technician did him the favor of printing out the text of his speech so he wouldn't have to read from the screen of his laptop. Then Jim and Anniek got some fast food and sat outside on a park bench to eat, while he made finishing touches in pen on the printout, not quite reaching the end.

Dr. James E. Hansen is almost universally regarded as the preeminent climate scientist of our time. He has been director of NASA's premier climate research center, the Goddard Institute for Space Studies, for twenty-five years, and he has been a member of the National Academy of Sciences for ten. During a series of talks that was seen as the "main event" that afternoon, he delivered his Keeling talk to an overflow audience in one of the larger conference rooms in San Francisco's Moscone Convention Center. There was a sense of history, a sense that the torch was being passed. As Ralph Keeling noted in his introduction, "The importance of Jim's work . . . was not lost on my father, who held him in very high esteem for his integrity and tenacity. In fact, just minutes before my father died, he was engaged in discussions with my brother Eric on Jim's recent paper in *Science*."

Many people stood for the forty minutes that it took Jim to read, somewhat haltingly, into the microphone. The light at the podium wasn't great; he couldn't see his text well.

His written abstract reads:

> The Earth's temperature, with rapid global warming over the past thirty years, is now passing through the peak level of the Holocene, a period of relatively stable climate that has existed for more than 10,000 years. Further warming of more than 1°C [about 2°F] will make the Earth warmer than it has been in a million years. "Business-as-usual" scenarios, with fossil fuel carbon dioxide emissions continuing to increase about 2 percent per year as in the past decade, yield additional warming of 2 or 3°C this century and imply changes that constitute practically a different planet.
>
> . . . Earth's climate is nearing, but has not passed, a tipping point, beyond which it will be impossible to avoid climate change with far ranging undesirable consequences. The changes include not only loss of the Arctic as we know it, with all that implies for wildlife and indigenous peoples, but losses on a much vaster scale due to worldwide rising seas. Sea level will increase slowly at first, . . . but as Greenland and West Antarctic ice is softened and lubricated by melt-water and as buttressing ice shelves disappear due to a warming ocean, the balance will tip toward ice loss, thus . . . causing rapid ice sheet disintegration. The Earth's history suggests that with warming of 2–3°C . . . sea level will [rise about] 25 meters (80 feet).

. . . Real world data suggest substantial ice sheet and sea level change in centuries, not millennia. The century time scale offers little consolation to coastal dwellers, because they will be faced with irregular incursions associated with storms and with continually rebuilding above a transient water level.

The grim "business-as-usual" climate change is avoided in an alternative scenario in which growth of greenhouse gas emissions is slowed in the first quarter of this century, primarily via concerted improvements in energy efficiency . . . and then reduced via advanced energy technologies that yield a cleaner atmosphere as well as a stable climate. The required actions make practical sense and have other benefits, but they will not happen without strong policy leadership and international cooperation. Action must be prompt, otherwise carbon dioxide–producing infrastructure [mainly coal-burning power plants] that may be built within a decade will make it impractical to keep further global warming under 1°C.

In the end, he had decided to include the following:

There is little merit in casting blame for inaction, unless it helps point toward a solution. It seems to me that special interests have been a roadblock wielding undue influence over policymakers. The special interests seek to maintain short-term profits with little regard to either the long-term impact on the planet that will be inherited by our children and grandchildren or the long-term economic well-being of our country.

The public, if well-informed, has the ability to override the influence of special interests, and the public has shown that they feel a stewardship toward the Earth and all of its inhabitants. Scientists can play a useful role if they help communicate the climate change story to the public in a credible understandable fashion.

Since he aimed to communicate not only to the public but also to his scientific colleagues, Jim buttressed these statements—including those regarding a practical solution—with copious evidence from real-world measurements and with rigorous analysis, based on his nearly forty years of experience studying the climate of our own planet and that of our neighbor, Venus. Indeed, this talk succeeded in connecting the dots for the first time in the minds of many geoscientists. One might assume that the thousands at this meeting would all be experts in global warming; however, most actually specialize in one or two specific aspects of the enormous field of geophysics. Very few—probably none—have the broad view of Earth's climate system that Jim Hansen does. A number of leading scientists, for instance, Paul Crutzen, who had won a Nobel Prize for his work on atmospheric ozone chemistry, told Jim that he had put together just the sort of comprehensive and convincing presentation that was needed. Many began using the charts from his talk, which he later placed on the Web, and a few suggested that he turn it into a paper and publish it in an academic journal. In a way, he would do that, about a year and a half later. By that time, however, his thinking had moved on, and it took six papers to get it all down.

Among those who gathered around immediately after the talk were a BBC reporter and a technician. "One of them just held a microphone in front of my face," Jim recalls. Other media requests began arriving by e-mail. Back in New York, his assistant, Darnell, and his institute's public affairs officer, Leslie McCarthy, also began receiving e-mails and telephone calls.

Jim and Anniek remained in San Francisco through Thursday evening, whereupon they caught a red-eye back to New York and Jim returned to science.

Jim leads an ascetic life. He and Anniek keep a tiny apartment a few blocks from his institute, the Goddard Institute for Space Studies (GISS), which is located on the campus of Columbia University. On the days when he doesn't get up at 4:30 A.M. to catch a train to Washington for a meeting at NASA headquarters or the Goddard Space Flight Center in Greenbelt, Maryland, he tends to spend the early morning thinking and writing in the peace and quiet of the apartment. Until recently, it had no Internet connection, which he saw as a good thing. If Leslie, Darnell, or one of Jim's scientific colleagues or fellow managers needs to reach him, she or he will call on the phone. At some point in the morning, when a meeting or some other pressing duty calls, he will rush downstairs and walk—more exactly run—a few blocks south to GISS, where he will work into the night. He claims that his only regular exercise comes from running up the stairs to his seventh-floor office. He and Anniek also own a small farm in rural Pennsylvania, to which he commutes by car about once a week—less in winter. Indeed, the old Volvo that they keep on the street in New York bears some resemblance to a farm vehicle. The one time I rode in it, the backseats and floors were covered with straw.

He works virtually all his waking hours. If he wakes in the night, he will put a few hours into his latest writing project or scientific paper. This is not busywork. Jim has a profound ability to focus. He moves from project to project, apparently shooting from the hip but hitting the bull's-eye nearly every time. As we shall see, it is difficult to keep up with him. Over the next few critical months, he would play a major role, sometimes in the background, in a dazzling number of crucial events that would finally put global warming back in its rightful place at the forefront of public concern.

The morning he and Anniek returned from the AGU meeting, Jim caught a few hours of sleep, then posted the words he had said and the images he had shown on the personal page he keeps on Columbia's Web site. He holds dual appointments at Columbia and GISS. Aside from directing the institute he is an adjunct professor in the Department of Earth and Environmental Sciences at Columbia and an active participant in the Columbia Earth Institute. GISS is also quasi-academic. Many of the NASA scientists at the institute hold dual appointments, some full-time Columbia scientists do their research there, and many Columbia students are involved in GISS research as well.

That afternoon, Jim sent an e-mail to a list of scientific and media contacts, to let them know that he had posted his Keeling talk on the Web. It's not as if he didn't realize that he was walking the political line with some aspects of the talk. This was his way of presenting it as a personal statement, disassociated from his position as a government scientist. Since Jim has been walking the political line to greater and lesser degrees for about twenty-five years—since 1981, to be precise, the first year of Ronald Reagan's presidency—he is probably as aware as any of NASA's 18,000 employees of the agency's stipulation that any statements that might relate to government policy must be presented as personal opinion.

The seeds he planted that afternoon quickly took root. . . .

The biggest headlines on the global warming front that particular week arose not from the statements of scientists in San Francisco, but from the behavior of a delegation representing the George W. Bush administration in Montreal. Representatives from nearly 200 nations were meeting in that city to discuss the next steps in the halting international effort to cut greenhouse gas emissions that had commenced seventeen years earlier, right around the time Jim had told the Senate that global warming had arrived.

Owing to the complexities of greenhouse policy, two parallel sets of negotiations were taking place in Montreal. The larger of the two was aimed at extending the voluntary 1992 United Nations Framework Convention on Climate Change, which had been negotiated during the term of the current president's father. The 189 nations that had eventually signed the Framework treaty, the United States among them, were discussing future, nonbinding agreements aimed at improving the treaty's effectiveness and enticing developing nations to join in the emissions-curbing effort. The second, smaller set of negotiations in Montreal involved only those developed nations that had signed the 1997 Kyoto Protocol. President Bill Clinton had signed the Kyoto treaty, but Congress had refused to endorse it; and when George W. Bush rejected it in March 2001, he ensured that the United States would be the only major developed nation besides Australia not to commit to the binding agreements of Kyoto. (The only other developed nations not to sign were Monaco and Liechtenstein.) The Kyoto signatories were working to develop a new set of more ambitious goals and timetables that would come into force after the Kyoto treaty lapses in 2012. Since the United States had not signed the treaty, the U.S. delegation was not party to these "post-Kyoto" discussions, of course.

Although it might seem that there was little to be risked in the nonbinding discussions, the lead negotiator for the United States, one Harlan Watson, spent nearly his entire two weeks in Montreal attempting to undermine their very premise. Stating quite openly that his aim was to end, right then and there, all international discussions even of nonbinding emissions limits, Watson fiercely resisted the efforts of the other 188 signatory nations even to start a new round of informal negotiations. This was very much in keeping with the goals of the oil giant ExxonMobil, which had recommended him for a place on the negotiating team shortly before President Bush, evidently taking the company's cue, appointed him leader of the team in 2001.

After midnight on the final day of the Montreal sessions, with a proposal for a new round of informal talks on the table, Dr. Watson is said to have uttered, "If it walks like a duck and talks like duck, it's a duck," and walked out of the room. A confused delegate from another country evidently stated, "I don't understand your reference to a duck. What about this document is like a duck?"

Slightly more than twenty-four hours later, again in the wee hours of the morning and only after the other signatories had agreed to two huge escape clauses—that any future talks would be "open and nonbinding" and that they would "not open any negotiations leading to new commitments"—did Watson agree to add his signature.

The United States received much criticism for Watson's antics—and not only from environmentalists. A front-page article in *The Washington Post,* published on Saturday, December 10, a few hours after Watson finally relented, read, "At times this week, Washington and its traditional allies seemed on the brink of divorce, especially after Canadian Prime

Minister Paul Martin told reporters . . . 'To the recalcitrant nations, including the United States, I would say this: there is such a thing as a
global conscience, and now is the time to listen to it.'"

The unique thing about global warming as a policy issue is that every
once in a while our planet itself decides to make a statement. Indeed, the
third intensifying factor that early December was the season. November
30 marks the end of the so-called meteorological year. Since weather stations generally report their results monthly, meteorologists and climatologists have found it convenient to divide the year into four three-month
seasons. September, October, and November are designated as fall; December, January, and February as winter; and so on. Sometime around
the second week of December, then, the three major research groups that
track global weather-station data—the Hadley Centre at the University of
East Anglia in Britain; the U.S. National Climatic Data Center, which is an
arm of the National Oceanic and Atmospheric Administration (NOAA);
and Jim Hansen's group at GISS—release their estimates of the Earth's
average temperature for the meteorological year just ended. They update
the reports in early January to provide laypeople with estimates for the
calendar year, which are rarely much different.

Jim's and the British group are the longest standing of the three, having both published their first global temperature estimates in 1981. All
three groups constantly improve their methods and their coverage of the
planet and report these improvements in scientific journals as necessary.

Owing to the intense interest of news organizations in this annual taking of the planet's temperature, the three groups coordinate with one
another and all release their data on the same day. Interest was especially
high this particular December because a race was on: since mid- to late
summer, the scientists in all three groups had been telling their friends
and acquaintances, including those in the news media, that 2005 might
turn out to be the warmest year on record—since about 1880, that is,
when station coverage first became global enough to permit a meaningful
estimate.

*   *   *

So there was a lot of interest in climate just then. Reporter Eli Kintisch from *Science* magazine, which along with *Nature* is one of the world's two leading scientific journals, sent an e-mail to Leslie McCarthy, GISS's public affairs officer, promptly on November 30. Kintisch noted the significance of the day and asked, "How can I find global and U.S. average temperatures for the year to see how this year stacked up with the previous years on record?" He probably had the date marked in his calendar, since his magazine tends to report the new numbers every year. In the past, Jim had sometimes made his formal announcement of the year's temperature in letters to the editors of *Science,* cast in technical language accompanied by graphs or tables—letters that amounted to terse scientific papers.

Leslie checked with Jim, who responded, "We'll do our usual end-of-the-year presentation. There's no stopping *Science* and *Nature* from trying to write something based on the data through November. I would be glad to give *Science* something once we are satisfied that we understand the data. We may have data as early as December 9, but likely it will be the following week." So Leslie suggested to Kintisch that he check back on the week of the twelfth.

The pressure was beginning to build. Mainstream journalists were approaching a watershed as well.

Two days after the Keeling talk, with Jim and Anniek still in San Francisco, ABC News journalist Bill Blakemore published in an article on ABCNews.com that focused on the psychology of global warming: our natural and in some ways healthy tendency to retreat into denial in the face of bad news.

"Journalism has no precedent for a story of the scale or seriousness of global warming," Blakemore began. "The vast majority of credible climate scientists—well over 95 percent, according to specialists in assessing scientists' opinions—agree that the average temperatures of the oceans, the land surface of the planet, and the lower atmosphere (anything lower than the tip of Mount Everest) have been climbing at an accelerating rate.

"The same specialists say that nearly as many scientists agree that manmade greenhouse gas emissions are a significant factor—and a good many say the only significant factor—in the dangerous global warming now under way.

"If ninety-five of the world's best, most experienced experts in child well-being were to tell you that your child was under lethal attack—and with dramatic signs already visible if you only look—would you say, 'I think I'll wait until the other five experts are convinced before I do anything about it?'

"It would be the other way around, and yet that is how a lot of people—and some parts of what's called 'the mainstream media'—often seem to be reacting to what the vast majority of scientists are telling us."

Blakemore did not pick his opinion estimates out of thin air. He had spoken to Granger Morgan, a physicist and policy expert at Carnegie Mellon University who has made a specialty of determining what constitutes consensus among scientists on any given question and had done an in-depth study of the consensus on global warming.

The title of Blakemore's article was "The Psychology of Global Warming: Alarm-ist Versus Alarm-ing: One Expert Warns Temperatures Could Climb to Highest Level in 500,000 Years." Jim Hansen was the expert in question, and Blakemore had taken this statement directly from a draft of the Keeling talk. He cited Jim as "one of the Galileos of global warming."

In the more than thirty-five years that Blakemore has been reporting for ABC News, he has covered, depending how you count them, twelve wars. He covered the entire twenty-seven-year papacy of John Paul II. He wrote several documentary hours about the pope as well as the major article about him in the *Encyclopaedia Britannica*. He has covered hostage sieges, earthquakes, volcanoes, the wedding of Prince Charles and Lady Diana, the arts, science, education, the environment. (He draws the line at national politics: "I've always stayed away from the Washington end of it. Just boggles my mind.") He's received numerous awards.

And a story he had first reported more than ten years earlier had recently ignited an interest in global warming. In 1994, he had done a news spot on the mysterious extinctions of a few species of exotic and colorful amphibians, such as the golden frog and the harlequin toad, in the Monteverde Cloud Forest Preserve of Costa Rica. Eleven years later, in the spring of 2005, he had paid a second visit to the scientist who had studied these extinctions and learned that they were no longer a mystery. There was now solid evidence that both plants and animals in the forest were being killed off by global warming, primarily through its effect on the clouds of mist that gave the Monteverde preserve its name.

Blakemore spoke with scientists working in Madagascar who had observed similar climate-related extinctions. He read surveys in *Nature* demonstrating that the phenomenon was global. The authors of one such survey, encompassing five continents, predicted, "on the basis of midrange climate-warming scenarios for 2050, that 15–37 percent of species in our sample of regions and taxa will be 'committed to extinction.'"

"I immediately got into global warming," he says, "and discovered, my goodness! How vast is the gap between the reality out there of the nature of the story and what all of the mainstream media, all the networks, all the newspapers, with very few exceptions, were doing. We'd obviously been very badly and successfully spun . . . and I felt very embarrassed for our profession."

Then he met Jim.

About two months before the Keeling talk, Blakemore paid a visit to his alma mater, Wesleyan University, to moderate a symposium entitled "Where on Earth Are We Going?" As coincidence had it, Jim delivered the opening talk. Blakemore walked up afterward, introduced himself, and, with a suddenness for which he later apologized, asked Jim if he would be interested in attending one of the regular lunchtime editorial meetings at ABC News, to brief the news president, David Westin, and various vice presidents and senior editors about global warming. (The ABC offices are on Manhattan's West Side, less than fifty blocks south of GISS.) The meeting took place in mid-November. Blakemore e-mailed Jim the next day, "I have already heard from several people at the meeting that they now get it—how real it is—and I believe that there was some serious journalistic realization going on yesterday."

But Jim had actually held back at that meeting. AGU was only three weeks away, and he wanted to make his major statement there, in writing, so that it would not be misconstrued. On the other hand, he and Blakemore had started a dialogue that would continue.

According to the ABC Web site, Blakemore "writes and lectures on the nature of professional journalism and how it differs from propaganda." He had published a law review article on this subject after reporting from Baghdad during the 1991 Gulf War. This may explain the e-mail he received from Jim as Jim was agonizing over his words on the afternoon before his Keeling talk: "I do not intend to make it political, but I think I need a couple of sentences regarding special interests, to help explain why we are not taking sensible steps—I'm still struggling with this aspect, how to remain an objective scientist."

Blakemore responded:

> Jim—Just an observation, but speaking on behalf of my own profession...it strikes me that [your] statements in the last two paragraphs of the abstract are statements of fact or of your belief...and do nothing to detract from your function as an objective scientist....What makes the difference between a propagandist on one side and a professional journalist or scientist on the other is not that the journalist or scientist "set their biases aside" but that they are open about them and constantly putting them to the test, ready to change them. I base this on a close study of the modern philosophy of science, especially that of Karl Popper and Peter Brian Medawar—and this is all aside from the fact that no one is going to object to a serious scientist trying to alert the public about the import of alarming news....I find your last two paragraphs straight-

forward and unassailable—and no more a "matter of
opinion" than the more numbers-supported para-
graphs above. . . .

At 2:54 P.M. on December 8, the day Blakemore explored the psychology of global warming in his ABCNews.com article, Leslie McCarthy
received a voice mail from a producer for *On Point,* a National Public Radio news program produced at WBUR in Boston. Tom Ashbrook, the
show's host, wanted to interview Jim live on the air the following Monday.
Leslie sent an e-mail regarding the request to Jim and to her public affairs
counterparts at GISS's parent organization, the Goddard Space Flight
Center, and to NASA headquarters in Washington.

She saw this as a professional courtesy. Leslie was *coordinating* with
Goddard and headquarters, giving them a heads-up; she was not asking *if*
Jim could give the interview. For all of her twelve years in NASA public
affairs, which included a few at headquarters, it had been standard operating procedure for scientists and engineers to speak directly to the news
media. Virtually every career public affairs officer in the agency sees her
or his role as being one of service, not control—of facilitating and focusing interactions with the media, not granting approval for them. Public
affairs officers will schedule different announcements so that they won't
vie for the spotlight, but aside from minor editing for clarity and the like,
they do not *control* information. And they have nothing to say about content. One senior headquarters veteran states the cardinal rule quite suc-
cinctly: "Don't fuck with the science."

But this is exactly what had been happening with increasing impunity
over the previous few years. The diddling had been directed by political
appointees at the highest levels of the agency, and it had focused pretty
much exclusively on the science of climate and global warming, with iso-
lated incidents in other areas.

Don Savage, a friend and colleague of McCarthy's who had recently
moved to Goddard as deputy chief of public affairs after eleven years at
headquarters, says, "What was going on at that time was kind of crossing

the line from the 'notification' into the 'asking permission' stage. We were getting that more and more; that was the way things would be for certain topics." Asked which topics, he responds, "Well, Earth science was pretty much it. The whole topic of global warming seemed to get a lot more attention. If anything came up in that arena, [headquarters was] definitely much more interested in knowing about it."

For this very reason, McCarthy, Savage, and their public affairs colleagues at Goddard and GISS were especially careful to notify headquarters about every announcement and upcoming event "in that arena."

One of the people who received Leslie's message about the NPR request was a recent addition to the public affairs staff in the Science Mission Directorate at headquarters, a young presidential appointee named George Deutsch. According to his résumé, Deutsch had earned a bachelor's degree in journalism from Texas A&M in 2003 and had continued to work at the university's student newspaper through 2004. He had gone straight from the newspaper to an internship in the "war room" of the 2004 Bush-Cheney reelection campaign, from there to the Presidential Inaugural Committee, and from there, in February 2005, to a public affairs position in another branch of NASA. Then, in early September, he was hired by the Science Mission on the recommendation of Dean Acosta, one of the top two political appointees in Public Affairs. Acosta held dual positions as deputy assistant administrator of the department and the NASA administrator's press secretary. His boss was David Mould, the assistant administrator for public affairs.

It was highly unusual, possibly unprecedented, for a so-called political to hold a "line office" public affairs position in Science—or any other mission for that matter. Since the position Deutsch held requires specific skills and knowledge, it was usually filled by a career civil servant. In fact, his presence in that position stood as a prime example of the increased impunity with which Dean Acosta had behaved since George Bush's reelection about a year earlier.

At age twenty-four, Deutsch was proud of being a political appointee and a Republican. He was thinking of running for public office and thought highly of the president. In fact, he had a George Bush screen saver on his computer. His first supervisor in the Science Mission, Dolores Beasley, recalls having corrected him more than once for saying that his job was "to make the president look good." She would point out that "he worked for NASA; he didn't work for the president, directly."

Headquarters is always a stressful place, but it was especially so at the end of 2005. Administrator Michael Griffin had been confirmed by the Senate only in April, and he had proceeded, naturally, to install new people in important roles. One was Dr. Mary Cleave, who became associate administrator for the Science Mission just a month before Deutsch shifted in. Shortly after Deutsch's arrival, Cleave replaced his boss, Beasley, with another career civil servant, Dwayne Brown.

Dwayne claims that he has actually seen "people get rolled out of here [headquarters]—and this is serious—get rolled out of here on stretchers because of stress." Dwayne is good for a quote. He plays the bass in several contemporary jazz groups and has a home recording studio. An esteemed scientist at the agency claims that he missed his calling as a Southern Baptist preacher. But Dwayne assures me that he is not speaking in hyperbole. He has "literally" seen people "go out on stretchers."

At the end of November, only two weeks into his new job, Dwayne had given Leslie what she remembers as a "solicitous" phone call, wanting to say hi because they would now be working together, and to discuss how they would coordinate with each other, owing to Jim Hansen's reputation as something of a maverick. Dwayne also mentioned a special twist to the general insanity that was infecting his workplace at the time: "Heavy politics here at headquarters. The only emphasis is not to make the president look bad. Leslie, I've never seen it this bad."

Dwayne hadn't sought the job in Science. Nearly everyone in public affairs had long seen Earth (as the agency's Earth science effort is affectionately known) as a trouble spot. Being a "good soldier," on the other hand, Dwayne did what he was asked. And on top of it all, he continued to fill the role of lead public affairs officer on a special project, the New Horizons mission to Pluto, which would be launched in January 2006. "It's a launch that requires White House approval," he observes. "I mean it's a monster. . . . You can make literally a career out of it until launch." The reason it needed White House approval was that the satellite carried a nuclear power source, a so-called RTG, a radioisotope thermoelectric generator. Solar power wouldn't suffice, owing to Pluto's extreme distance from the sun. Mary Cleave, the head of the Science Mission, was also extremely preoccupied with New Horizons. She says her perspective "would have been 'priority number one, New Horizons; everything else, after that.' I had never signed off on a nuclear launch before, and I was very, very focused on it."

So Deutsch "had the Earth side of the house," in Dwayne's words. "He would come to me and say, 'Hey, this is what's going on. What do you think?' Then, you know, I would give him what I thought, and then he would go off and do what he needed to do." Leslie, too, remembers dealing mostly with Deutsch during this period.

Dwayne refers to Dean Acosta as "the gatekeeper." Deutsch was constantly scampering up to the so-called Ninth Floor, where the offices of the administrator and the other senior managers are located, taking the latest news to Acosta and returning with his directives. Deutsch "would relay the fact that he was there to let Dean and David [Mould] know what was going on in Science," says Leslie. Some called him Acosta's "eyes and ears," others his "lapdog."

On the Thursday that he received Leslie's message, Deutsch ran it upstairs to Acosta, and Acosta instructed him to divert the NPR interview to one of the two senior administrators in Science, either Mary Cleave or her deputy, Colleen Hartman (neither of whom resides on the august Ninth Floor). Both of these women are accomplished individuals; both have doctorates, and Cleave has flown two space shuttle missions. However, Hartman has no background in climate science, and Cleave has very little. Cleave's graduate work at Utah State University bore some connection to carbon dioxide uptake by Earth's plant life, but that was about it—and she hadn't been a practicing scientist for decades. She had gotten involved in spacecraft design at Goddard about twenty years earlier and decided she'd rather "enable" other scientists to do their work than go back to doing science herself. Furthermore, neither Cleave nor Hartman had any particular familiarity with Jim Hansen's work.

Deutsch's e-mails indicate that Acosta (and whatever other senior managers he may have conferred with) went first to Hartman, the less qualified of the two: "Hey, Colleen, we just had this request sent to us and the details are below. We discussed it with the Ninth Floor, and it was decided that we'd like you to handle this interview."

Deutsch was nothing if not persistent. When Hartman balked, he sent out another request to both her and Cleave. "Please let us know which of you two ladies would like to tackle this one and we'll discuss this—we'll speak with the NPR folks and discuss the logistics and get back to you. Our main concern is hitting our messages and not getting dragged down into any discussions we shouldn't get into."

By the end of the day he seems to have resolved the issue, in his own mind at least, as he e-mailed Leslie to say, "It looks like Mary or Colleen will be handling it. I spoke with Dean about how best to broach this topic with Jim, and he said to simply say, 'Your boss would like to handle this interview.'" In a phone call the same day, according to the notes Leslie diligently records about most work-related discussions, Deutsch told her that management did not want Jim to appear on NPR because it was the "most liberal" news outlet in the country.

The actions of Dean Acosta and George Deutsch that day departed from NASA tradition in a number of respects. First, no one—even Acosta when he was later asked—would argue that it was up to public affairs to decide who should do the interview. Mary Cleave remembers refusing; she thought Jim ought to do it—and it was definitely her call. She says that she assumed the interview would then "flow" to Jim (although she actually played the game with Acosta for a while by suggesting a few other climate experts at the agency as substitutes). But under normal circumstances, this discussion would never have taken place. If NPR had called headquarters seeking an expert to interview about some general topic, it would have been quite appropriate to request a recommendation from Science, but it was highly unusual to take this route with a request to interview a specific scientist about his own work.

The word *tradition* is used advisedly here, because NASA's written policy was vague in this area. In fact, the civil servants at Goddard, GISS, and many other NASA centers had been pleading for months if not years for a clear written policy. On the other hand, the lack of a clear policy and the general lack of a paper or electronic trail served certain dark purposes very well—and this was another respect in which young George Deutsch broke with tradition: he left a trail with his e-mails. The headquarters veteran who spoke in plain language earlier about the cardinal rule says, "Little George was the toddler who shouldn't have been allowed so near the stove."

The next day, a Friday, Deutsch "offered" Colleen Hartman to NPR; but they refused. They still wanted Jim. (One wonders why they didn't just pick up the phone and call him.) According to Leslie's notes, she received warnings more than once from both Brown and Deutsch not to let Jim do the interview. And Deutsch seems to have forgotten his admonishments from Dolores Beasley. He told Leslie at least once that day that his job was to make the president look good.

But even his valiant attempts weren't doing much good on that particular Friday. That was the day Jim and Anniek arrived home on a red-eye and Jim posted his Keeling talk on the Web. That night, Harlan Watson stomped out of his meeting, ranting about ducks. And in the front-page news coverage about Montreal that appeared over the weekend, reporters frequently contrasted the points in the Keeling talk with the official position of the U.S. government. The following Tuesday, the *International Herald Tribune* would publish a brief adaptation of the talk, with Jim's byline but without his knowledge, under the title "It's Not Too Late." And, of course, Bill Blakemore had published his article on ABCNews .com the previous week.

Dean Acosta and David Mould viewed this rising tide with increasing consternation.

*   *   *

The fixation on NPR persisted through the weekend. Dwayne Brown remembers that on Monday he and George Deutsch were still "playing Ping-Pong" with the NPR folks, who were now getting a little angry. They'd figured out that Colleen Hartman had no background whatsoever in climate science, and, in any case, they wanted to talk about Jim's work with Jim. They finally gave up and sent either Brown or Deutsch an e-mail saying, in effect, "No Hansen, no NASA guest." But headquarters continued to suspect that the "confederates" at GISS might go behind their backs. After the negotiations with NPR broke off, Dwayne left a voice mail for Leslie threatening "dire consequences" if Jim went through with the interview.

Funny thing is that Jim had no interest in talking to NPR right then—and may not even have been aware of the request. He had not responded to Leslie's e-mail on the subject, which is one of his ways of saying no, and he felt that he'd done enough communicating for the time being anyway. He had been burrowed away since Friday, working on a major paper that he wanted to finish by the end of the year. He was also communicating with three GISS colleagues on the temperature data, since he had agreed with the leaders of the other two groups that analyze Earth's temperature that they would release their results simultaneously, three days hence. (That would be Thursday, the fifteenth, a date worth remembering.) Jim had informed Leslie of this plan, and Leslie had passed it on to a science writer at Goddard, who had posted a notice of the upcoming release on the Goddard Web site.

In the spirit of apprising headquarters in advance of everything that had anything to do with climate, Leslie and Don Savage set up a six-way telephone conference on Monday afternoon to discuss the coming week.

Since the summer, CBS's *60 Minutes* had been planning to do a show on climate change that would include an interview with Jim. The plan had been derailed when Hurricane Katrina struck New Orleans, but it was now back on track. Leslie had been keeping headquarters posted all along, but Dean Acosta had been stonewalling. Then again, before she had left Science, Dolores Beasley had given approval not once, but twice, for Jim to appear on the show. Nevertheless, Deutsch pronounced during this telephone conference that there was "no way Hansen would appear without headquarters approval."

The discussion moved on. *Vanity Fair* was planning to feature Jim in a "green issue" the following spring.

But Leslie and Don's main purpose in that Monday telephone conference was to notify headquarters about Thursday's pending release of the 2005 temperature data. Leslie pointed out that 2004's temperature analysis had been the most widely reported Earth sciences story generated by all of NASA, both nationally and internationally, and the most widely reported story of any type generated by Goddard in all of 2005. She suggested that there would probably be even more interest in 2006, since 2005 might set a record. Thursday's would be a simple data release on the Web, accompanied by a short explanation—a routine event that actually took place every month. There would be no big announcement and no press release, but even so, there would most likely be considerable media interest.

Indeed there already had been. Since Jim had alluded to a possible record in his Keeling talk, both *The New York Times* and *The Washington Post* had referred to the upcoming announcement in weekend stories about the negotiations in Montreal—the *Post* on its front page. The *Times* reported Jim as saying that 2005 was "nearly a sure bet to be the warmest year in recorded history."

Ed Campion, the news chief at Goddard, told his colleagues that ABC News had also expressed interest. He had received a call from producer Clayton Sandell, who had seen the notice on the Goddard Web site and was seeking someone to interview. Deutsch and Brown instructed their colleagues to direct all such requests to themselves at headquarters.

Don Savage had the sense that Dwayne was "trying very hard" during the telephone conference "to walk a tightrope to interpret what he felt were the marching orders from the boss"—Dean Acosta. Dwayne has the reputation of a survivor. When the boss says, "Jump," he asks, "How high?" He was also quite preoccupied with the Pluto launch; and, as he said, Deutsch had the Earth side of the house.

Virtually everyone who came into contact with George Deutsch during his career in the Science Mission describes him as arrogant, rough around the edges, and extremely ambitious. Even David Mould observes, after giving him an allowance for his youth, that "George had some strong opinions on things that he voiced, and had he asked me for coaching on expressing those opinions, I would have advised him to keep them to himself, because I think while, as an American citizen, he has every right to hold those opinions and express them, I'm not sure that it's the most productive thing to do at work, particularly when your work is here."

Dwayne Brown adds, "George even told me once, he says, 'What do you mean I work for you? You work for me.' You know, he was joking, but I didn't like it, okay? You don't joke with me like that. 'I've been here twenty-five years, Bucko, don't come flashing your Republican badge on me,' you know. I said to Dean, 'You need to talk to your boy. He needs to calm down because he won't listen to me."

Savage recalls Deutsch and Brown expressing a "big fear" all through the telephone conference that Jim would go behind their backs. "They were pretty spun up about it." Dwayne repeated his "dire consequences" remark a few times, and Leslie's notes record the two as reminding her yet again that the Ninth Floor did not want Jim Hansen on NPR. "Hansen can't say anything good about government," said Deutsch. "We can't have this anymore."

"[Deutsch] would have been easy to just blow off or put in his place had he just been acting on his own," recalls Savage. "Those sweeping kinds of statements . . . wouldn't be something that a lower level person would really be able to get away with. . . . All of us kind of felt that that was coming from higher up."

Regarding the data release, Savage adds, "We did everything we could to tell [Brown and Deutsch] that this was happening on Thursday, and that [ABC News was] very likely to do a story about it; they needed to do the story about it. We weren't planning to put a press release out; there didn't need to be a press release. Although we didn't know exactly what the content was going to be, we knew in general what it was going to say. What more do you need?"

Leslie even talked to Deutsch privately about the matter. Evidently, he didn't get the message.

On the morning after the telephone conference, Ed Campion, the Goddard news chief, followed his orders and shuttled Clayton Sandell, the ABC producer, over to headquarters. Sandell remembers speaking to Deutsch and/or Brown by phone the following day, Wednesday. He has a "very clear recollection" from that conversation of "how strongly they wanted to downplay the importance of this information being released." He had the distinct impression that he was "being waved off the story."

When the *Los Angeles Times* called, also on Wednesday, Deutsch sent them to Dr. Waleed Abdalati, a scientist at Goddard whose work focuses on the ice sheets and sea ice in the polar regions. Abdalati is a fine scientist, but he is not in Jim Hansen's reporting chain, does not study Earth's temperature particularly, and had no specific knowledge of GISS's latest temperature results. The newspaper never ran a story based on this interview. It *would* run a story on Friday, however, after the data release, based on an interview with Jim.

Like the folks at NPR, the reporters on the West Coast seemed to understand the importance of speaking to someone with a firsthand knowledge of the science they were hoping to report, but Deutsch and his managers on the Ninth Floor did not seem to understand this. Were they helping to communicate NASA's scientific work to the taxpayers who were paying for it, or were they burying it?

The bottom line is that Dwayne Brown and George Deutsch were told that the data release would be big news not only by their colleagues but by at least two national news outlets, yet somehow, in their desire to please their bosses and in their fixation on control, they neglected their most basic responsibility. They never told the Ninth Floor about the pending announcement. About a year later, Dwayne, ever the good soldier, would admit to this oversight, adding, "I would fall on my sword on this one."

* * *

As it turns out, Clayton Sandell is Bill Blakemore's producer—they talk on the phone many times a day—and Blakemore wasn't about to be waved off the story. On Monday, the day of the telephone conference, he did what most journalists would do: he went directly to Jim. "There is finally real editorial interest building here," he e-mailed, "and with word that NASA will be announcing 2005 hottest year on record on Thursday Dec. 15 (is this from your office?) we need to get a report ready while the interest is hot."

Actually, it was not yet clear where the year would come in. Jim and his three colleagues soon sorted that out, and on Wednesday morning Jim responded to the request Eli Kintisch had made of Leslie on November 30. He summarized the temperature results in a letter to the editors of *Science* magazine. This was not a press release; it was a scientific paper. It had the exact same title as a similar letter that Jim and the same three colleagues had sent to *Science* in 2002. Less than a minute after e-mailing it to *Science,* he sent it with no additional comment to Blakemore.

According to the GISS analysis, 2005 *had* set a record as the warmest year in the more than 100 years of instrumental measurement, although the statistical error in the estimate implied "practically a dead heat with 1998, the warmest previous year." Jim pointed out, nevertheless, that "record, or near record, warmth in 2005" was "notable" since 1998 had received a boost of about 0.2°C from the strongest El Niño of the twentieth century.

In the British analysis the year came in a close second to 1998, and in the NOAA analysis the two years were tied. The British ignore regions that don't have weather stations, while the two U.S. groups have different ways of estimating temperatures in the regions that don't have stations. The Arctic, which has few weather stations, had experienced an extraordinarily warm year, which the British had basically missed.

As for the differences between NOAA and GISS, the former interpolates linearly between stations, while Jim employs some most-likely sound physics related to "Rossby waves," which yields estimates for the temperature in a larger area of the Arctic and therefore provides a more realistic estimate of the region's warmth. When NOAA redid their analysis later in the year, they agreed with GISS that 2005 had set a record, and in mid-2006 an analysis of infrared satellite readings indicated that Jim's method of interpolation probably *underestimates* arctic warmth.

Thus 2005 probably did set a record.

"Global warming is now 0.6°C [1.1°F] in the past three decades and 0.8°C [1.4°F] in the past century," Jim wrote. "It is no longer correct to say that 'most global warming occurred before 1940.' More accurately, there was slow global warming, with large fluctuations, over the century up to 1975 and subsequent rapid warming of almost 0.2°C [0.4°F] per decade."

Put another way, whether it set a record or not, the warmth of 2005 meant that the six hottest years on record had occurred in the previous eight years, and the eighteen hottest years on record had occurred in the previous twenty-five.

"Recent warming coincides with rapid growth of human-made greenhouse gases," Jim continued. "Climate models show that the rate of warming is consistent with expectations. The observed rapid warming thus gives urgency to discussions about how to slow greenhouse gas emissions."

Chapter 2

"This Is Coming from the Top"

THE SPOT RAN AT TEN PAST SEVEN THURSDAY MORNING, close to the top of the first hour of *Good Morning America*. Anchor Robin Roberts led in with "This morning, NASA is announcing that this year, 2005, is tied for the hottest year ever," and added (imprecisely) that "for the fourth year in a row, we have seen the hottest annual global temperatures since reliable records started in the 1800s." Bill Blakemore's voice took up the thread: "NASA scientists say no natural climate cycles can explain it. The heat must be caused in large measure at least by greenhouse gas emissions."

This was an arresting lead, but even Blakemore remembers the spot as being "something of a grab bag." He did not touch upon the temperature record again, moving swiftly to other aspects of the problem: the stresses global warming is already placing on the world's poor, who are the least capable of adapting, and on other species. Then he moved to the dramatic changes in the Arctic, about which he would run another fine spot that evening on *Nightline*. Jim Hansen was not quoted, nor was his name even mentioned. Blakemore did, however, eloquently quote Harvard biologist E. O. Wilson. "Do we want to destroy the creation? That's the question. That's what we're doing at an accelerating rate."

The temperature announcement was certainly big news, but it was hardly a surprise. After all, three other groups around the world were announcing essentially the same thing at the same time. It was also purely a scientific story. It contained no discussion of policy whatsoever.

Blakemore believed strongly at that time that the mainstream media had been tricked into thinking of global warming as a "politics" story, when in reality, as he later said, "It's an event story, like when Mount Saint Helens blew up. You know. It's an event! It's happening! The atmosphere doesn't care about the politics." The few pieces of information for this spot that he had obtained from NASA had come from a scientific paper and a scientific lecture, the letter to *Science* and the Keeling talk, supplemented by a brief exchange with Jim to make sure the facts were right.

Blakemore shares Jim's belief in the need to connect the dots. "Part of the problem of doing [the global warming] story well, as professional skeptics and professional journalists, [is] helping everybody fit together all of the different disparate pieces from all over the planet, so to speak. I guess that was actually the logic of the December fifteenth piece. I didn't even think of it as a particularly sharp-edged scoop of a story, but a kind of a good routine story, covering the beat."

Evidently, someone rather high in the U.S. government thought differently. Leslie McCarthy's notes say that her colleague Dwayne Brown called at nine thirty or ten that morning to inform her that a "shit storm" was taking place at headquarters.

"What the hell happened?" Dwayne asked. His phone had been ringing off the hook. Nasty e-mails were flying around. An irate Mary Cleave had told him that Administrator Michael Griffin himself had received a complaint from the White House. Dean Acosta and David Mould, the two top dogs in public affairs, were also upset. (One was said to have heard the spot while shaving.) "You never told us you were doing a big release," Dwayne told Leslie. "This was big news!" Then he promised to refrain from finger-pointing.

There may have been two or even three calls from the White House that day. One public affairs insider who saw a lot of Dean Acosta confirms that Dean got one, too.

Leslie reminded Dwayne that this was not a big release; it was straight science—as she and Don Savage had told everyone during Monday's telephone conference. She also reminded him that Ed Campion had mentioned ABC's interest during the same telephone conference, and that all the folks at Goddard and GISS had warned Dwayne and George Deutsch that the news would probably generate interest. Dwayne advised Leslie that Associate Administrator Mary Cleave, the highest science manager in the agency, would soon be calling Jim to give him "counseling" on how to interact with the media.

Leslie took Dwayne's call in her office at GISS, in Manhattan, where she was working with the institute's deputy director, Larry Travis, on an unrelated task that morning. Larry walked in and out during the course of the call, noticing the look of concern on Leslie's face, and asked what was going on when it ended. She brought him up-to-date on the events of the past week: the diversion of the NPR interview, the general unhappiness at headquarters over all the news coverage about the Keeling talk, and the present shit storm. Recalls Larry, "When she got to the point of saying that she had been told that Mary Cleave was going to call Jim and give him some 'counseling' . . . I don't remember who said it first, but between Leslie and me, we just said, 'We'd better call Jim.' . . . At the very least, we wanted to be sure that if he really was going to get a call from Mary Cleave that he wasn't blindsided by it, and he would be prepared to have a rational discussion."

They reached Jim at his apartment, where he sometimes works in the morning. Until that moment, he had been entirely oblivious to these goings-on—even the NPR fiasco—and when he now learned of them, his first response was to laugh. He loved the "shit storm" phraseology. "Is that an exact quote?" he asked. When he heard that Cleave or her deputy, Hartman, now reserved the right to stand in for him in interviews, he observed that neither of them probably had the time to be his personal public affairs spokesperson.

Jim remembers his laughter as being a "Fat chance, what else is new?" kind of laughter, since he figured he would still be able to dodge restrictions and get his scientific messages out one way or another. Larry laughed along at first. However, Leslie, who was more in the direct line of fire, tried to impress upon them both her sense that things seemed to be different this time.

Indeed they were. GISS was planning to post the temperature data on the Web that day, along with a short summation, similar to the letter Jim had written to *Science*. (They had been observing an embargo, which Bill Blakemore had unwittingly broken, in order to synchronize the announcement with the other two groups.) Sometime before noon, Deutsch or Brown called Leslie to tell her not to post the data, and she conveyed this message to the institute's webmaster, who complied. Thus the institute's monthly routine of posting Earth's temperature data, and yearly routine of summarizing it, were interrupted for the first time in their quarter century of existence.

It seems odd that this message would have been passed on by public affairs. If it was justified at all, it should have been delivered by Mary Cleave directly to Jim Hansen, for it pertained specifically to science. Leslie gathered that Dean Acosta had initiated the action by first asking Cleave to review the data and then directing Brown or Deutsch to call GISS.

That was a long day for Leslie, as she remained in the line of fire. Numerous phone calls and e-mails went back and forth asking her for explanations and so on—while, tellingly, no one from headquarters even tried to reach Jim.

Meanwhile, at the behest of public affairs, the scientists at the top of Jim's management chain spent part of their working day checking out a simple and straightforward piece of scientific information. The review team comprised Cleave; her deputy, Colleen Hartman; and the head of Goddard Space Flight Center, Dr. Ed Weiler, a veteran of thirty years at the agency and one of its most highly regarded scientists. For twenty-seven of those years, Weiler had worked in various management capacities at headquarters, some as high as associate administrator, and he had been chief scientist of the Hubble Space Telescope the entire time.

The scientific managers unanimously agreed that the GISS Web posting was "all science" and should certainly be posted. Weiler remembers that "Mary and Colleen—it was usually Colleen I was dealing with—were always on the same side of these issues, but we always seemed to be overruled, if you know what I mean."

By whom?

"Somebody. Not Mike Griffin," says Weiler.

At five thirty that evening, Dwayne Brown called Leslie to tell her she could post the data, but George Deutsch, who seems to have been in Dwayne's office at the time, quickly countermanded him—and by extension Cleave, the top scientist at the agency—with the explanation that he was still awaiting confirmation from Dean Acosta.

Thus public affairs trumped science, and the data stayed down overnight.

Five minutes after this exchange, as Leslie was preparing to leave for home, Dwayne rang again to inform her that Acosta wanted to speak to her. She had children to pick up, so she asked for a few moments to call her husband and make arrangements. She also asked if she could have Don Savage on the line. Dwayne agreed and quickly called Savage at Goddard to ask him to stand by.

"So," says Leslie, "a few minutes later, Dean calls, who I had never spoken to ever, and has David Mould on the phone with him, who introduces himself. I said, 'Well, hold on a second, I'm going to dial in Don Savage.'

" 'That's unnecessary, we don't need him.'

"And I said, 'Well, wait a minute. Dwayne called me and told me you two wanted to talk to me. I would like to have somebody else on the phone here with me.'

" 'That's not necessary.'

"They wouldn't allow it."

Although Leslie didn't realize it (because she wasn't told), there were actually four people in Acosta's office that evening, behind a closed door, listening to her lone voice on the speakerphone. Along with Mould and Acosta were Mould's assistant, Jason Sharp, and, unsurprisingly, George Deutsch, neither of whom spoke during the call. All four were political appointees.

About a year later, when Goddard director Ed Weiler learned that this call had even occurred, he remarked, "They called her directly? That's inappropriate. . . . She doesn't work for headquarters."

Since Mould and Acosta's remembrance of this conversation would differ greatly from the notes Leslie hurriedly wrote down as the call was taking place, it is worth pointing out that Don Savage remembers standing by in Greenbelt all through this phone call and that Leslie called to brief him on it the moment it was done. His memory of what she said at that time jibes well with her notes, according to which, Acosta started the conversation by asking:

"Why were we blindsided?"

"By what?" Leslie asked.

"Good Morning America."

"You weren't. I can't control what *Good Morning America* picks up on. People use our Web site all the time. The data is quoted all the time."

Acosta asked why he hadn't been warned about the data release. She explained that headquarters had in fact been "warned," if that was the correct word, during Monday's telephone conference, which Dwayne Brown and George Deutsch had attended.

David Mould broke in, "This is policy from Griffin on down. No one takes direct phone calls." His point was that Michael Griffin, the NASA administrator, did not take calls from the press without first conferring with his press officer, Dean Acosta, and that "if it was good enough for the administrator, it had to be good enough for Jim Hansen."

Now, it may be that during the Bush years an attempt was made to institute such a rule at headquarters itself, but it had not been entirely successful even there. Ed Weiler, who left headquarters for Goddard in 2004, says, "Let me tell you a little secret. When I was the associate administrator and when I was a division director at headquarters, I didn't call up to the Ninth Floor, two, five, ten years ago, every time somebody called me up from CBS or ABC for an interview. I just did it. You know, I figured if I did something wrong, I'd get my wrist slapped." And Weiler was far from the only one. Moreover, there was no way this was standard operating procedure at the NASA centers. It would have been impossible. Goddard alone employs hundreds of Ph.D.'s.

Acosta then informed Leslie that he wanted to know about everything coming from GISS well in advance. Henceforth, she was to include him on all e-mails to Deutsch and Brown. She calmly repeated the plea that she and her fellow civil servants had been making for months: would he and Mould please lay these new procedures out on paper, because they seemed to be "a kind of moving target."

"Great idea, Leslie. We'll do it." She felt that they were being solicitous. Acosta said, "Your programs and projects are important—important to overall management. You must be a bit smarter. I recognize your challenges."

He was referring, as Leslie understood it, to Jim.

"There was always this attempt to say that they understood that Jim was kind of the wild horse who wouldn't be kept in the stable, and that they recognized that it was my challenge to control his behavior," she explains. "I don't try to control Jim Hansen. That's not my job. I don't want that job—I don't think anybody could do it, first of all. Jim Hansen's been the director here for twenty-five years, does a pretty good job of asking for help when he needs it, and when he doesn't, he handles things himself.

"That was a frequent issue. They would call here and complain about Jim, and I'd say, 'I am not Jim Hansen's boss. Franco Einaudi is. Here, let me give you his phone number.' It's much easier to call here and complain than to follow the chain up."

Dr. Franco Einaudi, the head of the Earth Sciences Division at Goddard, was indeed Jim's boss, and since Jim and a few others at GISS and Goddard who were directly affected by these events responded in quite the appropriate way, by discussing them with Einaudi, we shall meet him in a moment.

In the purest of ways, Leslie is touching upon the crux of the matter. The political appointees in public affairs seemed to believe that they held some sort of executive authority. (Dwayne Brown even remembers Dean Acosta "beating his chest" and threatening to fire Jim and a few others at GISS and Goddard that day. Dwayne replied, "You can't fire jack. It's not set up like that, Dean," as he thought to himself, "These Republicans really are tripping.")

Mould indicated to Leslie for a second time that Michael Griffin had been involved in at least some of the discussions that day. "The administrator is giving Mary and Colleen direction here. This is coming from the top. Specific rules and expectations of conduct and procedures will be spelled out by Mary to Jim."

Leslie heard the door to Acosta's office open and close as Dwayne Brown entered the room, fresh from a meeting with Mary Cleave. Dwayne had been sprinting all day. On top of dealing with the fallout from the *Good Morning America* story, he and Mary had been working on a presentation for the administrator about their highest priority, the New Horizons mission to Pluto. He had been hoping he might avoid the present discussion but, after twenty or thirty minutes, had decided he ought to "go up and give Leslie some support, because I thought about it and I said, 'Damn, I just gave her to the wolves. . . . I hope these guys don't start beating their chests, talking smack, and they can't do jack.'"

It seems that Dwayne, Mary—and quite possibly Michael Griffin—had discussed issues besides New Horizons, for Dwayne now announced that there would be two new "rules of engagement," starting immediately. First, all Web content would need to be approved, including journal articles.

"Let me get this straight," Leslie responded. "Jim Hansen has an article accepted by the *Journal of Geophysical Research*. I have to call the director of public affairs for the Science Mission and ask for permission to post this on our Web page when it's been approved by a refereed journal?"

"Yes, that's correct."

"Okay."

"All requests for interviews must go to Colleen and Mary with the right of first refusal, then they will be disseminated to the appropriate contact."

Leslie asked her friends at headquarters what they knew about the workforce at GISS, where she is the sole public affairs officer. "We have twenty-seven or so civil servants [NASA employees]," she pointed out. "We have thirty-some contract employees; and we have one hundred or so, at any given time, university personnel, who are a combination of researchers, postdocs, and students. Are these rules for the civil servants, for the university personnel—who are mostly Columbia, but not necessarily; they're from Rutgers, MIT, all over the world—or the contractors?"

David Mould jumped in to ask why she was asking so many questions. She felt he was accusing her of being insolent. She said it was because she didn't understand. "If I have a guy here from Columbia who's studying clouds, does he have to follow this rule?"

The answer was that the new rules applied to anyone with a NASA badge and/or getting NASA money. Mould did not seem to realize that the bylaws of most universities would prevent them from accepting money with such restrictions.

At about this point in the conversation, Leslie McCarthy sensed over the telephone and Dwayne Brown observed in Dean Acosta's Ninth Floor office that David Mould was getting angry. However, Mould is not one to raise his voice. He grew up in South Carolina and Tennessee, and he has a relaxed, Southern way of speaking. He is also far too professional to *display* anger.

He remembers that he thought he heard Leslie say something that took him by surprise, and that he even took a moment to write it down: "We don't have to do that. We are independent."

She utterly denies saying anything of the sort. Her actions over the previous week—passing along the NPR interview request, for example, and setting up the conference call the previous Monday—as well as copious electronic and written evidence from the weeks and months previous to this phone call, indicate that she could not possibly have believed that GISS's press operations (such as they were, since she embodied them in one person) were independent of headquarters. But this is what David Mould and Dean Acosta both claim to have heard.

"I don't remember her saying that," says Dwayne, "but she said *something* that ticked David off."

Leslie believes it was simply that she had the nerve to push back. Her notes record Mould as being the first to say anything about independence.

"We are tired of Jim Hansen trying to run independent press operations," he stated with measured calm. "He is not his own boss. This is intolerable. From now on I want to know everything Jim Hansen does." He then told Leslie that he wanted to be informed in advance of everything on Jim's schedule, especially his public appearances.

She pointed out that this would be quite a new way of doing business. Neither Jim nor the hundreds of scientists at GISS, Goddard, or the dozen or so other NASA centers had ever worked that way. She suggested that Mould and Acosta might want to check with the public affairs staff at Goddard. "Most reporters go directly to Hansen, [Gavin] Schmidt [a GISS climate modeler], and others, unless they can't find someone, they're new to us, or they need something outside GISS research," she said.

"This is unacceptable. How long has this been going on? This has to stop now. That procedure is not allowed in the administrator's office at headquarters, at Goddard, or at GISS."

The precise answer to Mould's question is that reporters had been speaking directly to NASA scientists since 1958, the year the agency was created. Leslie's boss, Mark Hess, the chief of public affairs at Goddard and a veteran of thirty years at the agency, eleven of them at headquarters, says, "I can tell you without a doubt that scientists talk to the media every day all the time [chuckle] and we have no idea. And you know what? It's no big deal, because what they're talking about is their science, and who better to talk about science than the scientists? There's no reason to get yourself in the middle of that . . . because, for the most part, a lot of these scientists and journalists have long-standing relationships. These are journalists who have been talking to these scientists for years. So, to suddenly have a public affairs person insert themselves into that process—I mean, what kind of a message would that send?"

As the call from headquarters came to an end, Leslie told Mould and Acosta, "I understand what you've told me, and I'm going to pass it along to Dr. Hansen."

They asked if GISS was going to follow the new rules.

"I wrote down what you told me and I'll pass it along to Dr. Hansen."

"That was as far as I was going to go," she says. Leslie had not seen the rules on paper, and she believed they reached far beyond the traditional role of public affairs.

Her long day was not over. She quickly touched base with Don Savage, who had been left hanging in his office at Goddard. Then she called Jim and her supervisor, Mark Hess.

Emotions were running high on that mid-December day, and since much confusion would later confound even the honest attempts of the mild-mannered congressional investigators who would eventually look into this matter, let us review the basic facts: (1) The proximate cause for the "shit storm" at headquarters was about three sentences uttered on national television regarding pure, unassailable, and unsurprising scientific information that was simultaneously announced by two scientific teams in addition to GISS—an organization that had been releasing similar information, routinely and without incident, for more than two decades. There was no interview with Jim Hansen; his name was not mentioned. (2) The public affairs officers at GISS and its parent organization, Goddard Space Flight Center, notified their counterparts at NASA headquarters, Dwayne Brown and George Deutsch, in advance that this data would be released. Based on their experience with a similar but less exciting release the previous year, they suggested that the pending release might make big news. Notification of the pending release was also posted on the Goddard Web site. (3) Based on this terse Web posting, ABC, the news outlet that later broadcast the three sentences, also contacted Brown and Deutsch in advance, and so did the *Los Angeles Times*. Others might have inferred from these inquiries alone the potential for significant media interest.

At some point on the morning of December 15, Dean Acosta asked George Deutsch to write an internal document called a point paper, which was cosigned by Dwayne Brown. Deutsch and/or Brown asked Leslie to provide details about "what had happened," and in her e-mailed response at 12:02 p.m., she described the Monday telephone conference. But there is no mention of the conference in this point paper, and the blame for a great many alleged breaches of NASA protocol is placed squarely on the shoulders of the public affairs staffs at Goddard and GISS. "In past discussions with . . . Leslie McCarthy, she has sent Headquarters mixed signals as to if/when this data would be released," Deutsch wrote. "Headquarters was unaware that Hansen would be releasing this data when he did. . . . No one from either GISS or GSFC [Goddard] could definitively confirm whether this information would be posted, and the likelihood of seeing any such announcement was continually downplayed by GSFC." The point paper confirms that ABC spoke to Brown and Deutsch on Wednesday, but it remains silent on the question of whether it might have been their responsibility to pass this information up to the Ninth Floor.

"Headquarters public affairs officers *granted* the L.A. Times an interview with GSFC scientist Dr. Waleed Abdalati yesterday evening" (emphasis mine), Deutsch continued, "and during the course of the interview Dr. Abdalati could not confirm 2005 as being the warmest year on record. Again, no one from GSFC/GISS has yet been able to confirm any data showing 2005 as the warmest year on record."

This is a strange pair of remarks. Abdalati would, as previously stated, have had no reason to be aware of Jim Hansen's temperature results before they were released, and Jim, the expert on this question, had definitely "confirmed" the likelihood of a record in the letter to *Science,* which Deutsch had seen by this point and mentions in his point paper. As Leslie points out, the point paper that Deutsch wrote and Dwayne Brown cosigned was factually incorrect at best and contained outright, purposeful lies at worst.

A little more than a year later, Deutsch would be called to testify before the House Committee on Oversight and Government Reform in a hearing entitled "Political Interference with Science: Global Warming." After a year's reflection, he seemed even more convinced that Abdalati had been better qualified to speak of Jim's work than Jim himself: "In [the *L.A. Times*] interview, Dr. Abdalati stated that he could *not* confirm that 2005 was the warmest year on record. Yet, on December 15, Dr. Hansen submitted a letter to the journal *Science* and conducted an interview with ABC's *Good Morning America* program concluding that 2005 tied 1998 as the warmest year on record." Beyond his complete ignorance of the scientific method and the concept of relevant data, this young man was having real trouble with elementary logic.

There is much talk of public affairs' responsibility for *approving* the release of scientific information in Deutsch's point paper. The word is mentioned six times in two pages. "The release of this data had not been properly coordinated with Headquarters and undermined the protocol, chain of command and flow of information channels in place. . . . Furthermore, GISS currently has the information ready to post on its Web site, but they have been told by Headquarters to not yet do so until the required approval is granted. . . . It bears mentioning that Dr. Hansen and GISS as a whole do not always follow Headquarters protocol and sometimes fail to give Headquarters adequate notice when they plan to release information to the public. This is not the first time Headquarters has had this problem with GISS."

"An amazing piece of work," says Don Savage with a laugh. "They were trying very hard to fashion Leslie into being the fall guy . . . and to blame her for misleading them and all of this, when, in fact, she was trying extremely hard not only to keep them informed . . . but to suggest to them that if they took a certain course of action, the very thing that happened was going to happen."

So much for not pointing fingers.

Over three decades in NASA public affairs, Leslie McCarthy's boss, Mark Hess, has gotten good at staying on point in interviews. He would seem to recall few specifics, and he responds firmly and frequently with the lines "I don't remember that" or "I don't remember this."

But he remembers the conversation he had by phone with Dean Acosta on December 16, the morning after the shit storm, quite clearly. Hess was visiting NASA's Wallops Flight Facility on Virginia's Eastern Shore that day. He remembers Acosta laying out for him the same directives that Leslie had transcribed in her notes the previous evening—and being quite as surprised by them as Leslie was. He and Leslie compared notes by phone that day; and on Monday, Hess composed an e-mail to Jim Hansen's immediate superior, Dr. Franco Einaudi, and Einaudi's boss, Dr. Laurie Leshin, Goddard's new director of sciences and exploration.

"At some point fairly soon," Hess wrote, ". . . I need to sit down with you and fill you in on the discussion both Leslie McCarthy . . . and I had with David Mould and Dean Acosta. . . .

"Leslie is putting together a note which recaps what HQs [headquarters] has directed (not asked) us to do with regard to 'monitoring' the work of GISS and Dr. Hansen in particular. . . . They are asking we keep track of his schedule, his speaking engagements, his media interviews, all the science papers being submitted from GISS, all the content on the GISS web site, etc., etc. . . .

"You should also be aware that Dean Acosta wants to have a meeting with me sometime in the next few weeks so he and David can again review those activities for which they believe we (Leslie and I) are accountable."

Hess explains that he and Leslie were "in good faith trying to find some reasonable accommodation between what [Mould and Acosta] wanted and what we felt was a reasonable thing to do. . . . I mean, if they literally wanted to know Jim Hansen's every move, every talk he was giving, every speech he was giving, every meeting he was having, . . . that's an area where I just said, 'Nope. Not us. We're not going to do that,' because it's not appropriate. Jim Hansen doesn't work for me, and if his scientific bosses want to do something different, you know, that's up to them, but I'm not going to get in the middle of that."

The reason he sent the e-mail to Jim's two supervisors was to place responsibility where he thought it belonged. Acosta and Mould "were not going to put public affairs into trying to be the thought police," he says. "If there were legitimate concerns between scientists in terms of how NASA communicates what it's doing, those are discussions that need to take place between scientists."

From a management standpoint, Hess didn't actually report to Acosta or Mould (and therefore neither did Leslie). He reported to Goddard's director, Ed Weiler. So he conferred with Weiler and Einaudi, and with their encouragement sent an exceedingly diplomatic e-mail to Mould and

Acosta on Tuesday. He says he was hopeful that once they saw their requests "in black and white," they might realize, "Well, this is . . . heh, heh . . . This makes no sense."

David and Dean:

Leslie and I have been consulting on a summary of the discussions we had with you last week concerning the folks at GISS and how we should be coordinating with Goddard and HQs.

We took a crack at this, but before Leslie sits down with Dr. Hansen to go over these procedures, we thought we'd send you what she plans to talk to him about to make sure it captures all the information and activities you want provided to Leslie and from there on to you all.

It basically falls into three areas: interviews, web content and meetings—if we've missed anything, please let us know.

Any edits or other thoughts you have would be most helpful so that we can talk to Dr. Hansen about this as soon as possible. Also, I'm here throughout the holidays, so if you want to get together to discuss, before or after, just let me know a good day and time, and I'll come down to HQs.

Best regards, and hope you both have a great Holiday.

Mark

PAO Procedures (to cover all scientists, including NASA civil servants and/or GISS contractors who receive NASA funding)

1) NASA policy from the Administrator is that all calls or e-mails from the news media for

interviews, comments or other information with NASA employees are to be immediately forwarded to the cognizant PAO for coordination with Headquarters Public Affairs. No comments or interviews should be granted until they have been coordinated and approved by the NASA HQs Science Mission Directorate and Public Affairs Office. If a reporter calls, or sends an e-mail directly to a NASA employee (or NASA funded contractor), the employee should immediately refer the call or forward the e-mail to the GISS PAO who will work the request with [Goddard] and HQs. These requests will be forwarded to HQ Public Affairs who will in turn, work them with Drs. Mary Cleave and Colleen Hartman. Drs. Cleave and Hartman will have the right of first refusal on all interview requests. They will provide direction back to HQ on who will handle the interview. All interviews with NASA employees should be reported on fully via the HQ Public Affairs "On the Record" procedure.

2) All content for the GISS webpage needs to be sent to Drs. Mary Cleave & Colleen Hartman, as well as HQ Public Affairs, for approval before posting. This includes the posting of accepted scientific journal articles, datasets, science briefs, and news/features.

3) Dates of coming speeches, data releases, scientific meetings/conferences must be provided to the GISS PAO with enough advance notice to be able to keep HQ fully informed of any activities which may generate significant media coverage.

Franco Einaudi points to the singling out of GISS in this list of directives. He claims, for example, that no other group or department in Goddard's entire Earth Sciences Division, which he directed, had ever been required to submit Web content to headquarters for approval. On the other hand, many of the scientists in the division—and virtually all the climate scientists—had felt the bite of censorship over the previous few years, so in one sense Hess's e-mail was just the latest attempt to get some rules in writing.

Also as in the past, Acosta and Mould left no fingerprints on this episode, nothing in the way of an electronic or paper trail. Even George Deutsch's point paper does not mention their names, although it was written at Acosta's request; no recipients are specified. That internal document would never have appeared in public, most likely, had not Deutsch, in one of his numerous bumbling maneuvers, made it available to a right-wing, Web-based news organization in April 2006 as part of a bizarre attempt to smear Jim Hansen.

As evidence of other, previous and subsequent, incidents of intimidation and scientific censorship at NASA—at Acosta and Mould's hands, as well as others at their level and above—would gradually come to light, and a modus operandi would be revealed. Censorship of climate science was not a written directive at the agency. It wasn't openly discussed; it is still not quite possible to censor science openly in this country. Those lower down on the totem pole, who say they were directed to do the dirty work—that is, the rewriting of press releases and the control or stifling of the spoken and written words of scientists—always received such orders orally, usually in closed-door meetings or in telephone calls that they attended individually, frequently outnumbered by the higher-ups, but in the absence of other, potentially troublesome witnesses at their own level. Mould and Acosta's denial of Leslie McCarthy's request to have Don Savage on the line on the evening of December 15 is a case in point.

Organizationally, this constituted a shadow chain of command within the space agency, which would occasionally manifest in such absurd forms as Mould and Acosta's commanding of Leslie—a seasoned professional, yes, but no holder of administrative authority—to tell the director of her institute what to do. It was easy, as she says, to call and complain to her, to attempt to intimidate her and the other public affairs officers in their department—but that was about as far as Mould and Acosta's true authority actually went.

*   *   *

Acosta was the more experienced at these shenanigans. He had come to the agency in 2003, after a fifteen-year career as a sportscaster, broadcast journalist, and investigative reporter. He was the institutional memory, which is probably why he got the call from the White House on December 15.

Not only was David Mould newer to his job—he had been there less than six months—but by all accounts he was not as involved in the day-to-day "monitoring" of scientific information. He was the more senior of the two, the head of public affairs for an agency that focuses mainly on space exploration, after all: rocket launches, shuttle missions, and the like; so he usually had bigger fish to fry. One can still understand why he might have become upset when a spot on *Good Morning America* caused an uproar in his department, however, especially since one and possibly three calls from the White House rolled in.

The real question is why the White House would bother to complain about a routine announcement of a new global temperature record—and Mould's very presence at the agency points in the direction of an answer.

Acosta, Deutsch, and many of the other presidential appointees at NASA during the Bush years had little relevant experience to recommend them for their positions. "The difference with the Clinton political appointees is *they* were all qualified for what they did," observes Leslie, who worked at headquarters during the Clinton era. "They came from public affairs backgrounds; they were communications officers; they were press secretaries on the Hill; they had worked in industry. . . ."

But Mould was the exception to the rule of the Bush years: he had worked as a space reporter at United Press International for about eight years, and not only had he worked in industry, he had worked in what some might regard as just the right industry: the energy sector, which generally argues for increased greenhouse emissions. Before joining NASA, he worked for about two years as a special assistant for strategic communications to successive energy secretaries, Spencer Abraham and Samuel

Bodman. President Bush appointed Mould to that post, too. Before entering government service, Mould worked for about five months at Griswold-Lesser, a Washington- and Atlanta-based public affairs firm that describes itself as offering "strategic planning that enables senior executives to maximize their company's success in the regulatory, legislative and media arenas." Before that, Mould was vice president of communications for PG&E, a developer of power plants and natural gas pipelines that is also the holding company of Pacific Gas & Electric in San Francisco. And during George W. Bush's 2000 presidential campaign, Mould held senior positions in public and media relations at the Southern Company of Atlanta, the second-largest holding company of coal-burning utilities in the United States—and for that simple reason the nation's second-greatest emitter of carbon dioxide. During the 2000 campaign, the company's executive vice president was named a Ranger, signifying that he'd raised more than $200,000 for the Bush-Cheney ticket. That year, Southern's contributions to the Republican Party were exceeded only by Enron's. And in the years since the extraordinary Supreme Court decision that placed George W. Bush in office, Southern Company has distinguished itself as one of the most uncompromising foes of environmental regulation in the energy industry. To choose the most pertinent example, while other coal companies have at least begun to acknowledge that the burning of coal contributes to global warming, Southern continues to emphasize the supposed uncertainties in the science—much like the president, actually.

About a year after the shit storm, Mould's story of the pivotal phone call to Leslie McCarthy would go like this: there *was* no shit storm. He wasn't upset in the least that day. He wasn't even *aware* of the spot on *Good Morning America,* although he did feel that he had been surprised a few too many times in recent days by stories about Jim Hansen, and he figured Jim had been granting interviews without giving headquarters the professional courtesy of a heads-up. Mould wasn't into details, such as the fact that Jim, as perhaps the most respected climate scientist in the world, had just given a major speech that was subsequently picked up by news outlets. When he was told that Jim had actually given only one interview—minutes after his Keeling talk, when the BBC stuck a microphone in his face—Mould said, "You know what? I don't know what they were, and, you know, that's really hairsplitting."

Mould claims that *he* initiated the call to Leslie after seeing a story about the temperature record on that evening's network news. (This doesn't happen to square with Leslie's notes, which put the call at about 5:35 P.M. Network news doesn't begin until six thirty.) And the sole purpose of the call was to ask Leslie politely to adhere to the agency's heads-up policy, going forward. He says that he did write himself a note when he was surprised by her alleged remark about GISS being an independent organization, but he wasn't upset at that either. That's all.

Acosta's story is similar. No one was bent out of shape. Mould initiated the call. Acosta says that it *was* actually precipitated by the spot on *Good Morning America* and that it had nothing to do with all the media coverage about the Keeling talk, but this might be ascribed to a difference of memories. He quickly brings up Leslie's purported "independent organization" remark. When he is then presented with facts indicating that she and her Goddard colleagues *had* given a heads-up to George Deutsch and Dwayne Brown and that if *they* hadn't, ABC and the *Los Angeles Times* had, he gently explains that he and Mould weren't *accusing* Leslie of anything during the phone call. Like the good reporter he once had been, Dean was simply looking for the facts in an attempt to find out where the breakdown in communication had occurred. He doesn't have an answer, if fact finding was his motivation, as to why he didn't ask any questions of Deutsch during the call, why Deutsch didn't pipe up once, or why Leslie was not made aware of his or Jason Sharp's presence in the room. But Dean has an innocent explanation for every other issue that comes up, and a few that don't. He's not as smooth as David Mould. He's trying too hard.

In the document that George Deutsch prepared in advance for his testimony under oath to the House Oversight Committee in March 2007, he described headquarters' reaction to the *Good Morning America* spot. "Senior NASA officials—specifically Strategic Communications Director Joe Davis and Press Secretary Dean Acosta—conveyed to me that they were unaware of the release of this information being coordinated with Headquarters or peer reviewed. That day, NASA Headquarters received a deluge of media inquiries on the matter, inquiries Headquarters was ill-equipped to handle because no one had been briefed on Dr. Hansen's findings. The same senior NASA officials were, to say the least, upset by this procedural breach, and Mr. Acosta asked me to document these events in an internal 'PAO [Public Affairs Office] Point Paper.'"

In addition to being David Mould's boss, Joe Davis was one of his fellow alumni from the Energy Department. He had been Spencer Abraham's spokesperson when Abraham represented Michigan in the U.S. Senate and moved with his boss when Abraham became Bush's first energy secretary. As a senator, Abraham had led the effort to prevent the Clinton administration from increasing fuel economy in cars and light trucks, and he had sponsored two bills to authorize oil drilling in the Arctic National Wildlife Refuge as well as a third aimed at abolishing the Energy Department altogether.

In April 2006, Deutsch passed his point paper to the right-wing Cybercast News Service (CNSNews.com) and agreed to be interviewed for a hit piece on Jim. Dwayne Brown was interviewed as well. According to this article, "Deutsch said the NASA public affairs staff met with senior leaders at the agency to discuss the problems with Hansen, and the topic of firing Hansen was raised, but the conclusion from the meeting was that such an action would have 'huge political fallout,' so the idea was rejected." Marc Morano, the author of the piece, stands by his reporting on the existence of an actual meeting to discuss the firing of Jim Hansen and confirms that both Brown and Deutsch told him about it. I have been unable to determine which "senior leaders" took part in this meeting, but it seems unlikely that Administrator Michael Griffin would not have been involved. Brown would not discuss this topic with me, and Deutsch never responded to my numerous attempts to reach him.

As a so-called SES or Senior Executive Service employee, Jim Hansen did not have civil servant protection. His employment could have been terminated immediately.

As Dwayne Brown remembers the pivotal phone call on December 15, Leslie McCarthy "had the entire Washington public affairs management structure basically telling her, 'This ain't working, and we're holding you accountable to fix it along with Dwayne,' and when I got up there, what I heard was, all this was going to be documented [by] Dean . . . and I don't know if he ever did. I never saw anything." Remember, Dwayne had also heard Dean threaten to fire Jim earlier in the day.

The stories of Dean Acosta, David Mould, George Deutsch, Associate Administrator for the Science Mission Directorate Mary Cleave, and NASA Administrator Michael Griffin do not cohere in more ways than it seems necessary to catalog here.

Dwayne wasn't the only one who never saw the new gag orders on paper. Mould and Acosta did not keep their promise to put everything they had told Leslie and Mark Hess in writing, nor did Acosta ever arrange the promised meeting between himself, Hess, and David Mould. Hess's two e-mails remain the only attempt to put the orders in writing—and a futile one, because Mould and Acosta never responded to the e-mail he sent to them. Nor did Mary Cleave or anyone else at headquarters ever try to contact Jim. (This became a running joke. When Leslie or Larry Travis would pass him in the hall, they'd ask, "Get your counseling call today?" and he'd respond, "Nope. No calls today.")

The rules *had* been spoken, however; and Hess had documented them after a fashion, so they generated much discussion among the scientists, scientific managers, and public affairs officers at Goddard and GISS for the next couple of months. Of the three specific acts of censorship that had taken place in the days before Hess saw fit to write his memos—the diversion of the NPR interview, the diversion of the *Los Angeles Times* interview, and the delay of the GISS Web posting about the year's temperature—the scientists viewed the last as the more fundamental, as it seemed a blatant attempt by political appointees to assert control over the release of pure scientific data. In the phone calls to Leslie and Mark Hess, Mould and Acosta had also placed a strong emphasis on the requirement that headquarters approve all Web postings from Jim's institute specifically, even peer-reviewed journal articles. In some ways this was the crux of the matter. The release had only been delayed by about a day, but an important precedent had been set. It was now "an implemented procedure," as Jim points out.

"There were several days or a week or so when we were trying to obey these absurd demands," he says. If a reporter called him on the phone, for instance, would he "have to hang up and then tell headquarters and then call back after getting their approval?" What if another BBC reporter were to stick a microphone in his face? Would he have to say, "Wait a minute, I need to get permission before I can speak"? And if the folks at headquarters really wanted to approve every peer-reviewed journal article and every other type of Web posting from every NASA center in advance, they would need to add a few full-time staff members—perhaps even a whole department.

"It became clear," Jim writes, "that they likely would have some success in muzzling, as evidenced by: (1) They forced us to take down our announcement of temperature for 2005 and even the data itself. Instructions, one way or another, got to our webmaster without going through me. (This was one of the examples that began to be questioned—wasn't Public Affairs beginning to inject themselves into the GISS-Goddard chain of command inappropriately?) We could only put this data announcement back up after it was personally examined and approved by Associate Administrator Mary Cleave. She responded within twenty-four hours, much faster than the treatment we got previously on offending press releases, which could sit for weeks until they became stale. I assumed that the important thing for them in this case, since the data had already got out, was to set a precedent that everything must be approved, and once that procedure was in place they could slow things down whenever desired—and thereby achieve a self-policing effect: if we want to get anything through quickly, we had better make sure that it is not offensive. (2) They established the precedent of 'right of first refusal' when they chose to deny the NPR interview . . . so no interview was done, which was their preference, of course. (3) They demanded that Leslie report on my schedule details, no doubt again with various objectives including self-policing. (4) They put in place an attack dog, with little food, so that he would be as vicious as possible—they did not have time to keep track of every detail of what I was doing, but now with (over)enthusiastic political appointees all the way down to the energetic 'fresh-out' level, they finally had pretty comprehensive means to muzzle."

The aggressiveness of these tactics began pushing Jim toward his own tipping point.

Chapter 3

"A Dirty Little Secret"

JIM THOUGHT THINGS THROUGH as he spent the holidays with his wife, his children, and his grandchildren. He discussed the situation with Anniek, who had been against his speaking out even in the Keeling talk, "fearing a big disappointment and worse," she says. She had seen it before. "Jim's credibility would be attacked, and I would not be able to bear it. Truth is, everyone who knows Jim can vow that he never thinks of saying anything but the truth. Lack of inspiration, perhaps, but it is so." They agreed that if he lost his job she would go back to work.

Ethical considerations also played a role in Jim's deliberations. All federal employees are required to take annual Web-based training exercises on ethics, and he decided this might be a good time to take them. Ironically, one pertained to the No Fear Act, which had been signed into law by the current president. The act calls for all federal employees to be notified of their rights under discrimination and whistleblower laws as well as their right to freedom from retaliatory actions such as firing or demotion for whistleblowing and similar activities. As he went through the exercises, Jim came across words such as *honesty, ethical behavior,* and *candor,* and he was reminded that government service is a public trust. He also discovered that the first line in NASA's mission statement was "to understand and protect our home planet." He would use this line frequently in the coming months.

At the start of the new year, he took the plainly appropriate first step: he discussed the new rules with his supervisor at Goddard, Franco Einaudi, and Einaudi's supervisor, Laurie Leshin. "It would be difficult to exaggerate the potential damage that could be caused by screening and controlling scientific information on climate change provided to the American public, in my opinion," he wrote to his supervisors. ". . . If NASA is to fulfill its mission of providing information that helps the public and policymakers understand and protect our home planet, if it is to uphold its public trust with integrity, it cannot knuckle under to political pressures."

Einaudi and Leshin supported him, and he knew they were trying to help, "but going through the bureaucracy never works very well," he writes. "At best you get a little salve, but at the expense of enormous energy and time—the good always gets dragged down by the bureaucracy."

In spite of his reputation for "outspokenness" (a word that would probably never come up if he worked for a university, rather than the government), Jim generally prefers not to go public, as it takes time away from his scientific work. "But there have been a few times when I get pushed to the edge," he writes, "and it seemed this was going to be one." He began to realize that he was going to have to defy the new rules and "make an issue of the matter."

Jim had actually been walking the political edge for about a year, as we shall see. This had given him the resolve to add some of the more controversial dots to his Keeling talk in the first place. But it is a measure of his reluctance that it had been about sixteen years since he had really crossed the line. That was in 1989, the first year in office of the current president's father, when then senator Al Gore asked Jim to testify at a hearing of the Senate Subcommittee on Science, Technology and Space, which Gore chaired. Jim had just published a paper in the *Journal of Geophysical Research* that concluded that the greenhouse effect was changing climate. He stated this conclusion in the written testimony he prepared in advance for the committee, a document that would be entered into the *Congressional Record.* Before the hearing, however, political appointees in the Office of Management and Budget rewrote his main conclusion to state that the cause was unknown.

Jim had made headlines once or twice before this time, especially with the legendary remark mentioned at the beginning of this book about how the greenhouse effect was here and was affecting our climate now. But in May 1989, he produced what have arguably been the most explosive headlines of his career by appearing in person before Gore's committee to disavow the testimony that had been rewritten by his bureaucratic overseers. Gore had informed the media in advance of OMB's editing job, and it was the lead story on all the major television networks that night.

But Jim found those first brushes with the media limelight—as well as the tendency among politicians to try to put words in his mouth—to be disconcerting. After the OMB experience, he decided to bow out of politics and the media and focus on science. He began declining all requests from the broadcast media and most requests from the print media, with the main exception, occasionally, of *The New York Times*.

A few years into this media boycott, he demonstrated the nonpartisan nature of his focus on science by angering Mr. Gore as well. Early in Gore's tenure as vice president, Jim refused a White House request to rebut a *New York Times* op-ed critical of Gore that had been written by a global warming skeptic. By that time, Jim felt Gore was spinning the science in the other direction, violating what he calls the "Feynman admonition" by seeing global warming everywhere he looked.

Jim often invokes a quote from the legendary physicist Richard Feynman to explain his own scientific philosophy: "The only way to have real success in science . . . is to describe the evidence very carefully without regard to the way you feel it should be. If you have a theory, you must try to explain what's good about it and what's bad about it equally. In science you learn a kind of standard integrity and honesty." Larry Travis points out that this approach "leaks" into Jim's ethical deliberations as well.

Jim still believes he took a greater risk in defying Gore than he did in defying George Bush the father—or than he might, this time around, in defying George Bush the son. Since Gore was nominally on Jim's side, Jim believes, it would have cost him much less political capital to fire him than it would have cost either of the Bushes. "The thing is, damn it, administrations think that federal employees are working for them," says Jim. "They don't think federal employees are working for the taxpayer."

*   *   *

So, it is an odd coincidence that Al Gore happened to phone Jim exactly one day after Mark Hess sent his memo off to Mould and Acosta. The call came in at about nine in the evening, as Jim was still gauging the depth of his new dilemma. It found him working in his office, as usual. This was the first contact between the two men in more than ten years.

Gore was working on a slide show about global warming that he had been presenting around the world for a number of years, and he wanted Jim to review it for scientific accuracy. He also had some specific questions about the 2005 temperature data, and he asked if Jim would be willing to meet early in January, when Gore was planning to come to New York to visit his daughter. Jim agreed to the meeting.

But the first item on Jim's calendar for the new year was the interview with *60 Minutes* that had been brewing since summer—although it had now evolved from the simple personality profile that had originally been planned. However, the attack dog was still on the scent. According to Leslie's notes, George Deutsch told her at least once in the days leading up to the interview that it would not be allowed. Putting aside her misgivings about the very premise of such a statement, she reminded him that she had been keeping headquarters informed ever since the initial contact from CBS and that Jim had received "permission" numerous times.

There followed a petty subplot involving headquarters' desire to tape the interview. For copyright reasons, CBS balked at this request—it would take them a while to air the show, and they didn't want to be scooped—but headquarters insisted: no tape, no story. Mark Hess stepped into the fray and worked out a deal with the legal office at Goddard whereby GISS could make a tape for "personal use only." The task fell to Leslie, and in the segment that eventually aired, correspondent Scott Pelley made note of this perhaps intimidating tactic as the camera panned to her. (For reasons that were never understood, Leslie's tape recorder malfunctioned during the first of Jim's two interviews, and when she confessed this to headquarters, they "went crazy," in her words. She mentioned her predicament to a member of the film crew during the second session, and he graciously arranged to get her a copy of their audio track.)

Jim spent the morning of the first interview, January 5, 2006, in his apartment, completing his e-mail about ethics to Einaudi and Leshin. He remembers feeling nervous as he walked the few blocks to his office for the filming. "I wondered if I shouldn't just talk about the science, but then I decided, 'To hell with this. This has got to be illegal.' I would be blunt and not hold anything back."

"You believe that the administration is censoring what you can say to the public?" asked Pelley to open the spot.

"Well, they're censoring whether or not I can say it," Jim answered precisely. He paused. "I mean, I say what I believe if I'm allowed to say it. . . .

"In my more than three decades in the government I've never witnessed such restrictions on the ability of scientists to communicate with the public."

Thus, after sixteen years, he crossed back in to the hurly-burly of the American discourse.

E-mail to Leslie McCarthy, Monday, January 9, 2006: "Could you please send us the entire transcript and/or the audio cassette tape from last week's *60 Minutes* interview with Dr. James Hansen? Management has requested it, and I left you voice mail to this effect. Thanks in advance, George Deutsch." ("'Management.' There are never names used," Leslie observes.) The e-mail was copied to Dwayne Brown and another career public affairs officer, but not to David Mould or Dean Acosta.

Over the phone, however, Deutsch insisted that Dean "had to have the tape transcript right away." But as Goddard's general counsel understood it, the agreement with CBS did not extend to headquarters, so Mark Hess paid for a transcript out of his budget. Leslie remembers him saying, "I'm going to hold it on my desk until Dean calls me, and if Dean calls me, then we'll have to get the headquarters and the Goddard general counsels together and they can work out the legalese about who gets it and when."

Dean never called.

In the days following the *60 Minutes* interview, headquarters began insisting that all interviews given by all GISS scientists be taped. Leslie simply refused. Mark Hess backed her with the argument that if they didn't have to do it at Goddard, they shouldn't have to do it at GISS. The pestering was carried out by George Deutsch, of course, who again claimed to be speaking for Dean Acosta. "Hansen is extremely disrespectful of government," he declared to Leslie over the phone. "This belief is shared by management." She recalls that in the many calls that came in during those days, Deutsch "kept quoting Dean." "Dean is asking about this. Dean wants to know what Jim Hansen said about what's been going on."

So Jim ended his sixteen-year boycott of the broadcast media in an interview with *60 Minutes.* But CBS took a while to put the spot together, as they had predicted. This was not the way the public learned about censorship at NASA. The tipping point in the public mind would be reached in a different way.

Jim met with Al Gore on the day after the first interview. Gore had wanted to drop by Jim's office, but Jim explained that he preferred to meet at Gore's hotel, the Regency on Park Avenue—famous for its power breakfasts as Jim discovered. They actually met for lunch, and the first thing Gore asked was "What's the matter? Am I radioactive?"

"Well, yeah, probably you are."

For, in a perverse way, Jim was still following the unwritten orders he had received from Mould and Acosta. He wasn't quite sure where he stood, and he was acutely aware that he did not have civil servant protection. He told Gore about having to give headquarters advance notice of his schedule but pointed out that he "didn't think that it was necessary to report when I went to the bathroom or out to lunch."

Gore quickly told him that he "wanted to apologize," presumably for his anger ten years earlier; but Jim cut him off: "Your insight was better than mine." He says he was "taken aback" by Gore's apology, and he now regrets cutting him off, because he'd still like to know exactly what Gore wanted to apologize for. He had simply stopped hearing from the White House when he had balked at their requests a decade earlier. There had been no explanation.

Since the planet had continued to warm in the intervening decade, Jim could now see through the lens of science what he realized Gore had accurately perceived through intuition. He believes the vice president "just assumed that the system is more sensitive than scientists are giving it credit for. Somehow, and in a sense, he was right, but you can't get to that conclusion that way. You've got to get to the conclusion by analyzing the science." Thus, if he were faced with the same situation today that Gore presented him with more than a decade ago, his deep belief in the Feynman admonition would probably lead him to respond in the same way.

They talked about their grandchildren, which neither had had on their last acquaintance; and as they stood to leave, Gore introduced Jim to the pair at the next table, talk show host Larry King and Norman Pearlstine, who had just stepped down from the position of editor in chief at Time Inc., the subsidiary of Time Warner that owns *Time* and other magazines. Jim remembers that when King heard what he did for a living, he said, "Nobody cares about fifty years from now." But when Gore mentioned the new restrictions, particularly the demand that Jim give headquarters advance notice of his schedule, Pearlstine, who was still acting as an adviser to Time Warner, asked Jim if he would be willing to go public with the story. Jim said he would. Pearlstine asked if he would let his name be used. Jim promised to send him a memo with the details.

He worked on it over the weekend. "I attach memos (A, B, C) that explain the administrative 'house arrest' (my phrase) that I am under regarding contact with media." Memos A and B were Mark Hess's two e-mails. Memo C was the e-mail on ethics Jim had sent to Einaudi and Leshin. There was also plenty of science in the thick package that Anniek delivered by hand to the Time Inc. offices on Monday the ninth of January, including a copy of the Keeling talk.

But it seems that *Time* didn't quite know what to do with the story. The package was passed down the line and finally landed in the hands of a science writer who called Jim about doing an interview on global warming sometime in the indefinite future. The censorship aspect was lost along the way. The tipping point wasn't reached this way, either.

During the week after his interview with *60 Minutes,* unaware that the transcript was lying on Mark Hess's desk unread by headquarters, Jim sent e-mails to a few other well-known climate scientists at NASA to ask if they were willing to step forward and describe instances of editing and intimidation involving their own work that had become more or less common knowledge around Goddard, GISS, and the Jet Propulsion Laboratory (JPL) in the previous year. (These are NASA's three main centers for climate research. JPL is located in Pasadena, California.) "I understand that some people at NASA HQ are likely to explode when they hear the tapes of what I said in an interview with *60 Minutes,*" he wrote. "In my chagrin about being censored I have gone pretty far out on a limb, and had better try to collect evidence to support the criticisms." His recipients voiced support for what he was doing, but they had nothing more to offer. One later admitted that he kept his silence out of fear that he might lose funding for a project he had been working on for a few decades—most of his career. This individual had seen how Al Gore had thrown his weight around when he was vice president, and he always kept his head down when politics came into play.

I have asked two of these scientists if they thought Jim might have scared himself with his outspokenness. Neither concurred. They agree that he doesn't scare easily.

On January 18, Jim was summoned out of a meeting at Goddard Space Flight Center in Greenbelt to answer a phone call from Goddard's director, Ed Weiler, who was actually calling from NASA headquarters in Washington. Mark Hess had, of course, briefed Weiler as the December events had unfolded, and while Weiler will generally defend the right of a NASA scientist to speak to reporters at every chance he gets, he advised Jim to stick to science and not stray into policy in an upcoming interview with Juliet Eilperin, the lead global warming reporter for *The Washington Post.*

"They were claiming that I was speaking about policy, which, of course, they didn't like," Jim remembers. "And, of course, that *is* the basic issue here." This puts him in mind of an incident that took place in 2003, involving a GISS climate modeler named David Rind. A Goddard scientist had just published a paper about the remarkable warming trend that is presently under way in the Arctic, and Rind had been asked to join a panel for a press conference on the subject. Before the press arrived, public affairs decided to hold a rehearsal.

As Rind remembers it, a few NASA folks who "happened to be just hanging around in the auditorium" began asking questions. "One person said as a question to me, 'Can the U.S. do anything to affect what's going on here?' And I said that, given that the U.S. is responsible for twenty-five percent of the greenhouse gas emissions, it would seem obvious that the U.S. could do something about it. At which point, this [public affairs officer] in the back stood up and said, 'That is a completely unacceptable answer!' So my response to that was, 'If you don't want that answer, don't give me that question.' So they said, 'Okay, this is what we'll do. All questions will be funneled through Waleed [Abdalati, the moderator of the panel, who would innocently acquiesce to a request from George Deutsch to speak to the *Los Angeles Times* about two years later]. If there is any question that seems to have policy implications, Waleed will respond that "these are scientists; that is a policy question. Next question please."'"

For better or worse, the question never came up during the actual press conference, which was filmed for NASA TV and ended up being the most widely reported "Earth Science Update" the agency had ever produced. It was picked up by CBS, *The New York Times,* the Associated Press, the *Los Angeles Times,* and *The Washington Post,* and it reached people as far away as India and Iran, for an estimated audience of 12 to 15 million people.

"That's the whole point," says Jim. "They're just trying to cut off the flow of information to the public. The public has no interest in technical scientific detail. It has no relevance to the real world—their real world. So Weiler was delivering this message, and I said, 'Yeah, yeah, whatever.' But it doesn't solve the problem, because there is no sharp line, and there's no way that I'm going to agree to mask the implications of the science. I mean, that's the basic argument that we're having."

At the most basic level, Weiler agreed with Jim. He even said, "We may have to put our positions on the line." But he added, strangely, "I'm not giving you any instruction here." Jim laughs at that comment because he's pretty sure Weiler was telling him that he didn't want to read about their conversation in *The New York Times*.

Administrator Michael Griffin may have encouraged Weiler to call Jim. Weiler has a vague memory of speaking to Griffin sometime before placing it, and he was calling from headquarters, after all. Jim, for his part, doesn't think Weiler would have relayed such a message "based on some lower-level person suggesting that he do that."

In a telephone conversation the following evening, Thursday, January 19, Jim's supervisor, Franco Einaudi, advised him to ignore the new restrictions altogether. But the next day, Jim replied by e-mail that this didn't "seem viable." On top of the advice he had just received from Weiler, he understood from the December phone calls and Hess's subsequent e-mails that both Griffin and Mary Cleave, the associate administrator for the Science Mission, had been "brought into or informed about the matter."

"Surely it is all right to mention the restrictions that Public Affairs is placing us under," Jim wrote in closing. "They would not expect this to be kept as a dirty little secret."

Meanwhile, he sought legal advice through the First Amendment Center, a nonprofit in Arlington, Virginia. "What are my rights?" he asked. "When I became a federal employee, did I forfeit my right to free speech on such matters? Am I within my rights if I speak with a journalist and specifically indicate that the information or opinions that I express are my own, and not agency or administration policy?"

No response. Legally, he seemed to be on his own.

The discussion continued with more phone calls and at least one more memo to Einaudi, in which Jim attempted to provide "a clear demonstration showing that our research inherently gets us into a gray area between science and policy." He pointed out that the Bush administration had seemed quite interested in the policy implications of his work during its first months in office.

"I was asked to speak twice in 2001 to the Administration's Task Force on Energy and Climate, chaired by the Vice President and including six Cabinet members, the EPA Administrator, and the National Security Advisor." (Yes, Dick Cheney himself sought Jim's advice.) "The policymakers clearly encourage us to provide as much policy-relevant information as we can, including comparison of alternative scenarios for future climate forcings. These scenarios implicitly and explicitly compare simulated effects of alternative policy choices."

But with the Bush administration ignoring the nearly unanimous warnings of climatologists not only in this country but worldwide, he pointed out, "The situation is analogous to that faced by an engineer who spots a flaw in the Space Shuttle, but finds his complaint ignored by management. He has the right, and responsibility, to make his concern known to the highest authority. In our case the spacecraft carries billions of humans and other life forms, and the highest authority, the only authority with the power to throttle the engine, is the public."

Franco Einaudi recalls advising, ultimately, "Do what your conscience tells you to do."

It was a strange time. On the twentieth of January, as it began to appear that *Time* magazine would let the story slip, Jim gave roughly the same information to an old contact, Andrew Revkin, the lead global warming correspondent for *The New York Times.* On the twenty-fourth, Larry Travis was hit and severely injured by a truck as he walked across Broadway on his way to work. Jim's car was also broken into around that time, and the house in New Jersey in which he and Anniek had raised their children burned to the ground. Darnell Cain, Jim's assistant, admits to being "sufficiently lazy and negligent to not update the NASA public records with Jim's new address when he moved to Pennsylvania, so the New Jersey address was on record still. . . . As a matter of fact, Makiko [Sato, a GISS scientist] and I told Jim . . . 'We all better watch our backs on the way to work.'"

On the other hand, while lying on his hospital bed, Larry gave Andy Revkin permission to use his words and his name, figuring he didn't have much more to lose since he'd already been hit by one truck.

Revkin broke the story on *The New York Times* Web site at midday on Saturday the twenty-eighth, and it landed on the front page of Sunday's print edition.

Mould and Acosta had done a good job covering their tracks. Revkin had seen Hess's memos and talked to him, Leslie McCarthy, and Larry Travis (a few days before his accident), but in his rush to make deadline, Andy's story devolved into a sort of debate between Jim Hansen and George Deutsch—as represented by Dean Acosta. ("Acosta shielded Deutsch completely from getting in touch with me," Revkin claims.)

The basic facts were there: that all Web postings now had to be cleared, that Jim had been told to provide headquarters with his schedule and so on, and that the NPR interview request had been denied; but it appeared that Acosta had played no role, and Mould wasn't even mentioned. Revkin quoted Acosta as saying that no one had tried to silence Jim. "That's not the way we operate here at NASA," Mr. Acosta said. "We promote openness and we speak with the facts." He presented the media restrictions as standard operating procedure for all NASA personnel and said the reasons for reviewing interview requests were, as Revkin wrote, "to have an orderly flow of information out of a sprawling agency and to avoid surprises." "This is not about any individual or any issue like global warming," Acosta stated reassuringly. "It's about coordination."

Revkin remembers that Leslie "was not willing to go on the record right up till like Friday." ("It wasn't that I wasn't willing. It was more of an 'able' issue," she responds.) Friday afternoon when Revkin presented her story to Acosta, and Acosta responded with his remark about openness, Revkin quickly saw an opening. "I said, 'There are midlevel people who would like to talk with me on the record in support of Hansen, and you're saying that you're all about openness, so obviously you'll let me speak to them on the record, and you'll say that in print, that no harm would come to them?' . . . He said yes, of course, because he'd kind of backed himself into a corner, essentially, which was kind of fun, and then luckily she had the guts to go with that fairly fragile sense of job security—whatever job security—that would provide."

Leslie courageously read from her notes as Deutsch characterized NPR as the "most liberal" media outlet in the country and asserted that his job was to "make the president look good."

"I'm a career civil servant and Jim Hansen is a scientist," she said. "That's not our job. That's not our mission. The inference was that Hansen was disloyal."

In Revkin's opinion, it was not Jim's "outspokenness" but the willingness of a typically silent midlevel civil servant to go on the record that caught his editor's attention and propelled the story to top of the front page.

Acosta told Revkin that Deutsch had "flatly denied saying anything of the sort" and pointed out innocently that he, himself, "had no way of judging who was telling the truth."

Chapter 4

"... Because the White House Has a No Surprises Rule"

AMONG THOSE UNCONVINCED BY DEUTSCH/ACOSTA'S ARGUMENTS was Representative Sherwood Boehlert, who was then chairman of the House Science Committee and probably the staunchest defender of scientific integrity in the Republican majority at the time. Boehlert was visiting his home state of New York that weekend. Upon reading Revkin's article on Sunday morning, he swiftly called the chief of staff of his committee, David Goldston, and told him he wanted "to do something on this right away." Starting Monday morning, Goldston and his staff placed calls to various senior managers on the Ninth Floor, including the top public affairs officers, Acosta, Mould, and Joe Davis; Griffin's chief of staff, Paul Morrell; and the newly appointed deputy administrator of NASA, Griffin's second-in-command, Shana Dale. That afternoon, Goldston drafted a letter for Mr. Boehlert and sent it to Griffin himself. The committee also produced a press release.

"Good science cannot long persist in an atmosphere of intimidation," Boehlert advised the administrator. "NASA is clearly doing something wrong, given the sense of intimidation felt by Dr. Hansen and others who work with him. Even if this sense is a result of a misinterpretation of NASA policies—and more seems to be at play here—the problem still must be corrected. I will be following this matter closely to ensure that the right staff and policies are in place at NASA to encourage open discussion of critical scientific issues. I assume you share that goal. . . . I would ask that you swiftly provide to the Committee, in writing, a clear statement of NASA's policies governing the activities of its scientists."

The Senate took a while longer to pick up the ball, but when it did, it focused specifically on what Jim sees as the essential question, a scientist's right—and indeed responsibility—to discuss the policy implications of his work. About two weeks after Boehlert sent his letter, Chairman Susan Collins of the Senate Homeland Security and Governmental Affairs Committee and ranking Democrat Joseph Lieberman sent their own letter to Griffin, in which they took issue with an assertion by Dean Acosta, reported by Revkin, "that policy statements should be left to policy makers and appointed spokesmen."

Alluding to some "extremely informative" testimony that Jim had given to their committee in 2001, the senators wrote, "Maintaining the integrity of science is essential both to scientific inquiry and to the policy-making process. To that end, we believe scientists should be free to discuss both the results and implications of their research with the scientific community, policy-makers, and the American public, and to do so in a manner fully reflective of the analysis and conclusions resulting from their work."

They closed by echoing the line from the agency's mission statement that had also intrigued Jim. "We look forward to working with you to ensure NASA's continued contributions to the understanding and protection of our planet."

Michael Griffin was on a ski vacation in Colorado when the story broke. One of his first impulses was to send an e-mail to Ed Weiler. All the top officials at NASA are provided with BlackBerrys, and this seems to be Griffin's preferred mode of communication.

Weiler "hates to admit this," but he read Griffin's message on his own BlackBerry as he was driving on U.S. Route 50 in Washington. With "one eye on the road, in cruise control," he shot back a message that he'd call Griffin the moment he got home, "because, frankly, an issue like this you're not going to explain with your thumbs on a BlackBerry." About fifteen minutes later, he reached Griffin in his hotel room.

"The first words out of his mouth were 'Ed, what the hell's going on here? I've been hearing all these stories. What's going on?' And I laid it out to him. I said, 'Mike, I think we've got a problem at headquarters public affairs' . . . and I gave Mike some examples . . . and Mike's reaction was, you know, I can't describe it in public, heh, heh, but he was pretty pissed off about it—and on the right side, I might add. . . .

"Mike was in gaga land on this one. I can say that unequivocally."

Two of the examples Weiler gave to Griffin that day had nothing to do with climate. They came closer to Weiler's own field of astronomy. One involved a personal and elective interest that George Deutsch—and, it seems, Dean Acosta—had taken in cosmology.

For about three weeks back in October, Deutsch's first boss in Science, Dolores Beasley, had been assigned to the Federal Emergency Management Agency (FEMA) in response to the Katrina disaster. While she was gone, Deutsch—who was all of twenty-four years old and had no background in science—had offered some fatherly advice to a science writer named Flint Wild, who was working on a NASA Web site about Albert Einstein.

"Okay, Flint, we've got a slight problem here," Deutch wrote in an e-mail. "These pieces . . . refer to the 'big bang' as if it were law. As you know, the theory that the universe was created by a 'big bang' is just that—a theory. . . . First of all, we have been given direction by our Deputy AA [assistant administrator; that would be Dean Acosta] that we are never to refer to the big bang as anything but a theory. . . .

"Secondly, it is not NASA's place, nor should it be, to make a declaration such as this about the existence of the universe that discounts intelligent design by a creator. . . . We, as NASA, must be diligent here, because this is more than a science issue, it is a religious issue. And I would hate to think that young people would only be getting one half of this debate from NASA."

The e-mail made the rounds, and when Beasley returned from her FEMA detail, she heard about it from several scientists. One asked if it was now NASA policy to include intelligent design in press releases.

"Hell no!" she responded. "That's crazy. Where are you getting this from?" When the scientist showed her the e-mail, she called Deutsch into her office, shut the door, and said, "Look . . ."

Weiler says he also "went ballistic on that one." He had been disturbed as well by an incident in mid-January that seems not, for a change, to have involved Deutsch directly. In a draft press release about a recent discovery by NASA's Spitzer Space Telescope of what appeared to be comet dust surrounding a collapsed star called a white dwarf, a Goddard astrophysicist named Marc Kuchner was quoted as saying, "We are seeing the ghost of a star that was once a lot like our sun. . . . I cringed when I saw the data because it probably reflects the grim but very distant future of our own planets and solar system." The scientists involved had written the draft in collaboration with the public affairs staff at the Jet Propulsion Laboratory, which manages the Spitzer project.

Headquarters removed Kuchner's quote from the release after Erica Hupp, who worked with Deutsch and Dwayne Brown, explained in an e-mail to JPL that "NASA is not in the habit of frightening the public with doom and gloom scenarios." Never mind that the notion that the sun stands to run out of fuel in about 5 billion years has been standard fare in astronomy textbooks for about half a century.

While Griffin may have expressed anger and surprise to one of his top scientific managers, it seems that he did not communicate similar sentiments to public affairs—nor make much of an attempt to rein them in. They continued, as Dwayne Brown might have put it, to "talk smack."

David Mould took the unusual step of attending Dean Acosta's daily 9:30 A.M. staff meeting on Monday morning, January 30, the day after Revkin's article, to announce that Deutsch "did not say those things." And on Wednesday, Dwayne Brown forwarded an e-mail to a long list of public affairs officers at NASA centers around the country, making a number of points, two of which stated for the first time in writing the policies that many of the civil servants saw as restrictive: "Any NASA employee speaking on the record, issuing a press release, or posting information on our website, must coordinate such activities with the Office of Public Affairs. No exceptions"; and "Media interview requests related to science coming from a major network/cable station, major daily newspaper/magazine/publication or radio program should be coordinated with me prior to the interview."

Meanwhile, David Goldston of the House Science Committee pressed forward with his investigation. His notes from a conference call on Monday with Mould; Acosta; Paul Morrell; Mould's boss, Joe Davis; and others record a comment by Acosta, in quotes, regarding December 15, the day of the shit storm: "Hansen was on ABC and Griffin wanted to know why." Since Acosta has also stated that Morrell and Davis told him of their dismay at being surprised by Bill Blakemore's *Good Morning America* spot on the morning of the fifteenth, the statement Acosta made to Goldston would seem to indicate that Griffin was not totally "in gaga land on this one," although it doesn't say anything about his knowledge of the details.

Acosta denies saying this to Goldston.

It seems that the severity of the situation had not yet dawned on Acosta. He was acting cocky that first week of February. On Thursday, the second, he told reporter Brian Berger of the trade publication *Space News* that neither he nor David Mould had ever received Mark Hess's e-mail. When Berger showed it to him, however, he called it "pretty consistent" with NASA's public affairs policy, "except where it talks about giving Cleave and Hartman the right of first refusal on interview requests."

Acosta told Berger, "When you get into [the part about] Mary Cleave and Colleen Hartman, obviously Jim Hansen is under their organization. The mission directorate leadership certainly has the prerogative to designate who they feel are the appropriate spokespeople on a subject matter."

In other words, he was giving credit to the science managers for diverting the NPR interview. This would indeed become his argument. Mary Cleave denies it.

According to Acosta, then, not only were Leslie McCarthy and Mark Hess misrepresenting the phone conversations of mid-December, but

Hess had circulated a fake e-mail behind headquarters' back. Further-more, and possibly because the statements Berger attributed to him would contradict others he made later, Acosta presently denies even that Berger showed him the e-mail. "Not sure how Brian [Berger] could have shown me a document, such as any e-mail, during a phone call," Acosta writes. "I'm certain he did not give me a copy of this so-called 'Hess e-mail.' . . . [The article] badly mischaracterizes what we said and misrep-resents anything we were trying to do—which was basic coordination of communications and nothing more." If Acosta is to be believed, he is sur-rounded by liars.

Mr. Berger stands by his reporting.

Jim may well have worked more than his usual eighty hours that week. In mid-January, he had included Rick Piltz, a former employee of the U.S. Climate Change Science Program, on the distribution list for an e-mail about the 2005 temperature data. Piltz had anticipated the present frenzy with his own appearance on the front page of *The New York Times* the previous June, when he had taken public a set of documents that revealed a comprehensive effort by White House officials to spin and doctor the scientific underpinnings of climate-related reports by the Environmental Protection Agency, the Climate Change Science Program, and other fed-eral bureaucracies.

Piltz responded to Jim's e-mail by pointing out that they would soon be appearing together on *60 Minutes*. He also informed Jim of a "watch-dog project called Climate Science Watch" that he had just set up "with the mission of holding public officials accountable for the integrity with which they use climate science and related research." Thus, on the Friday before Revkin broke his story, Jim sent Piltz the memos he had provided to Revkin and Pearlstine, in one of which he mentioned his failed attempt at getting legal assistance.

"Hi Rick, I have been absolutely snowed this week—Larry Travis get-ting hit by a truck (he will survive and be put back in shape)—plus stuff re attached memos, which may be of interest. Jim."

When Piltz saw Revkin's story hit *The New York Times* Web site on Saturday afternoon, January 28, he suggested to Jim that he seek legal help from the group he himself had used, the Government Accountability Project, the leading whistleblower protection organization in Washington, which also happened to be sponsoring his watchdog project.

Bill Blakemore contacted Jim the next day, Sunday, when the story appeared in print, and interviewed him on camera in his office at GISS for a spot that ran that evening on *World News Tonight*. Then, the following Friday, Jim finally gave the interview to NPR's *On Point* that had been denied by headquarters more than eight weeks earlier. He sought permission for neither.

The latter made for stunning radio. Tom Ashbrook, the host and interviewer, opened gleefully, "The media James Hansen was trying to talk to? Well, yes, it was NPR, but more specifically, it was us—*On Point*!"

Jim was charting new territory even for himself here, and what made this broadcast especially riveting was the obvious discomfort and hesitation in his voice as he was led by a direct and savvy journalist through a legal and political minefield that might well have resulted in just the "dire consequences" that had been threatened at the beginning of this adventure.

Early in the show, Ashbrook asked if Jim was afraid for his job.

"Well, yeah, I'm concerned," Jim replied, and laughed nervously. "The last few days I've been talking to counsel." . . .

"Are you now off the reservation?"

"Until I get an instruction in writing that tells me I can't talk to you, I am going to continue to speak out."

Ashbrook pointed out that he had originally requested the interview as a result of reading Jim's Keeling talk. "What turned our heads," he said, "was your saying we may be nearing a tipping point for the biggest change in climate in half a million years that would leave us with a different planet, and that if we don't act in this decade, which is increasingly growing short, it may be inevitable. Have we got you right on that?"

"Ah, yeah."

Jim sounded awkward and preoccupied as he toed the indistinct line between science and policy. He had made his usual disclaimer at the beginning of the broadcast that he was speaking as a private citizen and not representing NASA or the government, but at this delicate time, facing dismissal, he held back in a way that he rarely does. He was careful not to disagree openly with the Bush administration's policies, although he did reflect upon their implications from the dispassionate view of science. For example, when Ashbrook played a short excerpt from Bush's recent State of the Union address in which the president had outlined new initiatives for greenhouse-friendly energy technologies, none of which had any chance of coming online within a decade, Jim avoided saying anything about the policy per se, while pointing out that climate would pass the tipping point before Bush's initiatives could possibly have an effect.

He spoke haltingly but with great clarity, once drawing a surprised laugh from Ashbrook by asking him to repeat a particularly hazardous question. This was clearly not a performer, and it may have been just this that imparted such impact over the airwaves.

Reflecting upon the television spot the previous Sunday, Blakemore remarks that when "you see a guy there quietly saying, 'It was only on the phone, and I was told there would be dire consequences,'" it adds a "natural sensual fullness to what had only been in print. . . . He's transparently full of integrity. . . . You get the feeling that this is a guy to whom it wouldn't even occur to lie."

Jim has a plain, Midwestern way of speaking. He was born in 1941 on a farm in remote Charter Oak township in southwestern Iowa, the fifth child and first boy of seven children. His father, whose formal education ended with eighth grade, worked as a tenant farmer, paying the rent with a portion of the crops he raised on small farms. The small farm was becoming less and less viable at that time, and the family often moved. When Jim was about four, his father finally gave up and moved them into a tiny house in the small town of Denison, supporting them first through bartending and then as a janitor in the hospital. Jim's mother worked as a waitress in a local fixture that still exists named Cronk's Café.

Even in town, Jim says, "we still had an outhouse, we had no refrigerator, it was still a very meager existence." The seven children slept in two rooms. After a couple of years, "we had a septic tank put in with a toilet in the basement and a sink in the kitchen, which also served as the place to wash, wash hair, et cetera. We survived that way until I was in high school, when a bathroom was added upstairs."

He feels lucky to have grown up "in a simpler place and time." When he was in third grade, his sister gave him part of her paper route for the *Omaha World-Herald,* a job he would keep through the end of high school, taking on larger and larger routes and finally becoming a distributor for the paper. This is how he saved for college.

Jim was and remains a huge sports fan. He played basketball and baseball as a kid, and he followed the Sioux City Siouxs, a baseball team from that nearby town, on the radio. He also followed a Yankees AAA farm team named the Kansas City Blues, when he could. Having had the pleasure of hearing an Oklahoma sensation named Mickey Mantle play with the Blues for a month or so just before leaving for a life of fame and glory in Yankee Stadium, Jim admits to being an "extreme Yankee fan."

"I could hear Kansas City sometimes, depending on the weather. They had a Murderers' Row with Bill Skowron, Bob Cerv, and Mantle for a short time. I knew of him before Kansas City because he was already much ballyhooed by 1951, when I was ten, and therefore strongly booed whenever he came to the plate, at least on the road. I would buy glossy baseball magazines with him on the cover—fifty cents, which was a lot for me, because I was pretty frugal—at the Candy Kitchen, attached to the Ritz Theater, where the lobby was decorated with Donna Reed photos. [Actress Donna Reed was born in Denison.] . . . I cut out box scores (Yankees only) and did Yankee statistics from about age ten to junior high."

Until he was in high school and the family got their first TV, he and his younger brother sometimes skipped school to watch the World Series on the set in the lobby of the Denison Hotel. Jim still spends the lion's share of the scant moments he dedicates to the newspaper of a morning, before diving into work, on the sports page.

He was a lackadaisical student, but he tested well and always earned the highest scores in his class in math and science. One of his sisters tells him that when he was in seventh grade, everyone in his school, which went through twelfth, was given an IQ test, and Jim got either the highest score or tied for the highest. The pithy character summation that appears near his senior photograph in the 1959 Denison High School yearbook reads, "Wisdom comes naturally." His scientific career would unfold with simplicity as well.

On the basis of his test scores, he was awarded a scholarship to the University of Iowa. Tuition was free, but room and board wasn't, and freshmen were required to live in a dormitory that cost $1,000 for the year. This ate up half his savings. He managed to get through the final three years without having to do too much work on the side by renting a room for $25 a month and providing for his own food.

He often employs the word *lucky* in connection with his life in Iowa. He was lucky that the state had such a strong educational system; he was lucky that his test scores overcame his grades and earned him a college scholarship; and he was lucky at the University of Iowa "to come under the personal influence" of the legendary James Van Allen, chairman of the department of physics and astronomy.

"Van Allen was such a gentle man," Jim writes, "calm demeanor, not in a hurry, smoking his pipe, curious about how things worked. In retrospect he was an incredible role model, one who can be emulated but not reproduced. I don't see how he could be so calm and aware of others, yet so productive scientifically."

Van Allen would become Jim's mentor and remain a powerful influence for more than forty years. (He died in August 2006, six months after Jim's muzzling hit the headlines.) Surprisingly, however, Jim never took a course with the great man. He says he lacked confidence. "I didn't want him to know how ignorant I was."

In his junior year, in a general astronomy course taught by Professor Satoshi Matsushima, Jim became friends with a fellow student named Andy Lacis, who had transferred to the university just that year. ("I first noticed him sitting in the front row, very attentive, and I was in the back of the room, kind of laying low," says Andy. These relative orientations still seem to hold.) The two did so well in Matsushima's class that the following year he suggested they take the graduate qualifying exams in physics—a brutal two days of testing that is generally administered to second-year graduate students. Unexpectedly, both of these undergrads passed. This not only ushered them straight into graduate school, it also earned them financial support in the form of NASA graduate traineeships. Iowa had been awarded a large number of these traineeships, owing mostly to the presence of Van Allen.

Those were the early days of space exploration—or the space race, to be precise. The Soviet Union had started things off by launching *Sputnik I* during the International Geophysical Year, in October 1957; and just shy of four months later, the United States had responded with *Explorer I,* which carried a Geiger counter designed by Van Allen. As the first satellite ever to be launched by the United States soared into space, radio signals from the counter revealed the presence of two belts of charged particles encircling the Earth, trapped by its magnetic field, which came to be known as the Van Allen belts.

NASA was formed later in 1958, only about five years before Jim and Andy won their traineeships, the purpose of which was to help develop a new generation of planetary scientists and aerospace engineers. Matsushima became Ph.D. adviser to them both, and during a total eclipse of the moon on December 30, 1963, he introduced them to the, in this case, frigid art of astronomical observation.

Indonesia's Mount Agung had erupted the previous spring, and the enormous burden of dust and aerosols that the eruption had added to the atmosphere was expected to affect the brightness of the moon during this eclipse.

"At that time, the University of Iowa didn't really have an astronomical observatory," Lacis recalls. "What it was, was a converted corncrib out in the middle of nowhere that had a kind of a crappy little telescope in it. . . . It hadn't been used in years. When we went there, I think the day before, to check it out, all the bugs in the surrounding forty-eight acres had come in to roost for the winter there, so we had to shovel all the bugs out and try to set the place up so we could make some measurements. Then at night we came back to do this lunar eclipse measurement . . . and that was the coldest day of the year. The wind was blowing; it was minus thirty; we were just freezing out there."

Andy testifies that this "definitely" cured both himself and Jim of any desire to become observational astronomers.

They produced a curve of the moon's brightness as it passed through Earth's shadow. Normally, the moon remains visible, a ghostly orange, during this passage, owing to the refraction, or bending, of the sun's light by the Earth's atmosphere. The dust and aerosols from Agung, however, scattered and reflected so many of the sun's rays away from their usual paths toward the moon that it more or less disappeared. This was one of the darkest eclipses on record.

According to Andy, "Matsushima didn't really know what to do with the data"—he wasn't much of a physicist. But Jim employed a theory of light scattering that had been developed by a Czechoslovakian astronomer named Linke to estimate how much scattering material Agung had sent into the stratosphere and provide some crude information about the size distribution of the particles involved. "It was a pretty good study," says Andy, and it formed the basis for Jim's master's thesis.

And although none of the three was thinking much about climate at the time, it just so happens that Jim's first bit of original work would form the basis for useful climatic calculations later in both his and Andy's careers. It turns out that the reflection and/or absorption of sunlight by airborne dust and aerosols plays an important role in determining Earth's equilibrium temperature. Volcanic eruptions tend to cool the planet for a few years, because the particles they send into the air reflect some of the sun's incoming energy back into space. The effect is something like putting a parasol over your head on a sunny day; in fact, it's known as the parasol effect. Benjamin Franklin actually pointed it out as early as 1784. About twelve years after their cold experience in the Iowa cornfield, by which time Jim and Andy, working together at GISS, had developed a computer simulation for Earth's climate, they collaborated on a study that demonstrated close agreement between their simulation of the parasol effect of the Agung eruption and the three-year cooling spell that actually occurred.

Although both young men were grateful to Matsushima for his support, neither had a particular rapport with him. They felt he was more of an academic politician than a scientist and that he was more interested in his own career advancement than in their education. In the end, Andy actually earned his doctorate under a different adviser. And Jim, despite doing his best to hide from Van Allen, found himself under Van Allen's wing, even as an undergraduate. As chairman of the department, Van Allen also appointed himself chairman of Jim's doctoral thesis committee. By suggesting to Jim that he might want to think about some interesting new data from Venus, Van Allen also pointed him in the direction of the topic that Jim eventually examined in his Ph.D. thesis.

New ground-based observations had shown that Venus was emitting a surprising amount of long-wave radiation. This meant either that the planet was very hot or that its ionosphere was radiating. Jim believes Van Allen, whose most famous discovery involved Earth's ionosphere, was intrigued by the latter possibility.

To get a doctorate at the University of Iowa back then, a student had to propose and defend an "original proposition." There was no requirement that it be correct. According to Jim, "You could make it 'The moon is made out of green cheese.' Then you had to defend that conclusion before a committee of professors and show that you understood the way the science worked and the way the analysis worked." Someone had already made a suggestion about the ionosphere of Venus, and a new young professor at Harvard named Carl Sagan had suggested that the planet might be heated by a runaway greenhouse effect. In his doctoral thesis, Sagan had proposed that the Venusian atmosphere might contain prodigious amounts of carbon dioxide. (This was how he first gained wide notice in academic circles. He later gained worldwide fame with his ability to popularize science.) No probes had yet been sent to the planet, however, so there was no way of proving either of these notions right or wrong.

Jim came up with a third idea: that high concentrations of dust in the Venusian atmosphere might be acting as a blanket, absorbing, reflecting back toward the planetary surface, and thereby containing the geothermal heat generated in the planet's core.

Even as he was defending his thesis, by the way, Jim was skeptical that his "original proposition" would prove to be correct, because he wasn't sure how the dust could remain suspended in the atmosphere. The science wasn't solid in this area. He did a lot of thinking and read a lot of books on the subject, but he couldn't prove either that it might float or that it definitely wouldn't. Thus, given the state of knowledge at the time, his proposition was plausible.

When the first satellites visited Venus in the late sixties and seventies, they found high levels of carbon dioxide in the atmosphere, thereby proving his proposition wrong and Sagan's correct. Correct answers are important in science, of course, but the purpose of the Iowa thesis exercise was to show that rigorous thinking will lead to correct answers. Besides, theory doesn't mean much at all without observational data.

Matsushima won a grant to visit Japan during Jim and Andy's third year in graduate school, and they both joined him there. This gave them an additional reason to be grateful, although Jim also points out that the main reason Matsushima invited them along "was that he didn't want to lose his students to some other professor" (though he did eventually lose Andy). Jim wrote most of his thesis in Japan, where he benefited from the insights of Professor Sueo Ueno at the University of Kyoto, an authority on light scattering. The young doctoral candidate had definitely caught fire by then, and he, unlike the laid-back Andy, was extremely focused on getting his degree. One day at the University of Kyoto, he noticed an advertisement on a bulletin board for postdoctoral fellowships at various NASA institutions. He wrote to them, got some information back, and decided to apply to the Goddard Institute for Space Studies in New York City, mainly due to its focus on planetary science and astrophysics. His fascination with Venus still held.

But Matsushima's idea of a good graduate student was one who would stick around for a while and produce a number of papers to which the professor might add his name. When he learned of Jim's exit plans, he hit the roof and refused to write a recommendation to GISS—something that was generally required from an applicant's adviser. He also attempted to delay Jim's thesis preparation and even resorted to a few tricks aimed at making him look bad in the eyes of Van Allen. But Van Allen saw through it all. He facilitated Jim's thesis defense and wrote a recommendation to GISS himself. Thus, in early 1967, doctorate fresh in hand, Jim packed his bags and headed for the big city. He was so excited to be working at a NASA research institute that he drove all the way from Iowa City to Manhattan without stopping to sleep.

He's been there ever since.

In addition to the integrity that Bill Blakemore perceives, Jim's upbringing in that simpler place and time seems to have given him the natural faith in humanity that is often attributed to Midwesterners. Looking broadly at his predictions over the past quarter century, for example, one finds the only real mistakes are in his estimates of mankind's response to the danger. Until recently, he has always assumed that we would begin to do something to help, when in fact we have done virtually nothing—at least by the bottom-line measure of global greenhouse emissions, which continue to grow every year.

This basic optimism, along with his scrupulous, somewhat trying, almost Gandhi-like insistence on factual accuracy, and his careful, even-handed way of speaking, have led some to call him naïve. Jim himself believes that he took a misplaced faith in the good intentions of Dick Cheney into the meetings of the climate change working group that he attended in 2001. But when the notion of Jim's naïveté is placed before Blakemore, he responds, "I'm not so sure it's naïveté. I know what you mean. It might look like it, but . . . I think it's rather the extreme opposite and closer to something that Yeats calls 'radical innocence.'" In Blakemore's opinion, this contributes not only to Jim's scientific brilliance, but also to his credibility when he testifies before Congress, for instance, "in that quiet, deliberate, 'I've done my homework' Iowa way.

"He's just constantly assessing his own veracity, which the great thinkers do. I think he's just watching it come and dealing with it as it comes, dealing with this, what I would call truly evil, knowingly evil, misdirection the way he deals with scientific data. I think it's the opposite of naïve."

In the week after Andy Revkin's front-page story in the *Times*, as his and other headlines blazed in print and over the airwaves, Andy also applied pressure behind the scenes. His "day one" story on Sunday had prompted NASA employees from around the country to send him their own stories of censorship and arm-twisting. He says he "got a huge input from all these scientists' Yahoo accounts." And it wasn't only scientists; it was also career public affairs officers who were disturbed and in some cases outraged by things they had seen or reluctantly done. It seemed that the drive for control had intensified at the beginning of 2004, at the start of Bush's ultimately successful reelection campaign—of which more in a moment.

On Thursday night and Friday, Revkin described some of these incidents in e-mails to Dean Acosta and a few other NASA managers, and asked them to comment.

Thus on Friday afternoon, February 3, just hours after Jim appeared on NPR, Griffin issued a public Statement on Scientific Openness, reaffirming the agency's commitment to "open scientific and technical inquiry and dialogue with the public"—as codified, he pointed out, in the Space Act of 1958. This statement also fulfilled Representative Boehlert's request for a swift, written statement.

Griffin said all the right things: "The job of the Office of Public Affairs, at every level in NASA is to convey the work done at NASA to our stakeholders in an intelligible way. It is not the job of public affairs officers to alter, filter or adjust engineering or scientific material produced by NASA's technical staff."

He addressed the statement to all 18,500 NASA employees, and he closed by encouraging them "to discuss this issue and bring their concerns to management so we can work together to ensure that NASA's policies and procedures appropriately support our commitment to openness."

Although Revkin received a copy of the statement, he pointed out in an article the next day (which also told of George Deutsch's interest in the big bang and intelligent design) that the *Times* had not received any direct comments about the other censorship stories he had brought to the attention of the Ninth Floor. The only reply had come from Dean Acosta via e-mail: "From time to time, the administrator communicates with NASA employees on policy and issues. Today was one of those days. I hope this helps. Have a good weekend." Acosta was also named as the point of contact in Griffin's Statement on Scientific Openness.

This irony was not lost on Jay Zwally, a distinguished climate scientist at the Goddard Space Flight Center who specializes in the use of satellite-based remote sensing methods to measure changes in the mass of the polar ice sheets. Zwally, who has a wry, "cut-up in the back of the classroom"-type sense of humor, relates that during the Bush-Cheney years, he had taken to prefacing his lectures, which generally presented clear evidence that the planet is warming and humans are most likely causing it, with the disclaimer "I want to make it very clear that as a NASA employee I'm not allowed to say that man's impact is causing climate to warm. So if you draw that conclusion from anything I say, that's your conclusion."

Late on Saturday evening, Zwally sent a one-sentence, half tongue-in-cheek e-mail to Acosta, asking, "Does this mean that I am no longer going to be warned by PAO [public affairs] not to say that man's production of greenhouse gases is causing climate to warm?"

Apparently Acosta did not see the humor. "Did a PAO warn you not to report your science? If so, please send me the evidence and I will personally handle it."

"That's not answering my question," Zwally responded. "I think there is strong scientific evidence for what I asked you if I can say. Can I say that as a NASA employee when I am asked?

"I must say I find your reply a little intimidating," Zwally added. "Yes, I was warned, verbally. By a civil servant, and I believe that within the climate of this NASA administration it would not be in the best interests of that person if I said who it was."

"First, I didn't know you had a question," Acosta shot back from his BlackBerry. "You made a statement in your last e-mail and I merely asked for evidence. I'm not sure how that is intimidating? Anyway, it sounds like you should bring whatever issue you may have with your direct supervisor."

Zwally decided to drop it.

There is not much evidence that public affairs read a message of openness, particularly, in the administrator's statement—nor, again, that the administrator made much of an attempt to mobilize the organization that had the main responsibility for translating his statement into policy. On Monday, February 6, Dwayne Brown complained to Leslie McCarthy that she hadn't been sending him a daily list of interview requests. She had decided it wasn't necessary, as she had not seen that rule in writing either.

Later in the day, the story took a dramatic—and, for some, a convenient—turn when a graduate student at Oxford named Nick Anthis revealed on his blog, *The Scientific Activist,* that George Deutsch had not actually graduated from Texas A&M. Anthis was well placed to figure this out: he had been a student at Texas A&M and even worked on the same campus newspaper as Deutsch before winning the Rhodes Scholarship that took him to Oxford to study biochemistry.

About a year later, Deutsch would tell the House Committee on Oversight and Government Reform, under oath, that when he applied for his jobs at NASA, "to the best of my recollection, I disclosed on various occasions the fact that I had not completed my college degree."

Evidently, one of those occasions was not his employment interview with Dolores Beasley, the person who hired him in the Science Mission Directorate. She recalls being confused when she read in Deutsch's résumé that he had worked at the student-run newspaper after having graduated, and that when she declared, "George, I can't tell when you graduated," he told her "point-blank" that he had graduated in 2003.

Beasley says she only had to "light into George" about three times in the three months that she supervised him: when she learned about his extracurricular interest in cosmology, the one or two times he said his job was to make the president look good, and, finally, in early November, when she offered him her place among the public affairs officers who would attend the AGU meeting in San Francisco, knowing she would soon be leaving Science. Not only would some see this as a perk, it might also be seen as a responsibility, and Dolores felt she was making him a generous offer to help enrich his fledgling career. Any such generosity was lost on Deutsch. He made some disparaging remarks about the city on account of its large gay population and refused to go.

This young man had all the makings of a scapegoat, and that is what he would become. NASA quickly announced that he had resigned.

The agency now had a genuine public relations disaster on its hands. On the day the so-called resignation was announced, David Mould, Dean Acosta, and Joe Davis held a video teleconference, or ViTs, for all of the roughly 350 public affairs officers in the far-flung agency. Mould dropped in on Acosta's nine-thirty meeting that morning to announce to the senior staff that the ViTs would be held that afternoon. When Acosta added that Deutsch had left because of "media pressure," according to Beasley, "everyone kind of averted their eyes, because we knew that wasn't why George had left." (After she had shifted out of Science, she had become lead public affairs officer—Dwayne Brown's equivalent—in Exploration.)

Acosta also told his staff not to talk to their colleagues about *any* of this—a directive so "very strange," remembers Beasley, that it was met with stunned silence and no one even bothered to ask if they were allowed to talk among themselves. She doubts anyone obeyed.

This policy of containment carried through to the ViTs, to which Leslie McCarthy listened by phone because GISS had no video connection. According to her notes, Acosta started things off by instructing his audience that the information to be discussed was for NASA public affairs and contract public affairs officers only. They were not to mention it to anyone else in the agency. He then turned the proceedings over to David Mould.

Mould was reading from a document that had three separate headers, each of which would seem to imply a certain concern with secrecy. The first: "PRE-DECISIONAL, INTERNAL, PERSONAL AND CONFIDENTIAL, NOT FOR PUBLIC DISTRIBUTION"; the second: "Pre-Decisional document"; the third: "CONFIDENTIAL INTERNAL COMMUNICATION NOT FOR DISTRIBUTION TO ANYONE."

Andy Revkin points out that in the George W. Bush era, federal agencies have learned to insert the word *pre-decisional* at the top of documents in order to exempt them from the Freedom of Information Act, that is, to shield them from public view. The trick can also be used to ward off congressional scrutiny. And it is a useful tool when words involving the control of public information *must* be written down, as in this case.

There are no names on this document and no date. It isn't even on NASA letterhead.

"I'm sure most of us don't like what we've seen in the news lately," Mould began. "I know I don't. These stories do not make our department look good, and they do not make NASA look good.

"I know for a fact—and so do many of you—that much of what these stories say and imply about all of us is untrue. I also know that many things in these stories are greatly exaggerated."

He seemed to be denying that anything untoward had actually occurred.

He proceeded to criticize the general quality of the work produced by his entire staff. Sounding something like a schoolmarm scolding her students, he chose to focus on their writing. Alluding to "misspelled words, bad grammar, and sloppy construction," he said that one of the reasons Griffin had brought him on board was to change all that.

Then he clarified the main policies of his department.

"Major media interview requests across NASA need to be coordinated with Public Affairs at Headquarters. Not all interviews, just the major ones. Your judgement should tell you which ones. . . .

"In addition, all press releases, fact sheets, Web postings—the Web postings we in Public Affairs produce, *not* the ones produced by science and engineering—and other communications produced by Public Affairs anywhere in the agency need to be sent to Headquarters in advance."

Why headquarters had ordered the webmaster at GISS to remove pure scientific data involving the previous year's temperature was never addressed.

Mould promised that headquarters would give a "quick and competent turnaround," focusing only on clarity, grammar, and so on. (Interminable delays, while press releases and decisions on media opportunities were run through the Ninth Floor, had been a source of frustration among the career public affairs officers—especially those in Earth science—since about the middle of the previous election year.) The edits at headquarters would NOT change meaning, he promised. (Many of the words in his document are typed all in capitals.) "We will NOT insert any political views . . . we will NOT insert any personal or religious views. . . . We will absolutely not tolerate improper conduct, and we will not let political or personal ideology—of ANY type—influence NASA's communications. . . .

"I do not want to believe that anyone in our department has intentionally censored or intimidated anyone at NASA. We will be looking into all aspects of these allegations very closely in coming days. Any mistakes we find, we will fix. Any misconduct we find, we will bring to an immediate halt."

They had not, evidently, discovered any misconduct thus far.

As he approached the end of his speech, Mould invited his audience to consider the many "brave and amazing people" at NASA "who do incredible things like discover new planets . . . design and build spaceships that go to the edge of the solar system . . . strap themselves to the top of rockets . . . and explore the Moon.

"They all seem willing to follow NASA policies, and play by the rules."

This is where Leslie began to feel that some of Mould's remarks might be directed at Jim Hansen and herself.

"What truly amazes me is that in an organization with all those brave and amazing people . . . there could be anyone—especially anyone whose responsibilities consist mainly of sitting at a desk and analyzing data, or doing public affairs work—who would consider himself or herself to be above the rules that all these other brave and amazing people are willing to follow. . . .

"Seeing these allegations in the news is extremely disappointing and offensive to me personally. Because they describe conduct—and they describe an atmosphere—that I would find sickening to ever see here. . . .

"Equally disappointing is seeing these allegations being taken to a reporter . . . before they ever came to me or anyone else in the NASA management chain."

What, then, had Jim Hansen, Franco Einaudi, Laurie Leshin, Ed Weiler—in other words, Jim's management chain all the way up to the head of Goddard Space Flight Center—been talking about for the past six weeks? And, of course, what about that e-mail to Mould himself from Mark Hess?

"Airing grievances in this way . . . without ever giving internal solutions a chance to work . . . is just as unprofessional as trying to insert political views into a press release. And just as unprofessional as basing a news story on hearsay and innuendo rather than a solid set of verifiable facts."

So David Mould seemed to be asserting, on behalf of NASA, that Jim Hansen's actions were on roughly the level of George Deutsch's and that *The New York Times* had done some sloppy reporting as well.

This speech did not go down well with Mould's staff, most of whom had never before seen him nor heard his voice. It was the first time in his seven months on the job that he had "talked to the troops." And Leslie McCarthy was not the only one to take his criticisms personally—nor, of course, was she the only one who had spoken to the media, although she was the only one who had been courageous enough to speak openly. Incidentally, the close correspondence between her notes and Mould's transcript demonstrate that she's a pretty good note taker.

Dolores Beasley says, "These were people who have *scads* of experience within NASA, twenty to twenty-five years of history working in public affairs at NASA; and to have someone whom they hadn't had a working relationship with come in and lay down the law at that meeting, . . . it made me uncomfortable." NASA employees outside of public affairs also noticed that this speech cast a pall over Mould's staff—and an especially painful one given the sense of hope that had been engendered just a few days earlier by Griffin's Statement on Scientific Openness.

Dolores, who is no shrinking violet, approached Mould afterwards. "Since you have an open-door policy," she suggested, "I think what would be helpful is if you used your opportunities to bring people together, because obviously there is a communications problem here or else people wouldn't be leaking, so rather than get mad at people for leaking, let's find out why they feel they need to and work on that." This didn't help either. Mould simply read again to her from his notes. He stayed "on message."

Dolores believes pretty much everyone thought Mould was talking to him or her directly—and that this suspicion was probably justified, because, in her opinion, he and Acosta were using this forum "as an opportunity to get at everybody."

The ViTs took place on a Wednesday, more than a week after Revkin broke the story. The folks on the Ninth Floor had hoped they could ride out a storm of a single day, but headlines kept raining down; and Deutsch himself was not a whole lot of help. On Thursday he gave an interview on a conservative talk radio station back in College Station, Texas, home to the university from which he had neglected to graduate. In those comfortable surroundings, he accused Jim of having "partisan ties . . . all the way to the top of the Democratic Party and . . . using those ties and his media connections to push an agenda, a worst-case-scenario agenda of global warming. . . . There's no censorship here. This is an agenda. It's a culture war agenda. They're out to get Republicans; they're out to get Christians; they're out to get people who are helping Bush—anybody they perceive as not sharing their agenda they're out to get." He expressed similar views to Andy Revkin and in an e-mail to a wide list of reporters, including Juliet

Eilperin at *The Washington Post,* who quoted a few more of his incendiary remarks in an article that appeared the following Saturday, February 11.

Queried by Revkin, Jim said, "This is so wacky that it deserves little response."

This and Deutsch's other escapades now provided the Ninth Floor with a convenient opportunity to scapegoat him and hope *that* would take care of it. However, David Goldston and his colleagues on the House Science Committee had been calling around to find out "who said what when," as staffer Johannes Loschnigg puts it, uncovered Mark Hess's e-mails, and spoke to him and Leslie McCarthy. It seemed to the staffers that the folks from GISS and Goddard were telling a straightforward and coherent story, whereas Mould and Acosta kept changing their tunes. "We were still feeling and saying to the press to some degree that we didn't think Dean and David were telling a convincing story," says Goldston.

With this as a goad, NASA requested a meeting that eventually took place in Griffin's Ninth Floor conference room on Tuesday of the following week, which happened to be February 14. ("The St. Valentine's Day Massacre?" asks Goldston.) Representing the agency were Griffin, Deputy Administrator Shana Dale, Dean Acosta, David Mould, Chief of Strategic Communications Joe Davis, and Assistant Administrator for Legislative Affairs Brian Chase, the agency's congressional liaison. Goldston was accompanied by his Democratic counterpart on the committee, Chuck Atkins.

Griffin opened—again with the right words: they were trying to get to the bottom of this.

Shana Dale presented the argument that they hadn't known anything about Deutsch's activities and that when they confronted him with the news reports, he denied everything. Then they saw his e-mail traffic, realized he was lying, and fired him. (One of the staffers compares Dale's line of argument to the one House Speaker Dennis Hastert used later that year to distance himself from former Florida congressman Mark Foley and the congressional page scandal: "He lied to everybody. How was I supposed to know?")

Although Goldston isn't entirely certain, he believes it was taken as a given at this meeting that the White House had called Griffin on the morning of December 15 to express dismay at the *Good Morning America* spot on ABC. Goldston had also heard this rumor a number of times in the course of his investigation.

His notes paraphrase Griffin as saying, "Hansen does interview; biggest NASA story of the year. They feel burned"; and later, "At the end of the chain, I'm responsible. If it's bad, the White House will call me."

Although he is vague on other aspects of this meeting, Michael Griffin remembers quite specifically that the second of these remarks was hypothetical. He claims neither he nor anyone else in his office got a call from the White House that day. He maintains furthermore that he didn't hear a thing about the *Good Morning America* spot nor anything about any possible communications problem involving GISS and Jim Hansen until *The New York Times* broke the censorship story on January 29. As he makes these denials, Griffin offers an ambivalent suggestion/question, as if probing to find out how much the questioner knows: "Nobody in the administrator's office suite even knew what was going on. Right?"

Hardly. Dean Acosta says that he heard complaints from both Joe Davis and Chief of Staff Paul Morrell on December 15. And the agency's deputy chief of staff and White House liaison, an upbeat young man named J. T. Jezierski (of whom we shall hear more), states that he received either a call or an e-mail from the Office of Cabinet Liaison, a sort of clearinghouse for information in the White House offices, to express dissatisfaction at their surprise. It would have been Jezierski's job to warn them of all NASA stories that might make headlines. The concern at the White House arose from more than just the *Good Morning America* spot, he adds; it arose from the "sustained media presence throughout that day and the next day of Dr. Hansen." Jezierski remembers many discussions in the administrator's suite on December 15, as the senior managers were forced to accept that "Okay, this is our news cycle. We're dominating [chuckle] this news cycle today" and discussed why they hadn't been informed and how they should respond.

"I have a no surprises rule, because the White House has a no surprises rule," says Jezierski. "So that's what it was, to be able to say, 'Man, guys, first of all, if I get a call on this from the White House or whoever, that's gonna be bad, and if I don't have an answer, that's even worse.'" As Jezierski tells it, all the top people in communications and communications strategy at the agency—that is, Morrell, Davis, Mould, and himself—discussed these questions *on December 15* with Michael Griffin.

David Goldston writes, "My recollection and the implication of my notes is that the call . . . to Leslie [McCarthy on the evening of the fifteenth] was indeed because Mike had wanted to know about the ABC show."

As for the content of that call as well as the one to Mark Hess the following morning, Mould and Acosta gave their standard line: all they wanted was a heads-up. When Goldston produced a copy of the e-mail Hess had sent to them, both denied ever having seen it—thus, in Acosta's case, contradicting the report in *Space News* of the previous week. (The important thing is not when Acosta saw the e-mail, but whether, a week earlier when he seems not to have realized the severity of the situation, he had actually stated that the directives in the e-mail were consistent with NASA policy.)

And in the same way that Acosta casts doubt upon the reporting in that article, he and Mould cast doubt—both then and now—upon the authenticity of the e-mail. About a year later, Mould would argue, "It didn't look like any NASA e-mail that I had ever seen before. The format was different. It looked like somebody had typed it up rather than being sent over an e-mail system. . . . If I am going to put out some sort of firm procedures, I'm going to write them up myself and I will send them out myself, and the fact that a couple people would sit and conjure them up and then begin circulating it—I don't find that very professional, do you?"

"So," says staffer Johannes Loschnigg, "there's only two things that you can conclude: (a) Leslie is making up an unbelievably intricate story that she has these notes for . . . or (b) the folks at headquarters are just plain lying."

He adds that it's more than just Leslie's story; it's "a very intricate web that has various sources." These would include Larry Travis at GISS; Mark

Hess, Don Savage, Ed Campion, Franco Einaudi, Laurie Leshin, and Ed Weiler at Goddard; and Dolores Beasley and Dwayne Brown at headquarters.

Franco Einaudi and Laurie Leshin still have the e-mail Hess sent to them at about the same time, and they, in contrast, acted upon it by holding meetings and conversations via phone and e-mail. It never occurred to the managers at Goddard to doubt that Mark Hess and Leslie McCarthy were telling the truth, and they still believe they were telling the truth. Moreover, if they *were* telling the truth, they did exactly what they should have. What would motivate this busy group of people, who have dedicated their lives to rather more inspiring matters, to conjure up extra work for themselves?

The only NASA employee interviewed for this book who has not snorted or snickered upon hearing Mould and Acosta's claim about losing an e-mail is Administrator Michael Griffin. One senior scientific manager joked, "What was there, a solar flare that day?"

In the Valentine's Day meeting, the administrator and his staff expressed amazement that Jim, Leslie, and a dozen or so anonymous others had gone to the media with their concerns instead of working internally. (Griffin, Mould, and Acosta were saying the same thing a year later.) Goldston says, "I'm like, you know, 'You're staff is basically telling them not to talk. I mean, Hansen's gonna call the head of NASA about it?' . . . It was just ridiculously unrealistic."

Furthermore, although many people at GISS and Goddard discussed this topic all through the month of January, no one from headquarters seemed to see it as their responsibility to get involved in these discussions— or even to place a simple telephone call to Jim. This may have had something to do with an ambiguity in NASA's management structure. Since GISS is part of Goddard, Jim's direct chain of command goes through Einaudi and Leshin to Weiler, who reports to the administrator. But Jim was getting the grant money for his scientific work from Mary Cleave. According to Weiler, "Jim Hansen really doesn't answer to me in a scientific sense. . . . He gets his salary and his heat and lights and all that from

Goddard Space Flight Center, but on matters of scientific policy or scientific whatever, he answers directly to headquarters, whether it's the division director of Earth science, or Mary Cleave herself. . . . I'll let you be your own judge as to who has more authority over somebody, somebody who doesn't give them money or somebody that does."

Weiler himself talked to headquarters at least once or twice in December and January. When he bumped into Jim at a meeting at Goddard on February 8, the day George Deutsch resigned, for instance, he mentioned a conversation he'd had with Cleave and Mould when the three had taken a plane flight together back in December. "Someone was supposed to call me up and keep me 'on the data,'" reports Jim, "but . . . they decided that they were reluctant to do that, because they thought that if anybody called me, it might end up on the front page of *The New York Times*."

Well, if one of them *had* called at that early date and made a sincere attempt to craft a policy for the public communication of science at NASA, there would never have been a story for the front page. But public affairs would have had to participate in the crafting of such a policy, and if they *were* engaged in censorship, as it seems clear that they were, they would have had no motivation whatsoever to participate in an open discussion— for the very reason that their tactics relied upon secrecy and intimidation. The one person who could have stepped into the breach was Mary Cleave, who admits that she "might" have said she would call Jim in the middle of the shit storm on December 15. She didn't, and Jim eventually gave up waiting.

The silence from above seemed to many outside headquarters a tacit endorsement of the oral directives Hess had recorded in his e-mails, especially considering the history of silence and lack of written instruction that reached back through the long campaign of censorship that preceded this episode.

The House staffers were also struck by the lack of written and electronic evidence. Johannes Loschnigg remembers that they remarked later among themselves, "This was done very well. There's no paper trail here."

The only explanations presented by NASA's senior management in the administrator's conference room that Valentine's Day focused exclusively upon a twenty-four-year-old political appointee who worked in the Science Mission Directorate for a grand total of about four and a half months, yet seems to have garnered enough clout in that short time to cause rather a lot of trouble to themselves and many other people with vastly more experience and seniority than he.

When the discussion turned to different hypotheticals regarding the procedures for press releases and the like, Goldston quickly realized that the NASA folks, including Griffin, were telling conflicting stories in that very discussion. At times they spoke of wanting a heads-up, at others they spoke of granting approval. He pointed out that they were speaking out of both sides of their mouths; there seemed to be a need for a coherent policy.

Griffin tried to state one in general terms: "Scientists have a right to speak. Private opinions should be designated as such." (Jim would have breathed more easily during the NPR interview had he heard this from Griffin's or Cleave's lips.)

And Griffin and his staff repeatedly assured Goldston that Mould had articulated a "very clear" statement of policy during his infamous ViTs. Goldston hadn't read the transcript at that point, but when he did, he found it "abominable." "I wrote back later and said, '*Everything* is wrong with this. . . . I mean it basically pretends the problem doesn't exist. How are you going to solve the problem?'"

Goldston was not reassured to hear Griffin say in the meeting, "David and Dean are going to fix the problem. We don't want spin." A committee would be organized (NASA calls this sort of thing a Tiger Team) comprising scientists, engineers, public affairs officers, managers, and, of course, lawyers from headquarters and the different NASA centers to seek honest input and develop a clear and sensible policy going forward.

As Goldston sums it up, "Acosta's lines of argument were basically (1) we all had egg on our faces because we were caught off guard by the ABC appearance; (2) Mary Cleave was largely responsible for not having Hansen do the NPR interview; (3) the conversation with Mark Hess laying out limitations never occurred, and we never saw his e-mail that listed them. I found it doubtful that any of these lines of argument were accurate. . . .

"It was clear that we were never going to get a story that was vaguely believable to us, and Mike [Griffin] was not being helpful. His goal really was to make peace, but largely by defending his guys . . . and when it became clear to me that he was not trying to be an honest broker in the meeting . . . I just decided to give up. . . . [It] was basically me versus David and Dean, with everyone else sort of arbitrating in an effort to get me, on behalf of the chairman [Boehlert], to feel that these guys were on the up-and-up. It didn't succeed in doing that, but . . . we felt we'd gone as far as we could. Everything future-oriented looked like it was going in the right direction . . . and so we sort of left it there."

Goldston and his colleagues are more or less certain that Griffin and Shana Dale did not really know what Acosta, Deutsch, and Mould were up to in December and January, and that from the moment in mid-December that the *Good Morning America* story triggered a shit storm, nearly everything Griffin and Dale heard on the subject was filtered by Mould and Acosta.

The staffers also believe that, for a short time, Mary Cleave went down the road of requiring first refusal on interviews and approving scientific Web content, but that she was similarly misled by Mould and Acosta. She probably spoke with Michael Griffin about such notions on December 15, as Mould indicated to Leslie over the phone that day—but never with any real intention of censoring science.

Most everyone who knows Michael Griffin or was involved in this investigation believes he has a sincere interest in promoting scientific openness. Goldston says the desire to control global warming news "was probably a greater concern of the White House than it was to Mr. Griffin. This was not the stuff that he came to NASA to do." In reality, moreover, Griffin only had so much control over public affairs.

A self-described "political on the Ninth Floor, behind the glass doors at NASA" during the Clinton administration reminds us that the top three people in public affairs—Mould, Acosta, and Joe Davis—were White House appointees. "It's not really Mike's decision. Mike could, I suppose, go over to the White House and say, 'Listen, White House personnel, these guys you sent me are just terrible. Please send me somebody new.' He's not about to do that. It's a White House personnel issue." And, as we shall see, Acosta had been helping certain people in the White House censor climate science for at least a year.

The staffers met with Jim Hansen and Leslie McCarthy the day after the standoff at headquarters. Her inevitable notes record Goldston as assuring them that "if we find out that we're being lied to, we're going to have to insist on somebody's head; somebody's going to have to go." But when Johannes Loschnigg told them that there would be no public hearings, Leslie knew no one outside of Deutsch would be going anywhere. "I worked on Capitol Hill for ten years," she says. "I know if you're not having hearings on something, you're not serious about any kind of investigation."

Goldston argues that a full-fledged investigation would not have been helpful. He didn't want the matter to "blow up into the kind of political issue where everyone has to circle the wagons and get so defensive that no one is ever willing to do anything." He "absolutely" did not want to hold a hearing, out of fear that "all the conservatives and pro-NASA guys would feel the need to defend the agency, and then the message would be 'Well, maybe this kind of thing is okay.'" He may have been right. In the political atmosphere of that time, with Republicans controlling both houses of Congress, this sort of response would not have been unusual.

But Andy Revkin, who spoke to Goldston "many, many times" during this period, believes "he was trying to stamp out this fire. . . . The Republican moderates did not want this to become a big issue."

Chuck Atkins, Goldston's Democratic counterpart, was so "used to living in the minority" that he accepted the fact that he couldn't have had hearings even if he wanted them. However, in retrospect, he says, "It would have shone a lot stronger light and been a lot more of a shot across the bow had we done hearings and made a bigger, more public deal about that, yes. . . . I don't think it would have necessarily been counter-productive."

Be that as it may, both he and Goldston felt that they had made it clear to NASA's upper management that the House Science Committee would not tolerate any form of scientific muzzling or censorship, and that they would be watching to make sure genuine changes were put in place. They would keep the pressure on, remain in contact as the agency set up its Tiger Team, and watch the team's progress.

So Deutsch remained the fall guy. Goldston says that even Chairman Boehlert "was relieved that there was such a tidy story. . . . The general story line became pretty quickly that there was this rogue guy, and he's typical of young, partisan Republicans, and they got rid of him."

Indeed, the chairman's sense of relief seems to have been strong enough as to have stifled any desire to find out what actually happened. Goldston thinks Boehlert truly believed the tidy story, even though he was told "millions of times" that there was more to it than that. And the chairman's public remarks from that time forward would reflect his tidy belief.

Michael Griffin claims that he saw no reason to punish anyone in-volved in these incidents because he never saw "a piece of actual evi-dence." He would have been "the most irresponsible of managers," he claims, if he "were to harm [Mould and Acosta] based on an unsupported accusation. . . . People up at GISS were not disciplined; people at headquarters . . . were not disciplined, because it was not possible for me to determine if either of them should be." Griffin even claims that Deutsch wasn't disciplined: "George was confronted with the fact that . . . he had lied on his résumé and he resigned." When he is reminded that Shana Dale told Goldston during the meeting in his own conference room that Deutsch had been confronted with his e-mails and the lies he had told about them and fired, Griffin says, "I don't recall that."

In fact, there was plenty of evidence. Griffin is conveniently overlooking Deutsch's e-mails, Leslie McCarthy's notes, Mark Hess's e-mails, the verifiably false point paper that Deutsch wrote at Dean Acosta's request and that Dwayne Brown cosigned (grounds for the disciplining of all three, in and of itself), and other things.

Our "political" from the Clinton days guesses that Boehlert and his Republican majority on the Science Committee just "didn't need the trouble. . . . They all like and respect Mike over there. Didn't want to just go out, do a hatchet job, and embarrass him, you know. Probably more generally just 'We're all part of the same party, why do we want to share this ugliness?'"

So, in the end, Michael Griffin champions Mould and Acosta. To this day, he uses the same logic and the same arguments they do. Perhaps he wanted to avoid ugliness, perhaps he realized that if he were to give even the slightest credence to the notes Leslie McCarthy wrote during the pivotal phone call on December 15, *he* would be implicated in the attempt to censor Jim Hansen. The notes say that Mould and Acosta laid out their directives in his name: "This is coming from the top." And Goldston's notes have Acosta saying in his first cocky days after the story broke, "Hansen was on ABC and Griffin wanted to know why."

It is unlikely that Michael Griffin was ever truly interested in censorship, but it is not unlikely that he may have wanted to exert a modicum of control over an "outspoken" scientist after having been surprised by a news story and even heard about it from the White House. Griffin was relatively new to his job, and he may not have been aware of every little drama that was going on at his agency. As well, his subsequent actions and words indicate that he doesn't hold science or scientists themselves in particularly high regard. He seems to think of them as childish and unruly. In fact, a senior scientist who has recently left the agency claims that Griffin "hates scientists." Griffin may well have voiced one or two ill-conceived notions about communications policy on December 15 that sounded much worse when they emerged from Mould and Acosta's mouths.

Anyhow, Mould and Acosta weathered the storm.

* * *

"Never ascribe to malice that which can be explained by incompetence," as the saying goes. In this instance, there was probably an equal admixture of both. Johannes Loschnigg remembers sitting around with a few other Republican staffers and "kind of half-laughing about this in early February, just the fact that 'Congratulations, headquarters public affairs. You have made this a major story, when it would have been forgotten in a few minutes.' That's not to say that the 2005 temperature record wouldn't have gotten more press later on . . . but this story, as it is, is kind of their own creation. So, well done!"

The staffers may not have realized just how right they were. Shortly after the year ended, *The New York Times* published a list of the most frequently viewed stories on its Web site in 2006. Andy Revkin's "day one" story on January 29 came in fourth overall, with 1.1 million hits.

Chapter 5

"Gretchen, Do Not E-mail Me on This"

FIVE YEARS EARLIER, THE BUSH ADMINISTRATION had sought out Jim's views on policy.

Even at the time, few were aware that a few weeks into his first term and shortly after convening his notorious energy task force, Vice President Dick Cheney also convened a climate change working group comprising essentially the same people: Secretary of State Colin Powell, National Security Adviser Condoleezza Rice, Treasury Secretary Paul O'Neill, Energy Secretary Spencer Abraham, EPA Administrator Christine Todd Whitman, Interior Secretary Gale Norton, Agriculture Secretary Ann Veneman, and Commerce Secretary Donald Evans. In a sign that Mr. Cheney attached some importance to the meetings, he designated them "principals only," meaning that the cabinet officers and senior administrators themselves were to attend; they were not to send representatives. The working group met more or less weekly from the last week of March 2001—only two months after the inauguration—until mid-June. The first two meetings were dedicated to science. Jim Hansen was the only expert invited to both.

The previous August, as the Gore and Bush presidential campaigns had been waking from their summer slumber, Jim, Andy Lacis (his friend since college days), and four other GISS scientists had published a surprisingly optimistic paper in the *Proceedings of the National Academy of Sciences of the United States of America,* under the title "Global Warming in the Twenty-first Century: An Alternative Scenario."

Their argument was based upon solid estimates of all the major climate "forcings" of the industrial era. A forcing is basically equivalent to either turning up the brightness of the sun or turning it town. A positive forcing, such as a greenhouse gas, will heat the atmosphere; a negative forcing will cool it. An example of the latter would be the tiny particles called aerosols that spew forth from coal-burning power plants—sulfates mostly, which also cause acid rain. This type of aerosol cools the air through the parasol effect: by reflecting sunlight back into space. But another important industrial aerosol comes down on the positive side of the ledger. Black carbon soot, which is emitted mainly by household heating systems, diesel engines, and open fires, heats the air by *absorbing* sunlight, owing to its color; and its effect is amplified by the fact that some airborne soot eventually settles on mountain glaciers or polar ice sheets, darkens their surfaces, and enhances *their* absorption of sunlight. This not only speeds their melting dramatically, it also adds a positive feedback that enhances global warming; for in their white, pristine state, glaciers and ice sheets cool the atmosphere by reflecting sunlight away from the planet in the same way most airborne aerosols do. Not only does the soot on their surface reduce the reflectivity of the ice itself, but also, as the glaciers shrink, they expose the darker land or water underneath, which absorbs sunlight even more effectively.

The comprehensive view that was presented in this paper could be seen as Jim Hansen's trademark. In fact, the main contribution of his very first paper on the climate of Earth (as opposed to Venus), in 1976, was that it considered the effect of the so-called non–carbon dioxide or non-CO_2 greenhouse gases for the first time.

When the GISS scientists compared, side by side, the forcing power of all the main greenhouse gases and aerosols that have been added to the atmosphere during the industrial era, they discovered some low-hanging fruit. They realized that, while carbon dioxide has so far been the strongest individual contributor to manmade greenhouse warming, the total effect of the non-CO_2 greenhouse gases is about equal to carbon dioxide's. They also understood that realistic efforts to reduce carbon dioxide emissions, while essential, could only be expected to *slow* their growth, not stop it. Jim's "alternative scenario" proposed that we might make a significant dent in the greenhouse by focusing on the non-CO_2 gases for the next fifty years, particularly methane and ozone, and by limiting black carbon soot. This would supplement reductions in the emission of carbon dioxide, which is a much more difficult nut to crack both economically and politically, since this gas is an inevitable by-product of fossil fuel burning and, therefore, of the global energy infrastructure. "Combined with a reduction of black carbon emissions and plausible success in slowing CO_2 emissions," the authors wrote, "this reduction of non-CO_2 greenhouse gases could lead to a decline in the rate of global warming, reducing the danger of dramatic climate change."

Jim and his colleagues also noted some immediate side benefits to this scenario. Soot is linked to an increased prevalence of lung cancer and asthma. Ozone also causes asthma and other adverse health effects and hurts agriculture, for a total cost of about $10 billion a year in the United States alone. And in addition to the direct greenhouse benefit of limiting methane, which is presently the second most important greenhouse gas, this would in turn limit ozone, owing to active chemical processes in the atmosphere that eventually produce ozone from airborne methane.

The GISS group did not ignore carbon dioxide emissions; in fact, they stressed the critical importance of curtailing their exponential growth between now and 2050 and cutting them drastically in the second half of the century. They were simply making the optimistic suggestion that we might buy a few decades to develop new technologies to replace fossil fuel burning by dealing also with soot and the non-CO_2 greenhouse gases, while implementing a few sensible and not particularly painful strategies for energy efficiency and conservation that would limit carbon dioxide emissions as well.

Jim felt that he was simply following the Feynman admonition here: "Describe the evidence very carefully without regard to the way you feel it should be." "I don't see any harm in being broad-minded about the problem and looking at it from different angles," he says, "but the [international climate science] community got very upset about this, because they just wanted to focus on CO_2, which I think is limiting. I think we have to address the non-CO_2 forcings with much more intensity than we're doing. We need a full court press on both CO_2 and non-CO_2 forcings."

Thus, as the presidential election shifted into high gear, he found himself in the unusual position, for him, of being attacked by greenhouse activists and scientists and embraced by the fossil fuel lobby.

Jim recalls that, near the end of the first meeting of the climate change working group, Dick Cheney himself read a line from the alternative scenario paper aloud to the assembled experts and cabinet officers: "We argue that rapid warming in recent decades has been driven mainly by non-CO_2 greenhouse gases, such as chlorofluorocarbons [also known as freons], CH_4 [methane or natural gas], and N_2O [nitrous oxide], not by the products of fossil fuel burning, CO_2 and aerosols, the positive and negative climate forcings of which are partially offsetting." It appeared to Jim that Mr. Cheney interpreted this to mean that there was no need to worry about fossil fuel burning. The vice president then invited him back for the second meeting, indicating that he wanted to hear more about this sort of thing—not exactly a scientific aspiration. As it happened, Cheney missed the second meeting, as his attention was drawn to a diplomatic incident arising from the collision of a U.S. navy spy plane and the Chinese fighter jet that had been tailing it near the coast of China.

Although Jim remembers the meetings as being "pretty perfunctory," he was quite impressed at the knowledge and enthusiasm of Treasury Secretary Paul O'Neill, who told the group at the first meeting that he had spoken with President Bush the previous day and that the president had said he wanted the United States to take a leadership role on this issue. Colin Powell also seemed engaged, as Jim recalls, asking a question or two about soot. "The secretary of state is a logical person to be interested," he adds, "because he's the one who's going to take the brunt of the criticism from the rest of the world."

The administration was taking quite a bit of criticism that first spring it was in power. Only a week or so earlier, Bush had reneged on his campaign promise to limit greenhouse emissions from power plants and, more fundamentally, to classify carbon dioxide as a pollutant. Nevertheless, Jim felt that the group as a whole was somewhat open-minded. He was "hopeful that the administration would respond to a clear scientific story.

"Bush made a very reasonable speech in early June of 2001—it was right before he was going to Europe, and he knew he was going to get a lot of flack in Europe about global warming—a Rose Garden speech, as it's called, in which he said that although he had changed his position, he would remain open to new information as it developed; and, therefore, I was still hopeful that clear information might have a beneficial effect on U.S. policy."

But as Paul O'Neill puts it (apologizing for the cliché as he utters it), "the horse was out of the barn" before the working group even met.

Consistent with Jim's quick reading, O'Neill was probably the most well informed on the global warming issue of anyone in Bush's cabinet. As chief executive officer of Alcoa he had been one of the leading corporate advocates for addressing the problem, and he had actually passed out an Alcoa booklet on global warming at the new president's very first cabinet meeting.

In *The Price of Loyalty,* a book about O'Neill's tumultuous two years as treasury secretary that was written with his cooperation, author Ron Suskind relates that Bush asked O'Neill to "get me a plan on global warming" only three days into his presidency. This was somewhat awkward, as the issue rightfully "belonged" to EPA Administrator Christie Whitman. Nonetheless, O'Neill and Whitman did work, both together and separately, in the first few critical weeks of the new administration to "get" Bush a plan.

On February 17, 2001, less than a month after the president's request, O'Neill sent him the bare bones of a plan, suggesting that he "form an interdepartmental group, possibly in conjunction with the vice president's energy task force—'since energy and the environment are in many ways the same problem.'" (Cheney had wasted no time setting up his task force. Its first meeting had taken place the previous week.)

At the beginning of March, Whitman attended a summit with the environmental ministers of the Group of 8 industrial nations in Trieste, Italy, for the main purpose of discussing the Kyoto Protocol. Although Bush had not endorsed this first international agreement to limit greenhouse emissions during the campaign, there was still some hope that the United States might participate, since nearly every other industrial nation was participating and the Clinton administration had genuinely engaged in the most recent round of negotiations over the fall.

Whitman assumed that the president would honor his pledge—it is highly unusual for a president to disavow a campaign pledge in his first 100 days in office—and she had a strong personal belief in the need to address global warming herself. Indeed, she surprised her fellow ministers with her enthusiasm in Trieste. In her own book, *It's My Party Too,* she writes, "I assured my G8 counterparts that the president's campaign commitment to seek a mandatory cap on carbon dioxide emissions was solid and that the administration sincerely agreed that global climate change was a serious problem that demanded attention." But Bush was getting pressure in the other direction from industry, certain members of Congress, and sources within his administration who were strategically leaking internal documents to the press.

On her flight home from Italy, Whitman composed a memo to the president, which she transmitted the day she landed. (This is one of the documents that was leaked.) That same day, Bush received a memo from four conservative Republican senators, Chuck Hagel of Nebraska, Larry Craig of Idaho, Jesse Helms of North Carolina, and Pat Roberts of Kansas, urging him to oppose Kyoto and any and all regulation of carbon dioxide. Whitman and O'Neill received copies.

O'Neill remembers that they both thought the letter looked suspicious. Not only was it perfectly timed, the tone and even much of the substance seemed to have come "right out of Dick Cheney's mouth." O'Neill told Whitman he "wouldn't be surprised if you found out that the White House requested this letter of clarification and that the vice president was preparing the response."

Suskind writes, "O'Neill, like others who served with Cheney under different presidents, was almost always in the dark about his actual beliefs. But they'd sometimes pick up his method: quietly select an issue, counsel various participants, manufacture the exchange of seemingly impromptu letters or reports—the bureaucratic version of a media event—and then guide the unfolding events toward the intended outcome. This was the puppeteer's craft, all done with strings and suggestions.

"In the end, there are no fingerprints. No accountability."

Not unlike the tactics of censorship that would be employed at NASA a few years later.

Whitman swiftly requested a meeting with the president, hoping to engage in a dialogue. It was scheduled for Tuesday of the following week, March 13, at 10 A.M. She was not even given the chance to state her case. Bush informed her that he had already decided to oppose Kyoto and renege on his pledge to regulate carbon dioxide, and he read her portions of a letter that had already been composed to the four senators.

As she left the Oval Office, she bumped into the vice president. "He muttered a brief hello to me," she writes, "as he asked an aide who had come up behind me, 'Do you have it?' The aide handed him a letter, which he tucked into his pocket as he rushed out, on his way to Capitol Hill for his weekly policy meeting with Republican senators." This was the letter the president had just read to her, of course.

"It was a clean kill," writes Suskind.

This knockout punch to facts-based, consensus-built decision-making was delivered less than two months into Bush's first term and roughly one week before Cheney's climate change working group first convened and listened to Jim Hansen. Paul O'Neill would later see it as the first episode in "a rolling revelation of the way this administration was operating."

O'Neill was also astute enough to realize that Cheney's subterfuge had delivered a body blow to a decade's worth of international dialogue on climate change policy, a process that had begun with the Framework Convention on Climate Change, negotiated somewhat reluctantly by George H. W. Bush in Rio de Janeiro in 1992. As Princeton's Michael Oppenheimer, a scientist and policy expert who had worked on the issue for decades, told me about a month after George Bush Jr.'s change of heart, "We live in a very difficult time right now because of the attitude of the Bush administration. We will determine in the next coming months, really, whether the last ten years of trying to build a diplomatic solution to this problem . . . was all wasted time. And if so, that will put the world back in trying to solve the problem. It will mean a guarantee of a significant amount of additional warming before we bring the thing under control. The diplomatic process was very difficult, and there will be a lot of distrust no matter who the U.S. president is four years from now, and it will take a long time to rebuild. There will be a decade lost, I think." Now, in retrospect, with Bush's reelection, more than a decade.

Another ironical aspect to Bush's thumbing of the nose at his EPA administrator and treasury secretary, not to mention the entire international community (which responded lividly), was that it occurred just as the last reasonable doubt about the human origin of global warming was erased. In January 2001, the very month that Bush and Cheney were sworn in, the Intergovernmental Panel on Climate Change (IPCC) stated in its Third Assessment Report, "There is new and stronger evidence that most of the warming observed over the last 50 years is attributable to human activities," and added that "the increase in temperature in the 20th century is likely to have been the largest of any century during the past 1,000 years." The IPCC had been established by the United Nations in 1988, the year that Jim's explosive Senate testimony first raised broad awareness of the global warming issue.

Dick Cheney's energy task force swiftly produced a plan that promised to carry the temperature increase of the twentieth century on into the next. By the end of April, the vice president was proclaiming that the main thrust of his new energy policy would be to increase supplies: by drilling for oil in the Arctic National Wildlife Refuge, by opening other public lands, especially in the West, to coal, oil, and natural gas exploitation, and by building more than a thousand new coal-burning power plants— about the worst thing there is for the greenhouse—as well as nuclear power plants, which are greenhouse neutral, at least. "Conservation may be a sign of personal virtue," he famously declared, "but it is not a sufficient basis for a sound, comprehensive energy policy."

Much newspaper ink has been spilled over subsequent attempts to reveal (and hide) the process by which Mr. Cheney arrived at this policy, and plenty of evidence suggests that it was essentially written by the coal and oil industry, in which he had recently been employed. Among those who met with Cheney in early 2001—in task force meetings that were actually arranged by the Edison Electric Institute, the main lobbying group for the power industry—were the chief lobbyist and senior executives of the country's largest coal company, privately held Peabody Energy. When Peabody went public, an event that happened to take place within a week of Cheney's formal announcement of the plan, the company's stock rose 50 percent in one day. And the day before Cheney's announcement, a splinter group composed of six of the nation's most antiregulatory coal-burning utility companies—which included David Mould's employer at the time, the Southern Company—donated $100,000 to the Republican Party.

Jim now willingly admits that he may have been naïve to hope that he could have influenced policy with "clear information." But he tried his best.

Back in 1993, he had helped found the Institute on Climate and Planets, a joint outreach program between Columbia University and his NASA institute, GISS, aimed at teaching science to underprivileged urban high school and community college students by getting them involved in real research. Stimulated by his encounter with the policy makers, Jim defined a new task for the outreach team that he led during the summer following his meetings with Cheney's working group. He challenged the team to develop a plan that would meet the nation's growing energy needs, as forecast by Mr. Bush's (or, perhaps more accurately, Mr. Cheney's) own Department of Energy, while meeting the requirements of the alternative scenario. The eminently sensible plan that this group of students and teachers developed over two summers, as the leaders of their country did less than nothing on this issue, shall be described later.

Jim's next, and most likely final, direct interaction with the Bush administration took place in June 2003, when he was asked to give a talk to the White House Council on Environmental Quality (CEQ) and its unabashed chairman, the president's top adviser on the environment, James Connaughton. Jim reads Connaughton as being Bush's top adviser on climate science as well (with the possible exception of a certain science fiction writer). Connaughton is a lawyer. He was installed at the head of

CEQ by Mr. Cheney himself. According to Jim, physicist John Marburger, the director of the Office of Science and Technology Policy and the official science adviser to the president, has nowhere near Connaughton's clout—nor his Machiavellian intent. One of the tasks Connaughton undertook shortly after assuming responsibility for the quality of the nation's environment, for example, was to lead the White House Task Force on Energy Project Streamlining, which supported Cheney's energy plan by making it easier for oil and gas companies to obtain federal leases and drilling permits. His success in this area despoiled much of the landscape of the Rocky Mountain West over the next few years.

In the two years following Jim's previous White House session, in 2001, the most dramatic progress in the science of global warming had occurred in the understanding of its potential effect on the vast sheets of ice that cover Greenland and Antarctica. More than two miles thick in some places, the polar ice sheets comprise the frozen equivalent of about 70 meters, or 230 feet, of sea level rise. Since a significant fraction of the human population and many of our greatest cities are located within a few meters of the present level, Jim and others in the research community, including Michael Oppenheimer, had begun to realize, as Jim would put it in his CEQ talk, that the "need to preserve global coastlines . . . sets a low ceiling on the level of global warming that would constitute Dangerous Anthropogenic Interference." This last phrase comes directly from the 1992 Framework Convention, which set as its goal the "stabilization of greenhouse gas concentrations in the atmosphere at a level that would prevent dangerous anthropogenic interference with the climate system." The IPCC had been circling the issue of exactly how much greenhouse forcing would be dangerous, and the work leading up to this talk was Jim's first attempt to put the marker down.

It would be an understatement to say that IPCC assessments represent a conservative evaluation of the state of the art of global warming science. The process that produces them is arguably the most consensus-driven that has ever been applied to a scientific problem. All the nations involved, including Saudi Arabia, for example, have line-by-line veto power over the executive summaries at the beginning of each of the three sections of every assessment, which are all that most people read. By mandate, the panel may only consider relatively well-established conclusions from the peer-reviewed literature. Thus, pretty much by definition, its assessments are a few years out of date the moment they are released.

Even as the ink was drying on the 2001 assessment, it was becoming clear that science had a poor understanding of all the factors governing sea level—and even to some extent how to measure it. There was little doubt that it was rising, however; and the first few years of the new century produced some signs that the rate of the rise was probably on the increase.

In February 2002, a slab the size of Rhode Island on the Larsen B ice shelf, which floats on the Weddell Sea east of the Antarctic Peninsula, dissolved into a galaxy of icebergs in the space of about five weeks. It is unlikely that any of the polar ice shelves has undergone a collapse of this magnitude in at least 10,000 years. (This might be interpreted as the planet's response to George Bush's announcement that same month of an entirely voluntary program that would set no limits on emissions themselves, but would hopefully reduce the so-called greenhouse intensity of the U.S. economy, the amount of emissions per unit of gross domestic product. This plan guarantees a continued exponential growth in emissions, only at a slightly slower rate than the present.)

An ice shelf is formed as a land-based glacier flows onto the sea. This is the main way the Antarctic ice sheet, most of which is far too cold to melt, sheds the mass that it gains from precipitation farther inland. Now, the melting of a floating ice shelf will not in itself cause the seas to rise. (Archimedes' principle: the level in a glass of water doesn't change as the ice cubes melt.) However, the shelf acts something like a champagne cork. Its presence, especially at the water's edge where it is grounded to the land below sea level (glaciologists call this the plug), inhibits the flow of the glaciers on its landward, uphill side. When the cork pops, these inland glaciers flow more rapidly onto the sea, and this *will* raise sea level.

Ominously, there is reason to believe that the trigger for this form of ice sheet collapse may occur early in the global warming process, for it seems to be located in the oceans. Right now, most of the heat from the modern greenhouse buildup is being stored some distance below the ocean surface, at approximately the grounding level of these glacial plugs—the perfect depth for "tickling" the outlet glaciers in their most sensitive locations.

A few months after the Larsen B collapse, a group led by NASA's Jay Zwally published a study of outlet glaciers in Greenland, demonstrating that the increased surface melting that has accompanied the recent warming there has initiated another dramatic process: the rivulets wandering along on the vast aquamarine surface of the Greenland ice sheet eventually converge into streams large enough to carve dark, near-vertical (and quite terrifying, if you're walking nearby and consider the possibility of slipping and sliding in) shafts, called moulins, which deliver the water to the base of the ice sheet, thereby forming a lubricating sheet of water that will speed the skating of an outlet glacier into the sea.

In the months leading up to Jim's presentation at CEQ, many studies confirmed that the seaward flow of a number of outlet glaciers had increased in recent years, mainly by means of the "champagne cork" process in Antarctica, and by both that and what some now call the "Zwally effect" in Greenland. Scientists were beginning to realize that the ice sheets could collapse much more rapidly than had previously been assumed. The standard ice sheet models, which haven't evolved significantly in decades, treat an ice sheet more or less as an ice cube sitting on a table, melting at its edges as snow is poured on top. Most ignore even the most basic principles of ice sheet dynamics, and those that include any treatment at all of glacial flow still ignore the two explosive processes just mentioned. These models predict that the ice sheets will shrink very slowly, on the time scale of millennia, whereas Jim and a few others now suspected that the champagne cork and Zwally effects change the time scale to something on the order of a century—this century, for instance, or the next.

Jim had found confirmation for this explosiveness in the paleoclimate record: the most recent ice sheet collapse, which took place at the end of the last ice age about 14,000 years ago, sent sea levels up a grand total of sixty feet, at the rate of three feet every twenty years, for 400 years. The first three feet would be sufficient, incidentally, for the entire Mississippi River Delta, including New Orleans, to vanish into the Gulf of Mexico; for tens of millions of people in Bangladesh, one of the most densely populated regions on Earth, to be forced to migrate; and for rice-growing river deltas throughout Asia, a major source of food for the human species, to be inundated.

Jim named his CEQ talk "Can We Defuse the Global Warming Time Bomb?" In his typically holistic way, he integrated the new metric of sea level rise with his alternative scenario and the insights into the physics and history of climate he has accrued over the past three decades to come up with a complete science-based plan. The historical evidence told him that if we add enough new greenhouse forcing to the atmosphere to add about one more degree Fahrenheit, Earth will reach its highest temperatures since the Eemian interglacial period about 125,000 years ago. During the warmest phase of the Eemian, sea level was between about thirteen and twenty feet higher than it is today. So he outlined an alternative scenario that would hold the added greenhouse temperature rise to less than one degree Celsius (about two degrees Fahrenheit).

It was the same story he had told Dick Cheney: "(1) Halt or reverse growth of air pollutants, specifically soot, ozone, and methane, (2) keep average fossil fuel CO_2 emissions in the next 50 years about the same as they are today [that is, at the time of his talk, in 2003]. The CO_2 and non-CO_2 portions of the scenario are equally important. I argue that they are both feasible and make sense for other reasons, in addition to climate."

He remembers his reception in the CEQ conference room as being a cordial one. He had a good-size audience. "It went pretty well," he recalls, ". . . and it lasted an extra half hour, because they were asking questions and discussing things. So, it was the kind of reception you like to have from those kind of people, but . . . their response . . . was in some ways analogous to the vice president's approach, namely, they picked out the parts that they liked, methane and black carbon, and kind of ignored the fact that I'm also saying there's a problem with CO_2."

He had told them straight out that carbon dioxide would "be the dominant anthropogenic [manmade] forcing in the near future" and outlined a scenario that "would require a near-term leveling off of fossil fuel CO_2 emissions and a decline of CO_2 emissions before midcentury, heading toward stabilization of atmospheric CO_2 by the end of the century."

In response, they threw him and anyone else who would like to solve the problem a bone. About a year later, President Bush announced a new program called the Methane to Markets Partnership, committing $53 million to help other countries "work in coordination with the private sector to share and expand the use of technologies to capture methane emissions that are now wasted in the course of industrial processes and use them as a new energy source." (In other words, except for awarding federal money to a few private companies, it would have no effect whatsoever in the United States.) Over ten years, the program was projected to prevent an amount of methane with the greenhouse power of about 180 million metric tons of carbon dioxide from entering the atmosphere. At a time when worldwide emissions were more than 20 billion tons every year, this seems more like a crumb, actually, than even a bone.

In 2007, testifying alongside George Deutsch at the hearing before the House Oversight Committee, the ever-sunny Mr. Connaughton would trumpet the earnestness with which he had listened to Jim in 2003 by claiming that the Methane to Markets Partnership had evolved from the "Time Bomb" talk (although Connaughton was far too wily to call it that). Thus, the Bush administration had not only sought but also acted upon a policy recommendation from Jim.

It was exactly a week after the Time Bomb talk that stories about the administration's censorship of climate science began to appear in the news. On June 19, 2003, Andy Revkin and his colleague Katharine Seelye at *The New York Times* reported that none other than the Council on Environmental Quality had done some serious editing to a section on global warming in the Environmental Protection Agency's first-ever report on the state of the environment, which had been requested two years earlier by its now beleaguered administrator, Christie Whitman. "The editing eliminated references to many studies concluding that warming is at least partly caused by rising concentrations of smokestack and tail-pipe emissions and could threaten health and ecosystems," Revkin and Seelye wrote. "Among the deletions were conclusions about the likely human contribution to warming from a 2001 report on climate by the National Research Council that the White House had commissioned and that President

Bush had endorsed in speeches that year." (The 2001 report had been requested by Cheney's climate change working group. Jim helped write it.) CEQ's editing job was also covered in *Redacting the Science of Climate Change,* a report produced in 2007 by the Government Accountability Project (GAP). "Emails from CEQ Chairman James Connaughton reveal that he participated directly in the review, requesting to be apprised of every edit made to the EPA draft report," GAP wrote. In the end, the staff at EPA refused to agree to the edits, and the entire section on global warming was dropped from the state of the environment report. Christie Whitman resigned as EPA administrator shortly thereafter in May 2003.

E-mails I have found on the White House Web site indicate that Mr. Connaughton and his CEQ colleagues actively strategized with organizations funded by ExxonMobil and other fossil fuel concerns to discredit the sound, mainstream science of global warming and fight all action that might limit greenhouse gas emissions. For example, in May 2002, the Bush administration released a report about the potential consequences of global warming in the United States, as required under a United Nations treaty. In accordance with mainstream thinking, the report concluded that warming posed a significant risk and was caused by human activity. When it made the front page of *The New York Times,* the folks at CEQ became concerned. Connaughton's chief of staff, Philip Cooney, sought the assistance of Myron Ebell at the Competitive Enterprise Institute, an active organization in the global warming denial industry. According to a 2007 report by the Union of Concerned Scientists, the institute received about $2 million in funding from ExxonMobil between 1998 and 2005.

"Dear Phil," Ebell responded. "Thanks for calling and asking for our help. . . . I want to help you cool things down, but after consulting with the team, I think that what we can do is limited until there is an official statement from the Administration repudiating the report to the [United Nations] and disavowing large parts of it. . . . It seems to me that the folks at EPA are the obvious fall guys, and we would only hope that the fall guy (or gal) should be as high up as possible. . . . Perhaps tomorrow we will call for Whitman to be fired. I know that doesn't sound like much help, but it seems to me that the only leverage to push you in the right direction is to drive a wedge between the President and those in the Administration who think they are serving the President's interest by pushing this rubbish."

Ebell and his friends got their official repudiation just two days after he wrote this e-mail, when the president himself disparaged the report, saying it had been "put out by the bureaucracy," and reaffirmed his opposition to the Kyoto treaty.

According to a June 2007 article in *Rolling Stone,* internal White House e-mails obtained under the Freedom of Information Act reveal that Cooney then crafted a letter in response to the *Times* article, stressing the uncertainties in climate change science and asserting that Bush's do-nothing policies were therefore "appropriate." The letter was published over James Connaughton's signature, and it seems that both he and the president's political adviser, Karl Rove, helped write it. "Edits to the rough drafts of the letter were blacked out by White House censors," reports *Rolling Stone,* "but Rove's pithy endorsement of the final draft survived."

" 'Great,' he wrote in praise of Cooney's spin. 'Defends the report rather than staying focused on the policy.' "

And, of course, about a year later, the Competitive Enterprise Institute got its "fall gal" when Christie Whitman resigned.

Connaughton's troops were excellent propagandists. They read the literature, and it seems that they understood the true science very well, but they employed their reading and expert advice they got, including Jim Hansen's, as an aid in twisting and confusing the facts. Many of their e-mails went back and forth to the Office of the Vice President.

In early 2003, two ubiquitous global warming deniers, Willie Soon and Sallie Baliunas, funded partially by the American Petroleum Institute, published a paper in the peer-reviewed journal *Climate Research*. It challenged one of the main conclusions of the 2001 IPCC report, namely, that "the increase in temperature in the 20th century is likely to have been the largest of any century during the past 1,000 years." These two authors argued that it was warmer during an unusual climatic interval in medieval times than it is today. They submitted their paper to this rather obscure journal through one of its even more obscure editors, who lived halfway around the world in New Zealand and shared their contrarian views. Five other editors of the journal resigned in protest over the publisher's subsequent refusal to change the shoddy and easily manipulated peer-review process that had let the paper through without scrutiny of its faulty methods. One of these methods was to count any change in precipitation—to either wetter or drier conditions—as a rise in temperature.

Connaughton's group loved this paper. After it came out, Philip Cooney stated proudly in an e-mail to Kevin O'Donovan, special assistant to the vice president for domestic policy and Cheney's point man on climate, "We plan to refer to this study in administration communications on the science of global climate change. In fact, CEQ just inserted a reference to it in the final draft chapter on climate change contained in EPA's first state of the environment report. . . . It represents an opening to potentially invigorate debate on the actual climate history of the past 1,000 years."

This e-mail only came to light as the result of a sly maneuver by one of the Democratic congressmen on Henry Waxman's House Oversight Committee. In March 2007, when the committee heard testimony from George Deutsch, Philip Cooney, James Connaughton, a fourth staunch global warming denier, and a rather outnumbered Jim Hansen, Representative John Yarmuth of Kentucky read the e-mail aloud during the hearing. This prompted strong objections from a CEQ lawyer and James Connaughton himself. The ensuing conversation revealed that this was just one of a number of communications between Cooney and O'Donovan that the committee had requested for its investigation. (Cooney admitted under oath that he frequently "consulted" and "compared notes" with O'Donovan.) Citing executive privilege, CEQ had refused to turn over the documents but had allowed some committee staffers to read them. This is how Yarmuth got the quote.

Kevin O'Donovan eventually left government employ for a job with Shell Oil.

The day after Jim spoke at CEQ, a group from the Jet Propulsion Laboratory and Caltech that happened to include one of Jim's earliest collaborators published a paper in *Science* entitled "Potential Environmental Impact of a Hydrogen Economy on the Stratosphere." Based on simulations and atmospheric chemistry, they argued that the potential widespread use of hydrogen fuel cells stood to produce a multitude of changes in the chemistry of the stratosphere, including the destruction of stratospheric ozone, which would cause the hole in the ozone layer to grow. The nations of the Earth have been trying to reverse the growth of the ozone hole since 1987, when they signed the Montreal Protocol, which limits the production of ozone-destroying chemicals, such as chlorofluorocarbons, or freons. (We *want* ozone in the stratosphere, where it provides a shield against ultraviolet sunlight. We don't want it in the troposphere, which lies closer to the planetary surface.) The public affairs offices at JPL and Caltech worked together on a press release to coincide with the paper's publication.

Bad timing. George Bush had announced a major hydrogen fuel initiative in his State of the Union address the previous January, and Energy Secretary Abraham was planning to visit Europe the week after the paper's publication to sign a major international agreement to develop fuel cells. Headquarters summarily killed the NASA press release, thus guaranteeing much less attention to the study.

About four months later, in October 2003, Jim's GISS colleague David Rind was told that it would be "unacceptable" to suggest that the United States might slow global warming by cutting back on fossil fuel use.

NASA was led at that time by Sean O'Keefe, a personal friend and protégé of Dick Cheney's. The majority of O'Keefe's public service prior to his confirmation as NASA administrator had been in various financial capacities at the Department of Defense. At the beginning of George H. W. Bush's term in office, during which Cheney was secretary of defense, O'Keefe was appointed comptroller and chief financial officer of the department. Near the end of the senior Bush's term, he was appointed secretary of the Navy. An accountant by training, O'Keefe is the only administrator in NASA's history to have had no background in science or engineering. He was also openly and unapologetically partisan. As one senior insider at the agency puts it, "In came Sean, and then it became very clear NASA belonged to Sean, who belonged to Cheney."

O'Keefe's assistant administrator for public affairs (David Mould's predecessor) was Glenn Mahone. It probably is fair to call Mahone "O'Keefe's guy," because he had entered the agency as a Democrat, during the Clinton presidency under Administrator Daniel Goldin, and had changed his party loyalty in order to keep his job under O'Keefe.

"The only way he survived," says our insider, "was, when Sean showed up, Glenn had the keys to the building. He knew every trick in the book and knew every player in the game and immediately became Sean's best friend and said, 'I will be your chancellor to tell you everything about this place—and, by the way, I'd like to stay.'" When O'Keefe asked the White House transition team if he could keep Mahone, they agreed—for a price: Dean Acosta was installed as his deputy.

NASA civil servants point out that it is unusual for the two highest positions in public affairs to be filled by "politicals." Usually the deputy is an experienced civil servant who brings a knowledge of the agency and some institutional memory to the job. This may provide balance as well and give the rank and file the means to be heard at the highest levels.

Mahone "was clearly the boss [of public affairs] during his reign," says a JPL source. He ruled by fear and intimidation. A source from headquarters says he "showed no cards to anyone, and he was a master of pitting people against each other . . . and just playing with people." With no prompting, a third source volunteers, "We had a boss, Glenn Mahone, who I personally felt was the Antichrist."

Acosta didn't stand a chance; it was war from the moment he appeared. Even he admits that he was Mahone's deputy "in name only," that he was shuttled to the side and "given little projects to go and work."

Guess what one of those "little projects" would have been.

The lead public affairs officer for Earth science, David Steitz, remembers the Council on Environmental Quality as being a "big player" in the discussions about handling every emerging development in climate science at NASA. "Mahone would get on the phone with Jennifer Wood, who is now at EPA—what a coincidence. She was Mahone's special assistant. . . . Jennifer and Glenn and I would call CEQ." And the spokesperson for CEQ was—second coincidence—Dana Perino, eventual deputy press secretary for the White House and, finally, press secretary, when Tony Snow left the post near the end of Bush's second term. Steitz remembers that he, Mahone, and Wood got direction from Perino on killing the press release about the potential danger of hydrogen fuel cells.

Control intensified with the approach of the presidential election. In fact, much of the information Andy Revkin received from employees throughout the agency in February 2006, as a result of his revelations about Jim, focused upon this period. "The politicization of NASA became very intense in the run-up to the 2004 election," he says. "A lot of people within the agency provided me with convincing evidence that essentially the whole public affairs apparatus was turned into a campaign election apparatus."

For example (though this is not one of the stories Revkin heard), in January 2004 the agency scored a much needed success after the *Columbia* shuttle disaster by placing two robotic rovers on the surface of Mars. The Jet Propulsion Laboratory had built the rovers, so the lab made a video to commemorate the success. It was produced by Blaine Baggett, manager of the lab's Office of Communications and Education, who had previously had a distinguished career in public television. When Dick Cheney visited the lab as part of the celebration, he saw the video. Soon thereafter, he was inserted into it, over Baggett's objections, and it began playing continuously on NASA TV.

The same month that the rovers landed, President Bush announced a plan for manned missions to the moon and Mars that was dubbed his New Vision for Space Exploration.

"Starting early in 2004," wrote Revkin two years later in the *Times*, "directives, almost always transmitted verbally [sic] through a chain of midlevel workers, went out from NASA headquarters to the agency's far-flung research centers and institutes saying that all news releases on Earth science developments had to allude to goals set out in Mr. Bush's 'vision statement' for the agency." (The MO sounds familiar.)

Three years after the fact, scientists still tell these stories ruefully.

One of the more egregious instances of "product placement" for "the vision" was a case in which a false quote was attributed to a NASA scientist. A release describing research about wind patterns and the recent warming of the Indian Ocean included claims that the findings would "advance space exploration" by increasing the understanding of our home planet and that the technologies involved "may someday prove useful in studying climate systems on other planets." The claims were placed in the mouth of Dr. Tong Lee of the Jet Propulsion Laboratory.

The original draft of the release had been prepared by the scientists and public affairs staff at JPL. Headquarters had then inserted the offending phrases, and Lee had been called to give the okay. Reached in a hallway in the midst of a scientific meeting in Hawaii, he reluctantly agreed. But he soon reversed that choice, arguing that he had been rushed and distracted by the meeting. It was too late; the release had gone out.

His colleagues expressed shock and outrage. "Putting words into a researcher's mouth is censorship," wrote one. "Come on, this is embarrassing to Dr. Lee," wrote another. "Enough said. Are any of you 'managers' going to point this out to whoever injected this nonsense into a press release of some excellent scientific work? There are no planets in our solar system that have climates like Earth. Are there? Are we talking about some other solar system?"

Lee soon demanded that the release be removed from the NASA Web site. The JPL press office complied, but the original version remained on headquarters' Web site for more than a year, until Revkin asked about it in the course of his reporting. It then disappeared—but briefly. A year after that, only the offending version could be found in the primary archive of press releases on headquarters' Web site.

A month after Bush's new "vision" was announced, Glenn Mahone invited the public affairs directors from every NASA center to a two-day meeting at a Holiday Inn in Washington, about a block from headquarters, to roll out a "school visits strategy" aimed, ostensibly, at promoting the new idea. Many in NASA public affairs point to this gathering, and especially the moment when Sean O'Keefe pounded the table and declared, "We have only two or three months to sell this thing!" as the point when things really began to go downhill.

Gretchen Cook-Anderson, the director of the education division, had been tasked by Mahone to develop the school visits strategy. Oddly, however, and to the frustration and extreme anger of the educational staff, no one from that division was involved in its implementation. In fact, a source from JPL recalls being firmly told at the meeting not to let the educational staff "interfere" in the events, that is, make them educational.

There was grumbling at the meeting about its pointlessness. Mahone overheard the public affairs director from Johnson Space Center, an ex-marine named Dan Carpenter, suggest, "Why don't we stop complaining and do something about it?" He was out of his job in a couple of months.

In any event, from March until just before Election Day 2004, top NASA officials, including O'Keefe, visited dozens of elementary and middle schools in "key Congressional districts around the country where the administration needed to shore up its support for Bush's Moon/Mars initiative and re-election," writes Cook-Anderson. Mahone directed his headquarters staff to secure local media coverage for every event and to make sure that a NASA astronaut was always on hand to attract a crowd. This was an effective way to "pump up" local parents, officials, and townspeople both for "the vision" and for the Republican presidential ticket. The product placement that was simultaneously occurring in scientific press releases seems like small potatoes by comparison.

At the same time, Mahone began taking a personal interest in Earth science. David Steitz says his boss was "riding shotgun" over him, saying, "I want every Earth science press release to come through me." Having held his position since the end of the Clinton era, and harboring increasingly strong misgivings about having to soften and change the wording of press releases, Steitz decided he wanted out. He'd worked with many of his colleagues for more than a decade, he says, and "it got to the point where I couldn't stomach trying to work that beat, and I didn't want to lie to my friends."

Gretchen Cook-Anderson was Mahone's "golden girl" right then. She says he used to "brag on" her, compliment her on what a wonderful public affairs officer she was and how hard she worked despite having twin three-year-old boys. Most people think highly of Gretchen. She is bright, vivacious, and astoundingly energetic ("one hundred and ten percent all the time," says Steitz). In her spare time, she has published a novel and founded a business. Mahone assigned her to Steitz's post in April 2004, as Steitz moved to the newsroom.

Gretchen soon learned that one of her new responsibilities was to give Mahone and Dean Acosta the famous "heads-up" whenever an Earth scientist received an interview request from a major media outlet. This was a seat-of-the-pants affair; most of the communication was done by cell phone; and, as Gretchen learned, Mahone and Acosta received most of their directives from the Office of Science and Technology Policy (OSTP), Executive Office of the President.

In late June 2004, record-setting temperatures and a stretch of unusually dry weather helped spark large wildfires in Alaska and Canada's Yukon Territory. On the first of July, as the town of Fairbanks seemed threatened and homes were being evacuated, *NBC Nightly News* with Tom Brokaw arranged to interview Waleed Abdalati, to get his perspective on the climatic factors that might have been involved. Waleed was wearing two hats in NASA's cryospheric science effort at that time: he was acting manager of the agencywide program at headquarters and head of the branch at Goddard Space Flight Center. The cryosphere comprises the icy parts of the world, which are found mostly at high latitudes such as Alaska's, and Waleed is a poised and well-spoken individual who does most of his research on the Greenland ice sheet, so he has a good knowledge of arctic climate.

He was about to leave his office for his 2 P.M. interview when Gretchen reached him on his cell phone and advised him not to go on, because headquarters had not yet "gotten approval from OSTP."

Waleed told Gretchen he was uncomfortable with this. She said she was, too, but she had managed to delay the interview until four, so he should stall for a while. On the other hand, one can't exactly stall when an interviewer starts asking questions. As it worked out, "clearance" came through at three twenty, but Waleed remembers being so "self-conscious about all of this stuff" that he gave one of the worst interviews of his life. Of the many he's given, he recalls, this was "the only one that was just plain not used at all."

"I actually challenged public affairs on this," he says, "and the position they take is, 'Look, a potentially controversial story can come out. The White House is right to want a heads-up on it. They're not approving it, but we don't know that they've received the notification until they respond to us.'

"You see where that leads you? . . . I read that to be approval."

OSTP never called Gretchen directly. Her calls always came in from Mahone or Acosta, and they sometimes came in when she was at home in the evening with her family. The White House may not always have been involved. She believes her bosses sometimes anticipated that the White House might get upset and decided to err on the side of caution. In this particular case, the interview was not actually shut down, of course, but she does remember times when she *was* directed to shut down interviews. Admitting that she is "slightly hardheaded," she claims never to have followed through. ("One can always feign stupidity later. 'Oh, you know, I couldn't reach him. I tried. I called him. I couldn't reach him.'") She believes she was actually helping the agency by doing this, because the canceling of an interview would "if anything . . . spark the curiosity of the reporter as to, well, what happened?"

In August or September of 2004, as the presidential campaign was rekindling, Mahone and Acosta began to complain that Gretchen's division was producing too many press releases. This struck her as odd, for there had been no spike in productivity; the releases were coming out at pretty much the same rate that they always had. She was told to "scrutinize" certain releases, and it didn't take her long to realize that they all related to global warming or some other global effect of air pollution. For example, her division might be putting out two releases separated by a few weeks on different aspects of the ozone hole. She would be asked why there needed to be two. "The news was different," she says, but Mahone and Acosta "were unable—and never really even tried—to discern the difference between, maybe, two different press releases that may have had the same general subject matter. I was told, 'Well, it's just not news.' And I'm thinking to myself, 'What do you mean it's not news? Whenever we do something on ozone, typically it does get press.'"

In contrast to her bosses, she and her civil servant colleagues tended to be very interested in such differences, because they were fascinated with the science. Many of them, such as Rob Gutro, a writer at Goddard who holds degrees in both meteorology and English, took special pride in their ability to convey complex scientific concepts in layman's terms. Indeed, they saw this as the main function of their jobs. Gretchen would take home books and other materials that she borrowed from the scientists in order to increase her knowledge so she could write more intelligently. "I actually got to a point where I was—whatever you want to call it—a tree hugger. I began to love Earth sciences!" This made the stifling of the science all the more disturbing to her.

Only a small fraction of the agency's scientific output ever results in a press release. There is a formal "news mining" procedure, and, for one thing, only studies published in peer-reviewed journals are even considered. NASA scientists publish hundreds of peer-reviewed journal articles every year, most of which are of interest only to specialists. Gretchen's division only produced releases for the articles that were "saying something new," the ones that "we really knew would be more earth-shattering, so to speak—excuse the pun."

The majority of the agency's Earth science budget is devoted to climate research, and of all the federal agencies, NASA receives by far the most funding for such research—on the order of $1.5 billion in 2004. (This number had shrunk by about one-third by 2006, but more on that later.) Largely for this reason, the agency was making and continues to make a goodly portion of the important discoveries in the field; so, naturally, most of the press releases were related to climate. ("Basic logic," says Gretchen.) At one point she looked into the statistics: about 60 percent of Earth science funding focused on climate and so did "sixty percent or thereabouts" of the press releases.

But her bosses did not follow this logic. They began to express anger at the public affairs staff at Goddard in particular, which is the largest research center at NASA, suspecting that they were at the center of a "conspiracy" to "kick out as many climate research–related press releases as they possibly could," motivated by "a political agenda." Actually, a significant fraction of the offending material was coming from JPL, and some was emerging from other, smaller NASA research centers. In Gretchen's hearing, Mahone and Acosta often accused the Goddard scientists and public affairs staff of being a bunch of liberals.

In September, the two summoned her to a meeting in Mahone's office on the Ninth Floor. There, behind a closed door, they informed her that all climate related press releases — and no others—would now be subject to a special review procedure. It went like this:

The releases were composed on computers, of course, and up until this time, they had been sent through the various stages of review entirely by e-mail. Now, whenever Gretchen received a climate-related press release from any NASA center—and in her position she received them all—she was to print it out and carry the paper copy upstairs either to Mahone or Acosta. It was usually Acosta. One of them would then "notify" the White House about it. (Her bosses used this word carefully, and in the months that Gretchen was involved, they used it over and over again.) After a few days, a week, or even more, she would be summoned upstairs to retrieve the paper copy, which would now feature handwritten edits that invariably muted the danger of fossil fuel emissions or amplified the uncertainty of greenhouse science. The author of these edits was never identified (and Gretchen was wise enough not to ask). She remembers "at least" two scripts, and she assumes that the one she saw most frequently was Acosta's and that the other was Mahone's. She was directed to incorporate these changes into the electronic copy and send it back for review by the scientists and center public affairs officers with whom it had originated. She was also encouraged to destroy the paper copy.

"Glenn Mahone himself, he never told me anything about throwing anything away," she says. "That would have been Dean. I think Glenn was quite a bit smarter than that." ("Glenn was evil and smart; Dean was just evil," observes Steitz.)

This advance notification procedure applied to any activity related to climate science that stood a reasonable chance of attracting media attention. The White House was also to be notified whenever a climate scientist was planning to participate in an important meeting or was contacted for an interview on a subject related to global warming. (This all bears a certain resemblance to the set of directives Leslie Mc-Carthy would hear in a phone call from Acosta and David Mould, one late afternoon a little more than a year later.)

All communication associated with this procedure occurred either in person or over the phone. "Whenever I got a phone call, usually it was Dean—unless it was something super major, then Glenn would call himself—it was usually Dean who called, and he would summon me up-stairs to talk to him in person, and he would always say, 'Gretchen, do not e-mail me on this.'" She was also told not to talk to her colleagues about it.

Sometimes, when it was getting near time for a release to be issued, Gretchen would call or walk upstairs to check on its status. "There were times when I would hear, 'We have not heard back yet.'"

She was never told where the documents went at the White House, but she suspects that Bob Hopkins may have been involved. Hopkins, who had been a spokesman in the Midwest for George Bush's 2000 presi-dential campaign, was now director of communications at OSTP, respon-sible "for managing media relations, providing strategic communications support, and coordinating communications on science and technology is-sues across government agencies." To Gretchen's admittedly partial knowl-edge, Hopkins was the only member of the White House staff "who had a fairly regularized line of communication to NASA headquarters." He also led a weekly telephone conference with public affairs representatives from NASA and other science-oriented agencies to talk in general terms about what was happening in the world of science communication, such as it was, at the White House that week.

The most measurable effect of the new procedure was an immediate and dramatic slowdown in the review process. (When he reviewed ar-chives on the NASA Web site in 2006, Andy Revkin discovered that the number of Earth science–related press releases dropped by a factor of four between 2004 and 2005, from almost fifty to twelve.)

The frustration began to build at a few NASA centers right away.

Gretchen informed her bosses of this, and in a rare moment of openness, they allowed her to tell her colleagues some but not all of the details of the new procedure. She did this in a conference call with six or seven Earth science public affairs officers from around the country, sometime in September 2004.

"What I was asked to communicate," she says, "was that anything that was climate-related needed to come directly to me, and then I would go through it and it would be vetted with the research scientists at headquarters. I added that such drafts would then go directly to Glenn Mahone or Dean Acosta. I did not hide the fact that I was opposed to what I was being asked to do. I never hid that fact, which is part of what I was afraid would get me into trouble eventually."

This was a difficult time for Gretchen. Headquarters is always a stressful place; it's "a bit tricky" to know whom you can be candid with. She alludes to "a lot of shifting alliances and loyalties." She does not recall mentioning White House involvement during the conference call, but she did talk about it in the halls to one or two of her closest colleagues. In any event, as events would show, Rob Gutro at Goddard somehow found out.

The new style of editing was noticed as well. Drew Shindell and Gavin Schmidt at Jim Hansen's institute, GISS, had recently completed a study of Antarctic surface temperatures using a GISS computer model. In contrast to the planet as a whole, the main landmass of Antarctica, that is, all but the Antarctic Peninsula, has cooled in recent decades. Stratospheric ozone levels have been dropping, and this has had an especially strong impact on the frozen continent, because the hole in the ozone layer hovers above it. To demonstrate the validity of their computer model, Shindell and Schmidt first plugged in the greenhouse and ozone levels that have been measured over the last fifty years and showed that the model reproduced Antarctic cooling rather well. Thanks to the signing of the Montreal Protocol about twenty years ago, stratospheric ozone levels are expected to reverse course and begin growing in coming decades, while greenhouse levels have been growing exponentially since the start of the industrial revolution. Plugging in the expected changes in both over the next fifty years, Shindell and Schmidt found that the cooling trend stands to reverse in the next few decades, and Antarctic temperatures stand to rise "more rapidly than elsewhere in the southern hemisphere." This prediction might be deemed newsworthy, since Antarctic ice represents the frozen equivalent of about 63 meters or 207 feet of potential sea level rise. It would also raise a red flag for those who have denied the connection between human activity and global warming prominently in the news media, because the cooling trend at the bottom of the planet is one of their favorite counterexamples.

The paper summarizing this study was accepted by *Geophysical Research Letters,* and more than a month before the late-September publication date, Shindell and Schmidt began working with Gretchen, Rob Gutro, and a second science writer at Goddard, Krishna Ramanujan, on a press release. There was a lot of back and forth.

Their first working title was "Cool Antarctica May Warm Rapidly This Century, Study Finds." As Shindell (who had only a vague understanding of the reporting structure at headquarters) later wrote, "Headquarters staff, who were recently enlarged to include some staffers sent over from the White House, asked that it be 'softened.' The next suggestion from us was 'NASA Scientists Expect Temperature Flip-flop at the Antarctic.' That apparently wasn't 'soft' enough, so this time they gave us a title to use themselves: 'Scientists Predict Antarctic Climate Changes.' I objected, but was overruled, and that was the title of the release that went out. Not surprisingly, it generated relatively little interest."

Ironically, about a month after their paper was published and less than a week after the presidential election, Shindell and Schmidt would be included in *Scientific American*'s list of the top fifty scientists of 2004, recognizing "outstanding acts of leadership in science and technology from the past year." They were the first NASA scientists ever to be so honored.

The review process for this release took more than four weeks, enough time for it to come out after the paper itself. Goddard director Ed Weiler points out that "news is news because of the first three letters, *n-e-w*. If the people at headquarters sit on a press release two or three or four weeks and just can't find time to get to it, that's just as good as censoring it." Mahone and Acosta knew this. They would sometimes actually say to Gretchen, "Well, yes, we may have it back [from the White House] now, but there's really no point in putting it out now, because the news is old."

With their paper nearly a week old and still no press release, Shindell and Schmidt complained to their managers at GISS, Larry Travis and Jim Hansen. This resulted in a series of e-mails on October 5, 2004. At midmorning, Leslie McCarthy wrote:

> Jim and Larry:
>
> As you may know, Drew Shindell has been working extensively with Rob Gutro of GSFC and Gretchen Cook-Anderson of HQ PAO on a press release on his newest paper. The press release had been slated to be released on September 27 but has been held up.
>
> Here is an email from Rob Gutro about what the hold-up is:
>
> "According to HQ, there's a new review process that has totally grid-locked all earth science press releases relating to climate or climate change. According to HQ Public Affairs, 2 political appointees, Ghassem and the White House are now reviewing all climate related press releases...thus, the 4+ week review time for Drew's press release that was slated for issue on Sept. 27th. We're still waiting to get the release back from the WH. We'll let you know when it happens."
>
> Wanted to let you know about this important new change. Thanks.
>
> Leslie

Ghassem Asrar, the deputy associate administrator for Earth science, had been a champion of the Earth science program at NASA and of Jim's work in particular for more than a decade. However, his coworkers affirm that he softened press releases and scientific presentations to management during this difficult time. "Ghassem, evidently, read the reality in such a way that he felt it prudent not to object," says Jim's boss, Franco Einaudi. David Steitz likens Asrar's position to that of a "governor of a state in an occupied territory."

At about noon, Gutro responded to an inquiry from Shindell:

> Drew, Krishna—
>
> Still waiting on the release from NASA HQ. It seems to be caught up in the White House, now...and HQ can't get an answer to move it along.
>
> It seems endless...but we'll let you know when we hear something. It is possible that all climate related releases may not be issued until after the election...that's one of the things we've heard. Stay tuned.
>
> Rob

Perhaps this first backhanded appearance of the procedure in print had an effect, for the release was issued the following day. (The public affairs officers at the center level had been trying for weeks to get something on paper. "We continually asked for something in writing about how these things were being reviewed, and the Ninth Floor continually refused to provide that. Absolutely. They were very smart about it," says one.)

This doesn't mean the Ninth Floor was happy to see the new process in writing. Glenn Mahone gave severe dressing-downs to Rob Gutro, his boss, Mark Hess, and Gretchen Cook-Anderson when he eventually found out.

*   *   *

Jim Hansen was probably responsible for that. He had grown increasingly disillusioned over the previous three years at the Bush administration's pattern of inaction, doublespeak, and, lately, outright censorship. Earlier in the year, he had been approached about speaking to a group of "bigwig" potential donors to the Democratic Party, but he had declined, explaining that he "was not a Democrat and did not want to get involved in politics." This led to an invitation from Resources for the Future, a nonprofit, nonpartisan research organization in Washington; but as the election approached, they backed out. Jim's sense was that they had read the tea leaves and guessed that Bush would win and did not want to lose favor with the administration by identifying with him.

But now Jim *wanted* to make a statement. This was when he began to walk the edge. He got in touch with his lifelong mentor, James Van Allen at the University of Iowa, and Van Allen arranged for him to speak in the Distinguished Public Lecture Series offered by Jim's old department, Physics and Astronomy. His "Iowa talk" was essentially the dress rehearsal for the more momentous Keeling talk he would give in San Francisco a year later. He delivered it exactly one week before Election Day.

"The opinions and interpretations that I express today are my personal views," he began. "I am a government employee, but I am on leave today, I travel here at my expense, and I speak as a private citizen."

His scientific message was similar to the one he would deliver a year later; the fundamentals of greenhouse science are not changing all that rapidly at this time. He added a gracious tribute to Van Allen, who would be celebrating his ninetieth birthday that month, and thanked him for the approach to science Jim had learned through "osmosis" by working in his department.

Near the end, Jim described an interaction he'd had with Sean O'Keefe about a year earlier, when O'Keefe had visited GISS for a private viewing of the "Global Warming Time Bomb" talk. As Jim showed O'Keefe a photograph of a small river of meltwater rushing into a moulin in the surface of the Greenland ice sheet, under the title "What Determines

Dangerous Anthropogenic Interference?" and suggested that we may be closer to that threshold than is generally realized, "the administrator interrupted me," Jim told his audience. "He told me that I should not talk about dangerous anthropogenic interference, because we do not know enough or have enough evidence for what would constitute dangerous anthropogenic interference.

"It was several months later before the analogy with the NASA space shuttle tragedies dawned on me. There were engineers who suspected the 'O-ring' dangers with a cold shuttle launch, and there were engineers who were concerned about potential damage from foam insulation bouncing off the shuttle. But they were strongly discouraged from passing that information to the highest levels, where it might have been possible to prevent the tragedies.

"The highest level requiring information on climate change, it seems to me, is the public. They are the ones affected by climate change, and they must decide how seriously we take the issue."

He followed this with a few comments about the communication of scientific information. Showing an image of Leslie McCarthy's e-mail to himself and Larry Travis, in which Rob Gutro described the new review process and mentioned White House involvement, he made the mild observation that "communication with the public has become seriously hampered during the past few years." (Leslie says they all groaned when they found out that Jim had revealed their names.)

Jim then made an unusual disclosure about his political leanings. First he pointed out that he was registered as an independent and stated that his favorite candidate would have been Republican senator John McCain, had he been on the ballot. Then, while expressing reservations about John Kerry, Jim nevertheless indicated that he intended to vote for him in the coming election, because "overall, in my opinion, John Kerry has a far better grasp than President Bush of the important issues that we face."

This speech had nowhere near the impact of the Keeling talk. Jim had briefed Andy Revkin beforehand, and *The New York Times* was the only major news outlet to report on it. In an article that had appeared that morning, Revkin had written, "Dr. Hansen . . . acknowledged that he imperiled his credibility and perhaps his job by criticizing Mr. Bush's policies in the final days of a tight presidential campaign. He said he decided to speak out after months of deliberation because he was convinced the country needed to change course on climate policy."

Jim's research assistant and gatekeeper, Darnell Cain, remembers receiving a series of threatening phone calls that day from the office of NASA's general counsel, requesting a copy of Jim's talk. Darnell did not comply. He explained that he had no knowledge of it; all he knew was that Jim was out of the office that day. He doesn't remember the name of the person who made the call, but other sources suggest that it was Andrew Falcon, an associate general counsel at headquarters. Whoever it was said something about how Jim was "going to be in hot water" and may even have recited the familiar "dire consequences" refrain. Darnell, who employs an understated turn of phrase, says these threats were delivered "in an elevated tone. . . . There were several calls, two or three calls, and one in which the guy was rather caustic." Hoping to generate an electronic record, Darnell asked him to send an e-mail.

Did he get one?

"No. Of course not. And that's where it ended, literally."

Jim would mention this interaction in one of the e-mails he would exchange with Franco Einaudi in January 2006, when he was in serious fear for his job:

> You may suggest that there is the NASA General Counsel to whom I could go, but I am not confident that I would get good advice. For example, just over a year ago, when I was about to give a talk about climate change in Iowa City as a private citizen, one of the attorneys from the NASA General Counsel's office called my office and advised that I would risk punishment under the Hatch Act if I gave the talk. I gave the talk anyhow, and a friend of mine advised me that the Counsel's advice mischaracterized Hatch Act restrictions.

The Hatch Act is aimed at preventing federal employees from using the resources of their office or the authority of their position to engage in partisan activity. The Web site of the U.S. Office of Special Counsel states explicitly, however, that the act permits "federal and D.C. employees" to "express opinions about candidates and issues" and even to "campaign for or against candidates in partisan elections." In taking a day off and in paying his own way when the University of Iowa would have been happy to underwrite his trip, it would appear that Jim scrupulously obeyed this law. So it seems ironic that his office would have received threatening calls from NASA attorneys at a time when the agency's entire public affairs apparatus was campaigning more or less openly for George Bush, under the guise of an educational program. The Office of Special Counsel Web site also states that federal employees may not engage in political activity while on duty, in a government office, using a government vehicle, etc.

Shortly after the Iowa speech, Gretchen Cook-Anderson was summoned upstairs to Glenn Mahone's office, where she found Dean Acosta and David Steitz also in the room. After she entered, the door was closed, and in the presence of the two other men, Mahone commanded her to pick up the phone and call Jim Hansen, right then and there.

"I can't remember his verbatim words," Gretchen says, "but it was something to the effect of 'Make him go away. Make him be quiet. Make Jim Hansen be quiet. I want you to tell him to cease and desist.' And I argued with him. I actually argued with him for the first time. . . . I said, 'Glenn, number one, I don't know what makes you think that Jim Hansen is going to listen to me. I'm a senior level public affairs officer from headquarters, but I'm not his boss in any kind of way. I don't supervise him. I don't fund his research. I do nothing of the sort, but yet I'm going to call him and I'm going to tell him to stop what he's doing and he's actually going to listen to me? Number one. Number two, I am not in the business of committing career suicide, and I honestly, truly believe that that's what a move like that would be doing, because if I call somebody like Jim Hansen and I tell him to cease and desist talking to the media about climate warming and all of this kind of stuff, well, you know what he's going to do? He doesn't know me from Adam right now. . . . He's going to call Andy Revkin or someone else at a big paper, and he's going to tell them that he got some kind of mandate from headquarters through some public affairs officer, and then my name is the name that's going to show up in the paper.' And I said, 'And thirdly, I just don't agree with what you're asking me to do.'

"I said, 'The man has a right. He's a scientist and he's speaking out on what the scientific findings are telling him. I work with these scientists every day. I have to have their respect as a public affairs officer or they're not going to cooperate with me, and the last thing I need to do is contact someone at the level of Jim Hansen, telling him what you're wanting me to tell him, so that he can go back and report this to all of the scientists at NASA through some mass e-mail or something, so that I completely lose the respect of the people that I work with on a daily basis, who know that I personally completely disagree with what's going on.'"

Dean Acosta claims that he wasn't in the room. David Steitz's memory jibes with Gretchen's. She remembers exactly where everyone was sitting. Steitz remembers her as being "very, very upset" at having refused to obey Mahone. "I wish there were ways to show you how twisted that environment was at the time," he adds, "where you have a talented young woman being told to lie or compromise her morals and her ethics strictly from a boss who had no—I mean, what would an outsider looking at this say? This is crazy. Just on many levels. . . . These are vindictive people."

Indeed, that was it for Gretchen Cook-Anderson. The call was not made—for some reason Mahone did not want to make it himself—and in that one conversation she went from golden girl to the doghouse. Mahone rarely talked to her from that day forth; and although it is common for the public affairs folks to work from home and most do so regularly a few days a week, she suddenly lost that privilege, even on the days when one or both of her young twin boys was ill and had to miss school.

*　　*　　*

About two weeks after the election, Mahone held a second all-hands meeting for the senior public affairs staff, this time on the West Coast, in a large meeting room/ballroom at a Courtyard Marriott in Pasadena, not far from JPL. About a hundred people attended. They sat at round tables in groups of eight to ten. Those who were there don't seem to remember the agenda particularly, but a few vividly recall that the political appointees were on a "real high," openly displaying their elation at the election results, and that they dined together at their own tables, separate from the civil servants and contract employees.

In the eyes of nearly everyone, the most memorable moment of this day-and-a-half-long event was a speech by J. T. Jezierski, the agency's White House liaison. (He would take on the additional role of deputy chief of staff under Michael Griffin about a year later.) Different people in attendance have different takes on just how ominous Jezierski sounded (he's not an ominous-sounding guy), but most were taken aback at the directness with which he informed them that they worked for the president, that he had just received a new mandate, and that NASA was all about "the vision" now. One person in attendance believes he "stopped short of a threat." Another took him as saying that "if we didn't like the Bush administration, we should leave the agency." No one asked if J.T. had ever heard of the Hatch Act.

Like George Deutsch, J.T. is a sincere evangelical Christian. He was born in a small town in West Virginia. He earned his undergraduate degree from Wheeling Jesuit University in 1997 and then a master's in public policy from Regent University in Virginia Beach. Regent was originally founded as CBN University by Pat Robertson, the televangelist. The acronym stands for Christian Broadcasting Network. The school's motto is "Christian Leadership to Change the World." After Regent, J.T. worked for the Republican National Committee. Then he did a stop at the Institute for American Values in New York City, which describes itself as a "private, nonprofit, nonpartisan organization that contributes intellectually to strengthening families and civil society in the U.S. and the world." The institute views a healthy family as consisting very much of a married man and a woman and their children.

This background would have qualified him well for his first position in government, in the White House Presidential Personnel Office. The director of the entire United States Office of Personnel Management, the president's "principal advisor in matters of personnel administration for the 1.8 million members of the Federal civil service," was Kay Coles James, according to her biography. James is a former dean of the school of government at Regent University. She presently sits on NASA's Advisory Council.

Regent has boasted on its Web site of having 150 graduates working in the Bush administration. Another would be a graduate of the law school, Monica Goodling, the White House liaison in Attorney General Alberto Gonzales's Justice Department, who in March 2007 pled the Fifth rather than testify to Congress about her role in the controversial firing of eight U.S. attorneys the previous year. A few weeks later, she resigned.

Through J. T. Jezierski, the NASA administrator's office has a bizarre series of connections to the U.S. attorney scandal. As it happens, J.T.'s wife, Crystal, is the director of the Office of Intergovernmental and Public Liaison at the Justice Department. And when J.T. left NASA in 2007 to work on Mitt Romney's presidential campaign, he was replaced by Jane Cherry, a young assistant to Karl Rove. Cherry herself as well as her late mother were also implicated in the U.S. attorney scandal. The daughter had exchanged e-mails with Monica Goodling using one of the secret White House e-mail accounts that were also under investigation.

J.T. did not have a background in science or engineering, but he professed to a long-held interest in space. As a young person, he told me, "I watched *The Right Stuff,* and I loved *The Right Stuff,* . . . and I had my own little space shuttle club and everything, so I've been into space for a while."

NASA was in his "portfolio" when he worked in personnel at the White House, and he moved himself to the agency when he saw a good opportunity. As White House liaison inside NASA, he was responsible for placing presidential appointees, so he later played a role in bringing George Deutsch along.

One public affairs officer remembers J.T. actually informing them during his infamous speech that the White House required advance "notification" for all press releases having to do with Earth science, and that they should all go through him. J.T. denies this, although he does remember that nearly all the questions after his speech pertained to "the process" for such releases.

As the editing of climate science press releases devolved into what Gretchen calls "basically just general practice," her situation at work devolved as well. She remembers the first few months of 2005 as "definitely one of the most stressful periods" of her life. She was being asked to do things that were against her principles by a boss who hardly spoke to her and seemed to have it in for her—and then, on top of it all, she discovered she was pregnant. Between the "combination of hormones," the fact that she got extremely nauseous in her first trimester, and the pressures of her job, she would sometimes just sit in her office and cry. ("I'm sure if there were a way for them to use her pregnancy against her, they probably did," remarks Steitz.) One day in particular, she remembers falling apart completely. "I had to close the door and all I could think was 'I have to get out of here. I cannot continue to do this.' And it wasn't just the stress level; typically, I can withstand stress. I've been in other stressful jobs and that kind of thing. It was what the stress was coming from, the fact that I was personally so fundamentally opposed to what was going on, and that I knew that this stuff . . . would have consequences far beyond myself. It was very disturbing. I couldn't believe that I had somehow gotten myself into that position. How did this happen to me? How did I end up being the person who was being asked to do these things?

"I told myself then, 'I will not remain here through this pregnancy. I can't survive this level of stress and be pregnant at the same time.' I knew that I had to do something—essentially to leave, to find a way to extricate myself."

She had always made her discomfort with the censorship practices known to her colleagues, so they empathized rather than felt angry with her. She quietly put out some feelers and eventually found the position as a contractor at Goddard that she still holds today.

At the same time, after three not particularly distinguished years as NASA administrator, Sean O'Keefe was looking for a job as well. Maybe he felt that he had served his purpose now that the president had been reelected. Rumors of an offer from Louisiana State University in Baton Rouge first surfaced in December, and O'Keefe took the $500,000-a-year position as chancellor of the university in February. "One source" noted in *The Washington Post* that "O'Keefe had three children approaching college age and had had little opportunity to make any substantial money during a career largely devoted to public service." The *Post* itself noted that whoever "succeeds O'Keefe at NASA will inherit a turbulent but aggressively high-profile agency still recovering from the loss of space shuttle *Columbia* last year, even as it tries to restructure itself for President Bush's 'Vision for Space Exploration.'"

One wonders if the *Post* reporter was aware of the extent to which that turbulence reached into public affairs.

It was obvious, evidently, to prospective administrator Michael Griffin when he made his first rounds of headquarters during his selection process. Glenn Mahone had made enemies besides those in his education and Earth science divisions, and the buzz at headquarters was that Griffin wanted him gone by the time he arrived. Mahone left for the private sector exactly one day after Griffin was confirmed by the Senate. (He resigned just before noon, evidently, and Waleed Abdalati recalls running into a colleague about an hour later, who gave him a "somewhat relieved grin and said, 'The Wicked Witch is dead!'") To her credit, Gretchen Cook-Anderson managed to outlast Mahone. She moved to Goddard about two weeks after he left.

Thus, for a while, Dean Acosta represented the only "institutional memory" of the secretive editing and its sibling processes. He eventually replaced the whirlwind that was Gretchen with two people: Erica Hupp and, the following September, George Deutsch. David Mould inherited this situation when he came on board as Acosta's superior near the end of

June. And by strange coincidence, Dolores Beasley announced Deutsch's hiring in the same e-mail in which she passed on the good news to her colleagues that Gretchen had delivered a baby girl two days earlier. Dolores noted that "she sounded just fine, if a bit tired (understandably!)."

Deutsch's career stop in NASA's Science Mission Directorate may have been short, less than five months, but it was nothing short of spectacular. Although the agency's climate scientists had been dealing with various levels of censorship in various forms for a few years, his performance stands out strongly enough in their minds to obscure nearly all their previous frustrations.

David Mould (who seems exceedingly preoccupied with this sort of thing) claims that Deutsch was hired as a grammarian; he knew all there was to know about commas, semicolons, and the like. The scientists and center public affairs officers remember him mainly for his editorial work. They could scarcely have imagined things getting worse than they already were, but that's what happened the moment he arrived. They were told by their headquarters colleagues that he ran every Earth science press release straight up to the Ninth Floor. The reason his effect was so strong, according to one, was that "Gretchen, who is a fantastic public affairs officer, kept fighting the Ninth Floor to make sure the science was accurate. George Deutsch, on the other hand, was so right-wing that he *wanted* to issue the press releases with the wrong science that the Ninth Floor was inserting. . . . I don't think he knew what the Hatch Act was. . . . It was basically like having Dean Acosta on two levels."

The most memorable battle (and the one that set the tone) took place during Deutsch's first two weeks on the job, over a release about retreating sea ice in the Arctic—slightly more than one page of prose that was reputedly revised more than twenty times.

Waleed Abdalati was one of the key members of the team, which comprised scientists from Goddard, JPL, the University of Washington in Seattle, and the National Snow and Ice Data Center (NSIDC), which is based at the University of Colorado at Boulder. Just to make things more complicated, the funding for the project came from both NASA and NOAA, and the data was gathered from satellites operated by those two agencies and the U.S. Department of Defense.

The scientists had employed the satellites to track the size of the cap of sea ice that floats at the top of the world, on the surface of the Arctic Ocean and its neighboring seas. This layer of frozen seawater—covering more than 2 million square miles, about the size of the contiguous United States—grows during the northern winter and shrinks during the summer, usually reaching its minimum size near the fall equinox in late September. The yearly minimum is one way to measure trends, and the minimum for 2005 was just occurring. This press release was motivated by the realization that it was breaking the previous record minimum for the past century, set in 2002, by a large margin, and thus strengthening the significance of the shrinking trend of recent years. (Not much of a surprise, perhaps, since the various organizations that measure Earth's temperature were about to an- nounce that the year would set a record in that regard as well—and make note of remarkable arctic warmth in doing so.) The satellite record extends back only to 1978, but less accurate estimates based on observations from ships and airplanes reach back to the early twentieth century.

As scientist Mark Serreze of the University of Colorado put it, "The year 2005 puts an exclamation point on the pattern of arctic warming we've seen in recent years." It was also consistent with a trend that had persisted throughout the satellite record. From 1979 through 2001, the minimum had been shrinking at a rate of 6.5 percent per decade, and since 2002 the drop had steepened to 7.3 percent. In the years since that previous record-setting year, the area covered by ice in late September av- eraged half a million square miles less than it had over the previous two decades—the equivalent of about twice the area of Texas.

There is a natural pattern in atmospheric circulation above the Arctic that also causes sea ice to grow and shrink on the time scale of decades, but the scientists interpreted the rapid decline in year-round sea ice in recent decades as a sign that the top of the world could be entering a new climatic regime in which the natural oscillation will play much less of a role. It appears that a powerful positive feedback loop is setting in. White sea ice reflects sunlight back into space just as ice sheets do, thereby keeping itself and the entire planet cool, while the dark ocean surface that replaces it when it melts tends to absorb the sun's energy and heat the water below it, which then heats the planet. That this sort of positive feedback would tend to amplify the effects of global warming in the Arctic was first proposed by the Swedish physical chemist Svante Arrhenius in the very first theoretical treatment of greenhouse warming by carbon dioxide, which was published in 1896.

The size of the minimum is also important because it represents what remains of perennial, year-round ice cover. Because it persists and can be built upon year after year, the perennial ice is relatively thick and comprises many layers. But even if a warm summer is followed by a severe winter that allows the ice cap to grow, the new, relatively thin, single layer of ice is more vulnerable to melting the following summer. Thus only a string of cold summers will allow the perennial ice cap to grow.

These results bode well for the opening of the fabled Northwest Passage as a year-round shipping lane, for instance, but they do not bode well for polar bears, the indigenous peoples of the Arctic, nor indeed for the very concept of the Arctic in the human imagination.

The dozen or so scientists involved in this work held some conference calls to craft a rigorous and conservative statement, and the NASA group established an aggressive schedule for producing simultaneous press releases, to which the others agreed. Then George Deutsch got into the act.

A public affairs officer who worked on a few releases with Deutsch points out that he and Acosta strove to put something they called "balance" into releases, and that in practice "balance" nearly always meant "bad science." Abdalati noticed this immediately. He and his colleagues had gone through a number of iterations before submitting a thoughtful draft to headquarters, but "it came back in pretty bad shape." "There were some factually incorrect statements inserted. One thing that troubled me was, at the end of every paragraph the phrase 'but this is not certain' had been added. That was George's work."

Another of Deutsch's "balancing" attempts was so out of line that Abdalati admits sheepishly that it had him bamboozled for a while. The scientists' draft had talked about perennial ice being replaced by younger, thinner ice, but Deutsch had added something like "It can also be replaced with thicker ice."

"I was so perplexed by this," says Waleed, "that I read it to a colleague of mine, who said, 'That's just an absurd statement.' It gets to the point where you think, 'Am I?—this is so off the mark that maybe I'm wrong here.' I couldn't believe that such an erroneous change would be made. You start to question yourself, you know what I mean?"

He was livid. He called headquarters and told them they were inserting science that was just plain wrong and that it would make the agency look stupid.

After a tremendous battle, they ended up with almost exactly the wording that the scientists and writers from Goddard had originally submitted—"scrubbed" of a few touchy points, such as the observation that if the Arctic Ocean follows its present trajectory toward completely ice-free summers within the next century or so, it will be the first time this has happened in more than a million years.

It irks Waleed that after NASA set a schedule that his colleagues at the other institutions met, the machinations at headquarters delayed NASA's release, while NSIDC got its release out on time. Thus, when the news made the headlines—which it certainly did—NASA was conspicuously absent from most of the coverage.

Maybe Dean Acosta avoided a call from the White House that way.

Long after the Tiger Team that was formed in the wake of the "George Deutsch scandal" had finished its work, Michael Griffin would claim that they had looked deeply into all allegations of censorship at the agency and had not found "any such examples where anybody was censored."

Ed Weiler, who was on the team, contradicts Dr. Griffin. He says they didn't dig into the past so much as craft a policy for the future.

"The press releases are not the sole property of the scientist . . . ," Griffin told me. "Scientists can publish papers. If the scientist wants a press release issued, and if after, you know, *adult supervision,* it is decided that, yes, this is a good thing to write a press release about, NASA will release a press release" (emphasis mine).

So Deutsch helped with more than grammar, it seems. He also provided a firm guiding hand.

Was this an example of censorship? Probably, even though, when all was said and done, the scientists got most of what they wanted.

This story has a few subtle features in common with myriad others that turned out less well. One is the aspect of thuggery. Headquarters manipulated the language so aggressively that Waleed Abdalati, an excellent scientist, operating honestly and in good faith, who knew perfectly well what he was talking about, found himself questioning his own understanding of a basic physical concept. This is like a punch in the stomach. It is confusing; it makes a person hesitate. Aggressiveness of this kind occurs in a more bare-knuckled fashion in the news media, where it also takes the form of personal attack. Jim Hansen has experienced many of those.

Another is what Jim calls "self-censorship." While Waleed and his colleagues did manage to link retreating sea ice and warming temperatures in their press release, they did not take the step of relating warming temperatures to human activity: they did not "connect the dots." On the one hand, Waleed believes it is more elegant in a press release to stick to the science you've actually done: "It's for other people to make the link between greenhouse gases and warm temperatures." On the other, he admits, "There was a tempering, I will say, on my part of 'I don't even want to go there, because I don't want to have that fight.'"

This statement comes from a person who has spent his entire career in what is probably the most politicized scientific field there is. As such, it may demonstrate the pernicious effect that politics has had upon the culture of climate science. In virtually every other discipline, scientists routinely go a good distance out of their way to explain the relevance of their work to the everyday world.

Jim Hansen is unusual among scientists in that he *will* engage in that fight. And in the months after his most recent battle, scientists from around the country would come out of the woodwork to thank him for it.

Chapter 6

A Theory of Government We Must Vociferously Oppose

LOOKING BACK AT HOW QUICKLY events had unfolded after he had written his "day one" story on Jim, Andy Revkin remarked that Jim had been "vital, uncorking the bottle," but that it had been the career people, such as Leslie McCarthy, who had "provided the flowing champagne." "It's a rare thing for 'safe' career people to stick necks out like that," he told Jim in an e-mail. It was thanks to Leslie, "an unnamed ally of yours in headquarters who got me key paperwork," and other "careerists" at the Jet Propulsion Laboratory and elsewhere "who proved this wasn't *just* a Jim Hansen story."

It certainly wasn't. There was pent-up pressure in virtually every federal agency that had anything to do with science, so corks began flying from other bottles right away. The next to blow was the National Oceanic and Atmospheric Administration (NOAA), which is the parent organization of the National Weather Service among other things.

On February 10, 2006, the Friday of the week that George Deutsch resigned, Jim spoke at a conference on politics and science, sponsored by the New School for Social Research in Manhattan. (He was added at the last minute on account of his recent notoriety.) In a talk derived from the Keeling talk, which was now about two months old, he decided to add a brief discussion of tropical storms, because the topic was "especially relevant to this conference."

As anyone who followed the life cycles of hurricanes Katrina and Rita vividly saw, the heat stored in tropical oceans provides fuel to the storms that swirl above them. So it would seem obvious that if the oceans heat up, we should expect more intense hurricanes. (When all is said and done, the physics of this question is probably about as simple as that.) Jim told his New School audience that the GISS climate simulations, "which do a good job of matching observed global climate change, yield a human-made ocean surface warming in the region of hurricane formation that is equal to a large fraction of the observed warming there." The GISS simulation isn't the only one to show this. The notion that global warming has been heating tropical oceans for the past few decades is widely accepted by mainstream scientists, and there is near unanimous agreement that warmer tropical water leads to more intense, though not necessarily more frequent, hurricanes. Jim therefore suggested that greenhouse gases might be "responsible for a substantial fraction of the ocean warming that fuels stronger hurricanes."

But during the devastating hurricane season just past, he pointed out, officials at NOAA's National Hurricane Center had stated un-equivocally that "recent hurricane intensification is due to a natural cy-cle of Atlantic Ocean temperature, and has nothing to do with global warming." "NOAA took an official position that global warming was not the cause of hurricane intensification," Jim told his audience, "and as the public was glued to their television listening to reports from the Hurri-cane Center, that is the main message the public received. The topic is a complex one that the scientific community is working on, but it seems that the public, by fiat, received biased information. NOAA scientists were told not to dispute the Hurricane Center conclusion in public. I am not certain whether that is legal or not. Perhaps, by declaring the conclu-sion to be 'policy,' NOAA scientists can be prohibited from questioning it in public."

Alluding to the recent revelations about his own agency, Jim said he'd been "told by NOAA colleagues that their conditions are much worse than those in NASA. A NOAA scientist cannot speak with a reporter unless there is a 'listener' on the line with him or her. It seems more like Nazi Germany or the Soviet Union than the United States. The claim is that the 'listener' is there to protect the NOAA scientist. If you buy that one, please see me at the break; there is a bridge down the street that I would like to sell to you." (He quickly regretted his reference to Nazi Germany and, in the version of the talk that he later posted on the Web, simply wrote "the old Soviet Union," believing this phrase wasn't "as laden with emotions and possible misinterpretation.")

Jim ended this little sidebar to his talk by tying it to the subject of the conference. "There is a good rationale for preventing scientists from intruding in policy making," he said. "The converse is also true. Policy should not intrude in science, or it will destroy the quality of the science and diminish the value of the science to the public.

"The ultimate policy maker is the public. Unless the public is provided with unfiltered scientific information that accurately reflects the views of the scientific community, policy making is likely to suffer."

Censorship at NOAA probably wasn't news to any climate scientists who may have been in the audience. MIT meteorologist Kerry Emanuel had published a paper in *Nature* that linked warm tropical water to more destructive hurricanes just two weeks before Katrina had destroyed New Orleans. He had subsequently talked in the same session as Jim at December's AGU meeting. At one point in his talk, he had characterized NOAA's restrictions on its scientists as "censorship" and received a standing ovation.

Reporters from *The Wall Street Journal* approached Jim immediately after his talk at the New School, and he gave them some contacts at NOAA. Revealing articles soon appeared in the *Journal, The Washington Post,* and *The New Republic.* In the last, an expert from the Union of Concerned Scientists coined a phrase by noting that NOAA scientists were "being what we now call *Hansen-ized.*"

A story of outright censorship and negligence of duty gradually emerged.

On November 29, 2005, in the aftermath of hurricanes Katrina and Rita, NOAA published a statement and held a press conference about the recent increase in what they called "hurricane activity"—a vague phrase, since it doesn't distinguish between frequency and intensity. In both its written and oral statements, the agency officially linked the increase in activity that had been observed over at least the previous decade to a phenomenon they described as "the tropical multi-decadal signal," leaving no room for doubt whatsoever. This mysterious signal supposedly oscillates with a period of "twenty to thirty years or even longer," affecting both water temperature and wind shear (winds changing with altitude), and causes so-called hurricane activity to ebb and flow accordingly. The statement was entitled "NOAA Attributes Recent Increase in Hurricane Activity to Naturally Occurring Multi-Decadal Climate Variability." It claimed that "NOAA research" demonstrated that the multi-decadal signal "is causing the increased Atlantic hurricane activity since 1995, and is not related to greenhouse warming."

The first reporter to be called upon in the press conference that day asked the assembled NOAA experts if one of them might "talk about what extent, if any, global warming may have played in the storms this year." The question was taken by Gerry Bell, whom the agency describes as its lead seasonal hurricane forecaster. Bell denied any connection with global warming and insisted that the recent upsurge in activity was the result of "the twenty- to thirty-year cycles that we've seen since 1950." Never mind that it is statistically impossible to prove the existence of a twenty- to thirty-year cycle with only fifty years' worth of data. The reporter persisted, asking if there were any recent reports indicating that "global warming may have been responsible for the intensity of the storms?" There had, in fact, been two such reports, and they had been widely reported in the press: Emanuel's, which had appeared in *Nature* in early August, and another that had appeared in *Science,* four weeks after Katrina. Exhibiting either an astounding ignorance of the scientific literature on the subject of his expertise or a supreme fixation on sticking to his message, Bell repeated his assertion about the multi-decadal signal and again denied any connection to global warming. He would brook no discussion of it.

As for the agency's role in providing policy makers with "unfiltered scientific information," the statement released that day explained with a sunny lack of irony that Max Mayfield, the director of the Tropical

Prediction Center at the National Hurricane Center in Miami (and Gerry Bell's partner on the press conference dais) had "heightened awareness" of the multi-decadal signal in testimony at a congressional hearing in late September. Mayfield had also told the lawmakers that hurricane activity was "not enhanced substantially by global warming."

The scientific community *is* still working on this problem. Jim's statement to this effect at the New School reflected both his conservatism and his patient belief that the give-and-take of the scientific process will reveal the truth in the end. But the reality is that most climate scientists believe global warming *will* cause more intense hurricanes. The idea has been around for more than two decades; it is buttressed by sound theory and solid observational evidence; and both Jim Hansen and Kerry Emanuel were there at the beginning. Jim mentioned it, in fact, in the explosive 1989 congressional testimony that George Bush Sr.'s Office of Management and Budget tried to edit. Furthermore, the research of some of the most highly regarded climate scientists at NOAA—as distinct from hurricane and weather specialists—suggests, for example, that "a greenhouse gas–induced warming may lead to a gradually increasing risk in the occurrence of highly destructive category-5 storms."

This quote comes from a 2004 paper in the *Journal of Climate* that was cowritten by Thomas Knutson of NOAA's Geophysical Fluid Dynamics Laboratory (GFDL) in Princeton, New Jersey, and Robert Tuleya, who had recently retired after thirty-one years at GFDL and now taught at Old Dominion University. (Knutson was one of the contacts Jim shared with *The Wall Street Journal*.)

GFDL is the oldest and most venerable center for computerized climate modeling in the world. Its original forebear was conceived in the 1950s by the spectacularly brilliant Hungarian mathematician John von Neumann, who not only helped design one of the world's first computers, but also put it to use almost immediately to model weather systems and, not long afterward, global climate. In the sixties and seventies, GFDL scientists conducted the first modeling studies ever to demonstrate that rising carbon dioxide levels would increase temperature—and to estimate the strength of the effect: so-called climate sensitivity. It would be fair to say that most of the scientists who presently work at what is probably the premier climate research center at NOAA would concur, generally speaking, with Knutson and Tuleya on the connection between global warming and hurricane intensity.

Yet the official scientific statement on hurricanes that NOAA published in November 2005 did not mention Knutson and Tuleya's work, and it ended with an entire section that would lead the reader to believe that there was a "consensus" among NOAA scientists that the increase in hurricane activity was "primarily the result of natural fluctuations."

It is unusual, if not outrageous, for a government agency to ignore an alternative explanation on an unresolved scientific problem. Imagine, back in the 1980s, when debate raged over the possibility of a hole opening up in the ozone layer, if NOAA or NASA had held a press conference to state "officially" that there was no ozone hole.

Well, NOAA's actions in "heightening awareness" of its preferred explanation went a few steps further than that. The day after Jim spoke at the New School, *The New Republic* quoted Jerry Mahlman, a former director of GFDL, as saying that NOAA scientists who disagreed with the preferred explanation were "being intimidated from talking to the press and that their papers [were] being withheld from publication." "I know a lot of people who would love to talk to you, but they don't dare," Mahlman added. "They are worried about getting fired." Judith Curry of Georgia Tech, an author of the *Science* paper supporting the alternative explanation that had appeared just after Katrina, characterized the situation at NOAA as an "absolute disgrace . . . You hear about Hansen, but NASA is not really that bad. NOAA is really, really bad."

It's hard to choose, actually; for when they made these comparisons, neither Dr. Curry nor Jim was aware of the goings-on at the space agency in 2004. As we shall see, at least NOAA had rules, however draconian and unevenly applied they may have been. Rules can be worked with and changed. When there *are* none, pretty much anything goes. The fear that still echoed more than a year after Michael Griffin's Statement on Scientific Openness in the voices of the midlevel public affairs officers who had been ordered to implement the unwritten and whispered policies at NASA testifies to the effectiveness and creeping sense of menace invoked by the secrecy and ambiguity there.

As a direct result of Jim's speech at the New School, the champagne began flowing at NOAA, too. Within a week, *The Wall Street Journal* reported that "a growing outcry from climate researchers in its own ranks" had led the agency to back away from its official November statement.

One voice in that outcry was that of Ants Leetmaa, the current director of GFDL. Upon reading the article in *The New Republic,* he sent an e-mail to a wide list of fellow managers at NOAA, describing it as an embarrassment that could easily have been avoided if the agency had simply softened its position and taken a "more humble," less know-it-all approach (the approach that is usually taken by any decent scientist; if not, beware).

"It is disconcerting scientifically that synoptic meteorologists were making decadal hurricane projections based on a phenomenon (Atlantic decadal 'Oscillation') of which they know nothing and which might or might not in recent years be forced by anthropogenic [manmade] effects," Leetmaa wrote (*Atlantic Oscillation* being his name for the hurricane specialists' "tropical multi-decadal signal").

His point was that the hurricane specialists were going beyond their expertise, for their favorite oscillation is fundamentally a climatic phenomenon. With the global perspective of a climatologist, Leetmaa pointed out that the Atlantic Oscillation is forced by a similar creature called the North Atlantic Oscillation and that the recent "positive" phase of the Atlantic Oscillation had probably been triggered when its northern cousin had switched positive in the eighties and early nineties. "[A] number of factors can cause decadal trends in the [North Atlantic Oscillation]—can't preclude that this recent positive phase was not linked to anthropogenic effects—if so, then the official NOAA position is that we are seeing a human induced effect on Atlantic hurricane activity!! Surprise!"

He included a graph demonstrating that a GFDL climate model incorporating anthropogenic greenhouse increases mimicked the observed changes in Atlantic sea surface temperature over the entire course of the twentieth century. Sea surface temperature *has* oscillated on decadal time scales, as the hurricane specialists insist; however, its average value has steadily risen—owing almost certainly to greenhouse increases—and many of the oscillations, along with the steady rise, are seen in a similar graph of the entire Earth's average temperature. Noting that even the hurricane specialists tie hurricane activity to changes in sea surface temperature, Leetmaa concluded that it was hard to dismiss an anthropogenic effect.

And while it is probably fair to accuse the agency's hurricane specialists of being out of their league when it comes to climatology, it would not be fair to accuse the climatologists of the converse. It continued to "irk" Leetmaa that National Weather Service (NWS) press releases during the hurricane season consistently ignored the work of GFDL and its partners. The "GFDL model is what the forecasters look to as providing the most reliable forecasts," he wrote. Its "consistent record over the past 3–4 years" in predicting the paths of the storms "is unequalled in any forecast the NWS makes."

Jim had also given the name of Pieter Tans to the reporters, a specialist in carbon dioxide measurement at NOAA's Earth System Research Laboratory in Boulder, Colorado. Largely as a result of the example Jim had just set, Tans was now willing to tell his story on the record.

In an e-mail he sent to Jim the day after Revkin popped the cork at NASA, Tans described the situation at the space agency as looking "very familiar. . . . A few weeks ago, new rules were distributed in NOAA. In short, we need permission before talking to the press, . . . and there is a lot of 'sensitivity' to issues that may have potential policy implications, which practically includes all of climate change science."

Tans told of a development that was remarkably similar to the suppression of GISS's 2005 temperature data: the monthly posting of atmospheric carbon dioxide levels at Mauna Loa, Hawaii, had recently been "deemed sensitive" and was now "carefully controlled." The Mauna Loa data has been published continuously for an even longer time than the GISS temperature data—since 1958, when Charles David Keeling, in whose memory Jim had spoken at the AGU, set up his instrument on top of the volcano. Tans also spoke of "alarm" at NOAA over the "leaking" of preliminary data about Mauna Loa's average carbon dioxide level for 2005, to the British newspaper *The Independent.*

In September 2005, when he had organized a conference on atmospheric carbon dioxide, Tans had been forbidden from using the phrase *climate change* in any of the titles or abstracts for the talks at the conference. He ignored this restriction, he told Jim, not only out of principle, but also because it would have been essentially impossible to hold a scientific conference on the topic without using the phrase. The director of his laboratory had ordered the lab's webmaster to avoid referring to NOAA on the conference's Web site and even prohibited him from linking to NOAA pages, many of which held relevant scientific information that the organizers themselves had produced. (Tans would subsequently tell the Government Accountability Project of being informed a few months after the conference "that anything dealing with climate change had to be pre-approved at the White House level, including . . . website content.") Tans told Jim that they had planned to notify major news organizations about the conference, but NOAA public affairs had "buried it" and had also "squashed" a press release and an associated press conference regarding a journal article, on which NOAA scientists were coauthors, demonstrating that increased carbon dioxide levels are making the oceans more acidic. ("In a sense this is almost a no-brainer given that CO_2 is the gaseous form of carbonic acid," Tans remarked.) He also pointed out that in mid-2005, when the BBC had interviewed him on film, "what I call a 'minder,' something I associate with the former Soviet empire," had insisted upon sitting in. This individual, one Kent Laborde, flew from NOAA headquarters in Washington, D.C., first to Colorado and then to Mauna

Loa—all at taxpayer expense, of course—in order to discharge this responsibility. NOAA has described Laborde as "the public affairs person who focuses on climate-change issues."

One of Tans's larger points is very much worth considering. His main reason for ignoring the new restrictions, he told Jim, was that they damaged his credibility among his scientific peers. "For example," he wrote, "once people catch on to the control that is going on, why should anyone take seriously a government scientist downplaying a possible link between hurricane intensity and climate warming?"

Also inspired by Jim's example, Thomas Knutson went on the record in *The Wall Street Journal* with claims that he had been "censored by the NOAA public affairs office," because of his alternative explanation for the increase in hurricane intensity. In October 2005, the office had prevented him from participating in an interview on CNBC television. Public affairs had "called and asked what I would say to certain questions, like is there a trend in Atlantic hurricanes," Knutson told the *Journal*. "I said I thought there was a possibility of a trend emerging that tropical hurricanes were becoming more intense. They turned down that interview." Knutson also spoke of receiving an invitation to appear on a talk show on MSNBC television cohosted by Ron Reagan, son of the late president. Shortly before he was to appear, Knuston received a voice mail from public affairs informing him that "the White House" had turned the invitation down.

About two months after he spoke to the *Journal*, Knutson expanded upon the MSNBC incident to the Government Accountability Project. "Public affairs" in this instance turned out to be none other than Kent Laborde. In August 2005, about a week after the publication of Kerry Emanuel's paper on hurricanes, Knutson had received voice mail messages from both Laborde and a member of the production staff of Reagan's television show, regarding a possible interview. Having picked up the messages over the weekend after returning from a trip, Knutson called the staffer back to confirm his interest and suggest that they contact

NOAA public affairs on Monday. Monday morning he received two voice mails from Laborde, the first to notify him that the White House had "said no," the second to explain that Laborde had done him the service of calling the show to cancel for him, with the excuse that Knutson was too tired from his trip to undergo the strain of an interview.

As these and similar stories about NOAA began cropping up on the Web and in the print media, the agency's administrator, a retired naval vice admiral named Conrad Lautenbacher, issued a watered-down version of Michael Griffin's Statement on Scientific Openness in which he proclaimed his strong personal belief in "open, peer reviewed science as well as the right and duty of scientists to seek the truth and to provide the best scientific advice possible." He also denied that any tampering with this right and duty had transpired at his agency. NOAA public affairs officers interviewed by the *Journal* and other publications also denied the scientists' claims or insisted that they had misunderstood certain innocent words.

Jerry Mahlman, the former GFDL director, then released a response to Lautenbacher in which he disagreed "emphatically" with the admiral's statement. "It is quite distressing that Dr. Lautenbacher has chosen in his 'Message' to pretend that NOAA climate scientists have not been forbidden from speaking freely about their scientific contributions to global warming science," Mahlman wrote. ". . . From my recent personal experience, his contention is simply not true."

It was looking like a "he said/she said" of the sort that had stymied the congressional investigation at NASA. The difference here was that a journalist named Paul Thacker filed a Freedom of Information Act (FOIA) request that bore fruit some seven months later. Thacker recovered a "large batch of e-mails" indicating not only that NOAA officials had engaged in clear acts of censorship, but that their efforts had clearly been orchestrated by the White House.

To demonstrate that the freewheeling ways at NASA served to cover up censorship there even after Michael Griffin issued his Statement on Scientific Openness, both Thacker and Andy Revkin also made FOIA requests to the space agency near the beginning of 2006. NASA sources describe a large effort in a number of offices that succeeded in gathering plenty of damning evidence in response, yet Revkin received nothing of value and Thacker got nothing at all. In April of the same year, the Government Accountability Project filed FOIA requests to NASA, NOAA, and the EPA. They got nothing from EPA. NASA provided them with a copy of a nine-page policy statement that was widely available anyway. NOAA provided about 2,000 pages "marked with significant irregularities," such as the redaction of all responses by senior officials in e-mail chains.

One of the e-mail chains recovered by Thacker specifically confirms Thomas Knutson's story about CNBC. On October 19, 2005, the CNBC show *On the Money* requested an interview with Knutson on the subject of hurricanes and global warming. In the first e-mail of the day, Jana Goldman, the public affairs officer who handled the request, detailed both the questions that were likely to be asked and Knutson's probable answers. (Remember that he told *The Wall Street Journal* that public affairs had queried him by phone.) One of the recipients of Goldman's message was the same Kent Laborde who had flown across the continent and on to the middle of the Pacific to "mind" Pieter Tans's interviews with the BBC. Laborde forwarded the request to Chuck Fuqua, deputy director of communications in the Department of Commerce, which oversees NOAA. (Fuqua had recently directed media operations for the 2004 Republican National Convention.) "What is Knutson's position on global warming vs. decadal cycles?" he asked. "Is he consistent with Bell and Landsea?"

Chris Landsea, who works at the National Hurricane Center, is one of the more intransigent deniers of the global warming connection. In January 2005, he famously quit a working group preparing a report for the IPCC, when IPCC leaders refused his demand that the lead author of the report be reprimanded or removed for noting during a media conference call that the strong hurricane season of 2004 "may well be a harbinger of the future."

Knutson's rather subdued "take" on the matter, explained Laborde to Fuqua, was that "worst case projections of greenhouse gas concentrations" would lead to "a very small increase in hurricane intensity that won't be realized until almost 100 years from now." Even this was too much for Fuqua, who ended the matter with "why can't we have one of the other guys then?"

A daily media tracking log from NOAA public affairs recovered by Paul Thacker shows that on this particular day a request to interview a GFDL scientist about hurricanes and global warming was denied, for the reason that it was "routine, but sensitive." Blacked out are the names of the scientist and the media outlet involved.

A Government Accountability Project review of these tracking logs reveals that they "label 'sensitive' such topics as 'hurricanes and climate change,' 'percentage of CO_2 in greenhouse effect,' 'sea level rise,' 'global surface and satellite temperature measurements,' 'unusually warm lake temperatures,' 'amount of $$ spent on climate change,' '[Kerry] Emanuel paper,' 'climate change,' and 'arctic info.'"

The FOIA documents demonstrate that NOAA officials showed little compunction in restricting media access to any scientist who might go "off message," and that they erected an imposing organizational structure to implement these restrictions. This structure extended beyond the agency itself, up through the Commerce Department, and into at least two familiar White House offices: the Office of Science and Technology Policy and the Council on Environmental Quality. In one 2005 e-mail, Kent Laborde approved a request by Juliet Eilperin of *The Washington Post* to interview a scientist from GFDL: "CEQ and OSTP have given the green light for the interview." In another, Jordan St. John, NOAA's director of public affairs, discounted off-message research by another agency scientist: "This doesn't say anything new about the data, it's just a new way of tracking it. This was the CEQ-approved release that went on the NOAA Web site earlier this week."

The documents also show that as coastal Louisiana and Mississippi were reeling from Hurricane Katrina, the most destructive natural disaster and one of the deadliest hurricanes in U.S. history, and as the entire

Gulf Coast simultaneously girded for Hurricane Rita, senior members of the public affairs staff at NOAA spent their time and energy spinning science. Access even to "friendly" experts such as Landsea and Mayfield was closely monitored. On September 21, 2005, four weeks after Katrina had devastated New Orleans and with Rita churning toward Texas in the Gulf of Mexico, Scott Smullen, NOAA's deputy director of public affairs, asked Catherine Trinh, a press officer in Commerce, if Mayfield might give a live interview that evening on a media outlet whose name has been redacted. "Max would stick to comments related to his already cleared oral testimony [presumably to Congress]," Smullen assured her.

"Scott—let's pass on this one," Trinh answered.

"Can I have a reason?" he asked.

No response.

Two days later, with Rita one day from landfall in Texas, Smullen received cautious permission from Fuqua for an interview with Landsea. "Okay on this one. Please be careful and make sure Chris is on his toes. Since [blank] went off the menu, I'm a little nervous on this one, but trust he'll hold the course."

Five days after Rita made landfall at the Texas/Louisiana border, public affairs announced a clampdown. Jim Teet, a recent addition to NOAA's public affairs staff, e-mailed the following directive to all employees:

> Good Day All:
>
> I have been informed that any request for an interview with a national media outlet/reporter must now receive prior approval by DOC [Commerce]. Please ensure everyone on your staff is aware of this requirement.
> Any request for an interview requires the following information to be forwarded to me immediately, so this process may begin:
> The name of the reporter and their affiliation; Their deadline and contact phone number; Name of individual being requested for the interview and

```
purpose of the interview; Additional background
about the interview subject, and expertise of
requested interviewee on this subject.
    The request will be forwarded through NWS/NOAA
to DOC; however, the individual to be interviewed
ultimately will be determined by DOC.
    If any requests for an update concerning the
interview are received from the media, refer the
individual to me for a response via my cell
phone. . . .
```

Prior to joining NOAA, Mr. Teet had assisted Karen Hughes, the close friend of then governor George W. Bush, in defending Mr. Bush's National Guard record.

Queried at the time of Teet's directive, public affairs director Jordan St. John claimed that they were merely reiterating a policy that had gone into effect in June 2004 but had not been enforced. While this may not render the policy any less draconian, the statements of NOAA scientists and Thacker's FOIA documents do bear this statement out. NOAA had published a new media policy on June 22, 2004, but it had not been widely implemented, and many NOAA scientists expressed surprise upon seeing Teet's e-mail.

This policy, laid out in the middle of the election year in which there was also a clampdown at NASA, mandated unprecedented restrictions at the weather agency, including "approval" or "clearance" for virtually any kind of interaction with the media. "NOAA employees must notify [public affairs] before responding to news media inquiries whenever the inquiries . . . pertain to science or research having known or potential policy implications" or "involve the release of scientific or technical papers that may have policy implications or are controversial."

Climate science received special scrutiny. When GFDL's deputy director, Brian Gross, read that scientists had to notify the "servicing" public affairs officer in advance of all "official and non-official scientific and technical papers . . . that may result in media interest," he sought clarification from Jana Goldman. "'Official and non-official' pretty much covers every possible scientific and technical publication, right?"

"You betcha," Goldman answered, "especially in the current political 'climate' (pun intended)." Goldman's name crops up frequently, and her witty asides seem to indicate that she wasn't all that happy with the new rules. Demonstrating a hint of restraint in this case, she assured Gross that she had no interest in seeing papers until they had been accepted for publication.

Apparently this arrangement was a little too loose. Six months after the policy was announced, the rules for scientific papers were tightened: all NOAA research laboratories were directed to send Goldman a list of "significant" papers every two months, so that they could be tracked from the moment they were *submitted* for publication. Rick Rosen, the head of all NOAA research at the time, explained that this would "satisfy the needs" of both himself and Dr. James Mahoney, the Commerce Department's assistant secretary for oceans and atmosphere.

Press releases are a different matter, as they have much more potential to generate media and public interest. Thacker recovered a flow sheet, dated February 2006 (the month that Knutson, Tans, and others finally went public), that detailed a thirteen-stage review process for all press releases at NOAA. They were to pass through the agency's general counsel, its chief of staff, "leadership review," and, finally, Commerce. Since this process could take a month or more, it is no wonder that journal articles by NOAA scientists often beat their associated press releases into print, thus seriously diminishing the public impact of both. The scientists complained repeatedly, both internally and later to the media, that this sort of delay could effectively bury an important finding.

Sometimes releases were killed outright—as was the one that was intended to announce the much discussed paper on hurricanes by Knutson and Tuleya in the *Journal of Climate*. Informed reporters recognized the paper's importance anyway, but when Andy Revkin attempted to interview Knutson, he was told that a public affairs officer would need to listen in. Revkin refused to agree to this condition and interviewed only Tuleya.

In contrast, a few months later, research director Rick Rosen actually

proposed that a press release be drawn up for an article in the same journal written by Chris Landsea. "It challenges the conclusions reached by
Knutson and Tuleya (2004) regarding the potential for more intense hurricanes in a warmer climate," wrote Rosen to a fellow administrator. "It is
not likely to attract the same media attention as the original Knutson and
Tuleya paper, but we should consider drafting a NOAA press release
nonetheless."

Delays were especially effective at sabotaging interviews, because the
broadcast media moves so swiftly that the delay involved in checking for a
"yea" or "nay" from public affairs often means the chance will be lost.
Knutson called this a "pocket veto" and claimed to have experienced a
few. His GFDL colleague Ronald Stouffer, one of the more experienced
and sought-after computer modelers in climate science, estimated that
these pocket vetoes cut the number of his media requests in half.

Stouffer figures in the oldest document that Thacker recovered. On January 24, 2001, which would have been four days after George W. Bush was
first inaugurated, Stouffer received an e-mail from Goldman: "If you get
any press requests for IPCC please bump them up to public affairs before
you agree to an interview" (emphasis hers). Recall that the IPCC had just
released the first of its periodic assessments ever to confirm unequivocally
that human activity had caused temperatures to rise.

Stouffer may not have realized that he had entered a new world. "Can
I ask why this new policy?" he asked. "It seems cumbersome at best. If
this policy is implemented, it will greatly cut down on NOAA scientist
interviews." As an example of how fast the media moved, he explained,
seven reporters had called him on a day earlier in the week when he had
been out of the office. Upon returning their calls just one day later, he had
learned that all seven had "found someone else to talk to."

As the NOAA bottle continued to fizz, corks began popping across the
country. On February 18, 2006, only four days after NASA management

fought to a tie with David Goldston and Chuck Atkins in Michael Griffin's Ninth Floor conference room, molecular biologist David Baltimore, Nobel laureate, outgoing president of the California Institute of Technology, president-elect of the American Association for the Advancement of Science (AAAS), and, according to *Nature,* "arguably the most eminent voice in all of American science," spoke at the association's annual meeting. In a packed session that had been organized at the last minute by the Union of Concerned Scientists, largely in response to the revelations about Jim, Baltimore decried the widespread suppression of science under the Bush administration and called it "no accident." Upon learning of each new incident, he said, "I shrug and say, 'What do you expect?' ... It is part of a theory of government, and I believe it is a theory that we must vociferously oppose."

Baltimore was referring to the so-called unitary theory of government, which, at its most extreme, dispenses with the notion of balance of power and holds that the executive branch may run the country more or less single-handedly, especially in wartime. The word *imperial* is sometimes used. This old idea had recently caught the fancy of conservatives and bobbed up in the media during the confirmation hearings for Supreme Court judge Samuel Alito. Baltimore suggested that it threatened the independence of all science conducted by any agency in the executive branch. This would include NASA, NOAA, the National Science Foundation, the National Institutes of Health, the Food and Drug Administration, the U.S. Department of Agriculture, the U.S. Geological Survey, the National Park Service, the National Forest Service, the U.S. Fish and Wildlife Service, the Centers for Disease Control and Prevention, and not least the Environmental Protection Agency. In the course of Bush's tenure, complaints of ideological interference with the scientific process have emanated from every one of these agencies, and from some repeatedly.

One of the incidents in Baltimore's mind may have been the coercing of Tong Lee of the Jet Propulsion Laboratory into becoming a tout for Bush's "vision" for space exploration. Andy Revkin reports that Baltimore had become aware the previous fall of various acts of censorship at JPL, and that he and JPL director Charles Elachi had looked into the matter and "determined" that "such activities had occurred." As president of Caltech, which manages JPL, Baltimore was effectively general manager of the laboratory.

Near the end of the AAAS session, Dr. Susan Wood, a former director of the Office of Women's Health at the Food and Drug Administration, told the audience that administration meddling with science and the regulatory process had left morale at that agency at a "nadir." When she explained that she had resigned in protest the previous August, after the FDA commissioner had overruled an expert panel and withheld over-the-counter approval for Plan B, the "morning after" contraceptive, she was greeted with a standing ovation.

Chapter 7

Congratulations for Your "Non Award"

RICK PILTZ AND THE GOVERNMENT Accountability Project were paying especially close attention to the corks that were popping and champagne that was flowing in early 2006, partially because Piltz had sent the first cork high into the air about six months earlier. A political scientist by training, he had worked on climate change policy in the federal government for about a decade and for the final few years at the U.S. Climate Change Science Program, the bureaucracy that is charged with "integrating" the nearly $2 billion worth of climate research that is sponsored annually by thirteen separate federal agencies. "Final few years" because Piltz had quit the previous March.

In June, he had provided Andy Revkin with draft reports from the Climate Change Science Program and the EPA that bore numerous hand-edits by Philip Cooney, the chief of staff of the Council on Environmental Quality, whom we have already met. CEQ is perhaps the primary overseer of the Climate Change Science Program. Mr. Cooney's edits, like the ones Gretchen Cook-Anderson found on the press releases she got back from Glenn Mahone and Dean Acosta, invariably played up uncertainties in the science of global warming and minimized the dangers. For example, in a 2002 draft of one of the program's periodic summaries of federal climate research, Cooney crossed out a paragraph on the worldwide retreat of mountain glaciers and snowpack. Not only has this process been extensively documented, most climatologists see it as an enormous threat to the supply of freshwater in virtually every region of the globe that receives its water from mountain runoff. The American

West gets most of its water from mountains, for instance, and so does northern India, where about 500 million people, a tenth of the human population, get their water from the Ganges and its tributaries, which are sustained by frozen reserves in the Himalayas that are on course to disappear sometime this century. In the margin near his excision, Cooney noted dispassionately that the offending paragraph was "straying from research strategy into speculative findings/musings."

His hand was not light. According to a memorandum introduced at the 2007 hearing of the House Oversight Committee, at which he and his boss, James Connaughton, testified alongside George Deutsch and Jim Hansen, Cooney and a CEQ associate named Brian Hannegan introduced "at least 181 edits to the Administration's *Strategic Plan of the Climate Change Science Program* to exaggerate or emphasize scientific uncertainties. They also made at least 113 edits to the plan to deemphasize or diminish the importance of the human role in global warming."

Cooney had no scientific training. Like his boss, Mr. Connaughton, he was a lawyer. And like Harlan Watson, the Bush administration's lead negotiator in Montreal during the week that Jim gave his Keeling talk, Cooney was looked upon favorably by the fossil fuel industry. Prior to joining the White House in 2001, he had worked for ten years at the American Petroleum Institute, the largest lobbying organization for the oil industry. In his final position at the institute, as "climate team leader," he had focused much of his energy on the same sort of undermining of science that he would carry on at CEQ and on resisting any and all movement in the direction of regulating or limiting carbon dioxide emissions.

Two days after Piltz made his revelations, Cooney resigned. Five days after that, he took a job at ExxonMobil.

Established by the Bush administration in February 2002, the Climate Change Science Program is where it all comes together—or, perhaps, where all climate change science grinds to a halt. Some familiar names held positions in the program. Its overall director was James Mahoney, the assistant secretary at Commerce whose "needs were served" by the comprehensive tracking of climate research publications at NOAA (although Piltz and others remember Dr. Mahoney, who has now retired, as being well intentioned and trying to work within the system—the same sort of "governor of an occupied territory" as Ghassem Asrar at NASA). Harlan Watson was a senior official in the program, and he joined Philip Cooney in adjusting the wording of its reports. In a memo to Mahoney dated October 2002, Watson "strongly" recommended the excision of entire boxes of text summarizing reports by the National Academy of Sciences and the IPCC. He claimed that the statements of these organizations did "not include an appropriate recognition of the underlying uncertainties and the tentative nature of a number of the assertions." In fact, characterization of the uncertainties was a stated goal of both reports.

In *Redacting the Science of Climate Change,* the Government Accountability Project notes the apparent lack of productivity at the Climate Change Science Program in the years since 2004. The program "has cautiously produced and posted on its website only five fact sheets and two research summaries, all ranging from two to four pages in length. It issued eight press releases—three of which were administrative announcements—and held one workshop on November 14–16, 2005. Furthermore, with the exception of three press releases, [the program] has not produced any new material as of January 2006." This may be explained by the cumbersome approval process, reminiscent of the one for press releases at NOAA, that applies to all the program's "products." Indeed, familiar NOAA employees play roles in this approval process, including Kent Laborde and Scott Smullen. Similarly, all media and public contacts with the program must be routed either to public affairs at NOAA or to the loquacious James Connaughton himself.

In the weeklong media firestorm that accompanied Piltz's revelations, various White House officials defended Philip Cooney by arguing that his edits were part of a normal review process that all interagency reports must go through. As it happens, one of those defenders was Robert Hopkins from the Office of Science and Technology Policy, the former Bush-Cheney campaign spokesman whom Gretchen Cook-Anderson suspects of playing a role in the secretive editing at NASA.

As Piltz put it in an e-mail to a group of friends, "I finally decided that the administration had put so many political constraints on the policies and directions of the science program, in a way that was getting worse after the re-election, that it was impossible to work there any more without speaking out about the administration's integrity issues on climate change science—not just working behind the scenes in the program office to try to limit the damage, but speaking publicly, which one cannot do freely in this context unless one is ready to give up one's job. So I quit."

But Jim Hansen was hoping to speak publicly and keep his job.

He had communicated with Piltz just before his own story broke in the *Times,* remember, and for the next month or two, Jim got what he considered to be excellent legal advice from the staff at the Government Accountability Project (GAP). But they soon became "very intrusive," he writes, "advising me on what to say on an environmental radio program, . . . wanting me to co-write op-ed articles, etc. . . . I don't like anybody telling me what to say; I want to give the science exactly as I see it. And it seemed they were interested in using me for fund raising, and that it would be a time consuming proposition. . . . I think that their goals are meritorious, but they didn't seem to recognize that I am a very deliberate slow-paced person, so what they were asking would have a big impact on my ability to do science." Having spent a lot of time on the censorship issue since December, Jim was anxious to return full-time to his scientific work. He had no desire to take up whistleblowing as an avocation.

His concerns were heightened when he learned from GAP's president, Louis Clark, that he and Rick Piltz had been chosen to receive the Ron Ridenhour Truth-Telling Prize. Ridenhour was the Vietnam-veteran-*cum*-investigative-journalist who in 1969 wrote the letter to Congress that revealed the horrific events at My Lai. The award, which comes with a $10,000 prize, is sponsored by the Nation Institute, a nonprofit organization associated with *The Nation* magazine that also seems to be closely aligned with GAP. Jim began to wonder whether this "was really an award for me, or whether there were expectations that went with it," and when he learned that Mr. Clark himself had nominated him, he sensed a conflict of interest and began to consider how he might gracefully back away.

The other shoe dropped when he realized he was pretty much on his own anyway: the legal director of GAP, Tom Devine, whom he describes as "very sharp and a good guy," told him that the organization and its whistleblower clients had lost something like "122 out of 123 cases." Jim writes, "I can qualify my talks with 'my personal opinion' and 'under protection of the first amendment' as much as I want, but apparently those protections are actually very weak, and the best protection may be strong science and public visibility."

Besides, this approach seemed to be working. In the weeks following George Deutsch's unceremonious departure, Jim received no threats from the NASA counsel's office, headquarters, nor anyone else in the executive branch—although the deafening silence had ominous overtones as well. He feared for his job for a few months. Michael Griffin had not bothered to let Jim know that he had no intention of punishing anyone.

The beginning of March 2006 then offered an opportunity to test the administrator's Statement on Scientific Openness. Jay Zwally's group at Goddard Space Flight Center published a paper in the *Journal of Glaciology,* and the folks in public affairs decided it was worthy of a press release.

Zwally has been working quietly and in the background on what is arguably the most important question in climate science for more than thirty years. He's been at NASA about as long as Jim. He began working at Goddard over summers in the early sixties, when he was pursuing a doctorate in physics at the University of Maryland under the same sort of NASA fellowship that supported Jim and Andy Lacis at the University of Iowa. After two years as a program manager for glaciology at the National Science Foundation, Zwally returned to NASA in 1974, whence he began to nurture the fledgling science and increasingly sophisticated technology of measuring Earth's polar ice via satellite. This was only a few years after the field was born.

His fingerprints are everywhere. He basically started what he calls "the ice program" at Goddard, and he helped start the cryospheric research program at headquarters. He hired many of the leading cryospheric scientists who remain at Goddard and continue to publish cutting-edge studies about the threat to the polar ice sheets, the thinning and retreat of polar sea ice, and the like. Since a few of his early hires eventually moved to the Jet Propulsion Laboratory, he also played a founding role in the ice program there. And, remarkably, during his short stint at the National Science Foundation, he helped give birth to the entirely new field of high-altitude ice core drilling by awarding a small grant to Lonnie Thompson of Ohio State University and his mentor, John Mercer, for an exploratory trip to the 18,600-foot-high Quelccaya ice cap in Peru.

Mercer was the largely unrecognized genius who first connected global warming to a potential sea level rise back in the early sixties. Even that long ago, he suggested that a warming might endanger the West Antarctic ice sheet by melting its buttressing ice shelves—the explosive "champagne cork" process that Jim would describe to the Council on Environmental Quality in his Time Bomb talk. Thompson, who was just a graduate student when Zwally awarded the grant, drilled the first high mountain ice core on Quelccaya's summit in 1983. In the intervening decades, he has carved out a unique scientific niche for himself by conducting more than fifty similar expeditions to the great mountain ranges of the world, thus providing invaluable information from the equatorial latitudes to complement the ice core records from Greenland and Antarctica. In the mid-nineties, he helped spark a minor revolution in climatology by demonstrating that the lower latitudes have played a determining role in major climate changes of the past—a realization that shook the field, since most of the attention had been focused on the polar regions.

Zwally first collaborated with Jim Hansen in the late seventies, when Jim was heading up a study for an Earth observing satellite named

CLIMSAT. He then became in-house champion for a larger satellite called Ice and Climate Experiment (ICEX) that he and a team of scientists from outside NASA proposed. "Of course, ICEX never flew," he says. "When the Reagan administration came in in 1980, that sort of ended NASA's consideration of new Earth observing satellites for a while. . . . I used to joke that we should at least launch some of our viewgraphs in the shuttle, so we could get *some* of our ideas into orbit. . . . There was about a ten-year hiatus in which we just did planning."

Shortly after the first Bush administration came to power in 1989, NASA announced the Mission to Planet Earth, which featured a new program of Earth observation called EOS. After a few more years, the Ice, Cloud, and land Elevation Satellite (ICESat) was conceived, with Zwally as its lead or project scientist. This remains his primary responsibility. ICESat's main instrument is a laser altimeter, capable of measuring the altitude of a seventy-meter spot on the Earth's surface, directly beneath the satellite, with an absolute accuracy of about fifteen centimeters (six inches) and a precision, that is, an ability to measure differences, of less than one centimeter (less than half an inch). In January 2003—more than two decades after his first attempts to get this sort of idea literally off the ground—ICESat was launched into an orbit that enables it to scan and thereby measure the volumes of the entire Greenland ice sheet and nearly the entire Antarctic ice sheet. (It misses a small disk centered on the south pole, because it orbits at an inclination of ninety-four degrees relative to the equator.)

The altimeter sends out laser pulses forty times a second, illuminating spots at 170-meter intervals and producing successive transects of the surface as the planet rotates between successive, daily satellite orbits. When the transects are put together, they make a map of the region being scanned (which is actually the whole Earth, minus eight-degree disks at the north and south poles). Over its lifetime, which is hoped to be at least five years, ICESat is poised to track changes in the polar ice sheets with unprecedented precision.

Zwally did not twiddle his thumbs during the decades in which the satellite program languished. It was his traditional fieldwork in Greenland, for example, wearing warm clothes and tromping around on the ice, that led to the discovery of the so-called Zwally effect, whereby meltwater from the surface of an ice sheet seeps to the bed and forms a lubricating sheet that helps the ice slide into the sea (the second factor that puts Jim in mind of a time bomb). Zwally has also developed an impressive ability to crunch vast quantities of data at Goddard Space Flight Center—a job that involves more than Goddard's world-class supercomputing facility. In addition to advanced mathematics, sound data analysis requires insight into the physics of both the measurement process and the system under study. He employed these capabilities to produce the first estimate of volume changes in the Greenland ice sheet in 1989, based on what are now seen as primitive altimetry data from Seasat, the first civilian satellite to measure sea surface heights, and Geosat, a navy satellite that produced more than three years of altimetry data for the scientific community after it had accomplished a classified mission for its owner.

It was his analytical work that provided a test for Griffin's Statement on Scientific Openness.

The paper Zwally and his colleagues published in March 2006 summarized their analysis of about a decade's worth of radar altimetry on Antarctica and Greenland that had been conducted by a pair of non-NASA satellites, the European Remote-sensing Satellites ERS-1 and -2. Radar has trouble with steep slopes, so for the coasts of Greenland, where the ice drops off quickly in places, they incorporated measurements by NASA's Airborne Topographic Mapper, an airplane that performs the same sort of measurement as ICESat. The data spanned the decade from 1992 to 2002, so the period of study had ended about four years before the paper was published.

The volume of an ice sheet is not the important thing; it's the mass, because this tells you how much water is stored in the ice. (Snow has a lot of air in it.) And this analysis was the first to refine its mass estimates by taking into account the compaction of the so-called firn, the dense cover of snow from recent years that is slowly compacting into ice. Furthermore, it isn't so much the absolute mass but the "mass balance" of an ice sheet that is important: the annual accounting of how much water it has taken on as a result of precipitation and given off mainly through melting and the flow of its outlet glaciers into the sea.

Zwally's group found that during the decade under study, the ice sheet on Greenland had grown in its inland portions, where the ice is more than two miles thick and the surface is high and cold, while it had been thinning at its coastal margins. The growth outweighed the thinning, so the sheet as a whole was slowly gaining mass—and removing water from the sea. This seemed like good news.

The Antarctic ice sheet is about ten times the size of its northern counterpart, comprising the equivalent of about 63 meters or 207 feet of potential sea level rise, versus Greenland's 7 meters or 23 feet. The Transantarctic Mountain Range crosses the frozen continent and divides its ice into two main sheets: the West Antarctic ice sheet, which comprises about 5 meters or 16 feet of sea level equivalent, and the East Antarctic ice sheet, the mother lode, which comprises about 58 meters or 190 feet.

Zwally's group found that West Antarctica had been losing mass, while East Antarctica had been gaining. The loss was winning out at the bottom of the world, and it was greater than the gain in Greenland; so that, taken together, the planet's three major ice sheets had been adding a total of about 20 billion tons (gigatons) of water to the oceans each year. This is the equivalent of all the freshwater used annually for agriculture and in the homes and businesses of New York, New Jersey, and Virginia, combined. It may seem like a lot, but it would take almost twenty times that, 362 gigatons, to raise sea level just one millimeter.

So, according to this study, the polar ice sheets were more or less "in balance"; they were only adding about five one-hundredths of a millimeter or two one-thousandths of an inch to sea level each year—at least, as of 2002.

But Zwally points out that even though they had shown that Greenland had been in balance during the last decade of the twentieth century, the "significant thinning at the edges and significant growth inland [was] exactly the response of climate warming." The growth at high, cold inland elevations was the result of increased precipitation, which is expected

in a warming climate, simply because the atmosphere takes on more water as it heats up, for the same reason that it tends to be more humid in
summer than in winter. And the melting at the coasts was a direct result
of rising temperatures. This study also showed that the ice shelves around
West Antarctica were thinning. In other words, John Mercer's early fear
was coming true.

These somewhat subtle findings would have been perfect fodder for
spin—and, indeed, a few of the usual global warming deniers hooted
with delight at the fact that Greenland seemed to be growing. So Zwally,
his public affairs colleagues, Jim Hansen, and even Andy Revkin watched
closely to see how headquarters would respond.

Nothing happened. The press release sailed through the approval process with hardly a delay and no changes to the science; and, as Zwally
points out, he "was quoted in the press as saying this should not give consolation to anybody who doesn't believe in climate warming, because this
is a climate warming signal; and that's the way the press release was
cast."

Under the dire title "Impact of Climate Warming on Polar Ice Sheets
Confirmed," the release quoted Zwally's even more dire forecast: "If the
trends we're seeing continue and climate warming continues as predicted,
the polar ice sheets could change dramatically. The Greenland ice sheet
could be facing an irreversible decline by the end of the century."

Jim Hansen's outspokenness seemed to be working a change.

This was another of those moments when the planet seemed to be making a statement. Sometimes, as with hurricanes Katrina and Rita, it
speaks for itself; other times, scientists do the interpreting. In the weeks
before Zwally's press release, two groups using different methods had reported increases in the rate of loss both in Greenland and Antarctica in
the years since his study had ended. And just two weeks after the release,
Science magazine produced a special issue named "Climate Change:

Breaking the Ice," that featured a breathtaking image of icebergs floating in a Greenland fjord on its cover and no less than seven articles on the accelerating changes in Greenland and Antarctica inside. This made headlines around the world.

Isabella Velicogna of JPL and the University of Colorado and John Wahr of Colorado had analyzed data from one of the more ingenious satellite observatories, GRACE, to measure the mass balance of Antarctica. The Gravity Recovery And Climate Experiment, which is jointly administered by NASA and the German Center for Air and Space Flight, estimates the gravitational attraction of the ice sheets by measuring changes in the distance separating two identical satellites, nominally 220 kilometers apart, traveling in identical orbits. (They are nicknamed Tom and Jerry.) Since GRACE measures mass changes directly (in theory, at least), it finesses the need to estimate firn compaction. The measurement is complex to interpret, however; and it is confounded by a process known as postglacial rebound, which Velicogna and Wahr describe as "the viscoelastic response of the solid Earth to glacial unloading over the past several thousand years." In other words, the portions of the Earth's surface that were weighed down by ice up until about 15,000 years ago, when the polar ice sheets began to melt (a process that has so far raised the seas about four hundred feet), continue to rise like a sponge from which you've just lifted your hand.

Only six days before Zwally's press release, Velicogna and Wahr had reported online in *Science* that the mass balance of Antarctica had decreased between 2002 and 2005, owing mostly to growing losses in West Antarctica. They estimated that Antarctic ice was now contributing almost half a millimeter to sea level every year, about six times Zwally's estimate.

Eric Rignot of JPL and Pannir Kanagaratnam of the University of Kansas had just published a study in *Nature* that employed satellite-based radar interferometry to track the *movement* of the Greenland ice sheet. They had measured a significant increase in the flow rates of Greenland's major outlet glaciers over the past few years and had also found that the phenomenon was moving northward. The speed of the largest outlet glacier, the Jakobshavn Isbrae, had nearly doubled between 1996 and 2005—most likely as a result of the "champagne cork" process. The floating ice shelf created by the advancing glacier had progressively disintegrated over the course of the study, and the cork had popped—in other words, the buttressing ice shelf had completely disappeared—by May 2003.

In the special issue of *Science* that came out a few weeks after Zwally's paper, a group from Harvard and Columbia reported that the rate of glacial earthquakes in seven major exit systems in Greenland had doubled in the past five years. These indications of massive lurches toward the sea dovetailed with the findings of Rignot and Kanagaratnam.

All these studies were exploratory and cutting edge, and the numbers weren't all matching up; but taken all around, the data seemed to be saying that the balances at the top and bottom of the planet had just begun to tip.

In the same special issue, a group led by Jonathan Overpeck of the University of Arizona sought clues to the future in evidence from the distant past. After demonstrating with computer simulations that we are on track sometime this century to produce temperatures as high as those of the Eemian interglacial stage, about 130,000 years ago, Overpeck and his colleagues showed that sea levels were then "several meters" higher than they are today. They concluded by echoing Jim Hansen's warnings about our proximity to a tipping point. "Current knowledge cannot rule out a return to such conditions in response to continued [greenhouse gas] emissions. Moreover, a threshold triggering many meters of sea-level rise could be crossed well before the end of this century, particularly given that high levels of anthropogenic soot may hasten future ice-sheet melting [here they referenced one of Jim's papers on soot], the Antarctic could warm much more than 129,000 years ago, and future warming will continue for decades and persist for centuries even after the forcing is stabilized."

In an accompanying editorial, Donald Kennedy, the editor in chief of *Science,* observed that "accelerated glacial melting and larger changes in sea level (for example) should be looked at as probable events, not as hypothetical possibilities."

*   *   *

On the day of Zwally's press release, a petition began circulating inside NASA, expressing support for Griffin's Statement on Scientific Openness as well as support verging on admiration specifically for Jim. Third, it stated, "We, the undersigned, encourage all NASA affiliated scientists and engineers to openly present their expertise for the public good such that NASA's implementation of openness may serve as a model for all US federal agencies." It was eventually signed by more than 300 NASA employees, the vast majority coming from Goddard and JPL.

Jim was more than ready to admit that he had made his point. On Monday, March 13, six weeks and one day after the story broke in *The New York Times,* he issued an e-mail entitled " 'Political Inclinations' and 'Back to Science.' "

In the time since George Deutsch had made his "wacky" remarks about Jim's ties to the Democratic Party, his desire to "get Christians," and so on, Jim had received enough inquiries from the journalistic community to feel a need to respond.

"Political inclinations should have no impact on science analyses, but in any case the above description of my inclinations is inaccurate. I can be accurately described as moderately conservative. I am registered to vote (in Pennsylvania) as an Independent." He went on to enumerate every one of his infrequent and for the most part rocky interactions with politicians from both parties, as well as the two political contributions he had made over the years, with an evenhandedness that recalls Bill Blakemore's remark about "radical innocence." It is worth noting that the only politician for whom Jim expressed unreserved praise was the late senator John Heinz, a Pennsylvania Republican, who had died tragically in a plane crash and whose widow eventually married the 2004 presidential contender John Kerry. Jim had hoped Heinz "would one day run for President." His "rationalization for supporting Senator Heinz was his balanced support for the environment in the context of strong economic development.

"As for religion," Jim continued, "I was baptized and raised as a Reorganized Latter Day Saint. Our long-time Sunday school teacher, Sara Goeser, would be disappointed by the fact that I married a (Dutch) Catholic. By pure coincidence, both of our children married into strong Catholic families (Galileo, forgive them!).

"I will not respond further to personal attacks."

But the main purpose of his message that day was to inform his friends and colleagues that he was done with whistleblowing for the time being and wanted to get back to science. Drawing attention to the problems that still remained at NOAA and especially EPA, "where double-speak ('sound science,' 'clear skies,' . . .) has achieved a level that would make George Orwell envious," and admitting that the "battle to achieve open communication between government scientists and their employer, the public, is far from won," he described NASA's situation as "promising" and voiced admiration for Michael Griffin's clear and seemingly effective words. "If implementation by Public Affairs differs from that spirit, you will hear about it," he warned.

Jim declined the Government Accountability Project's Ridenhour award, observing that "it would be most useful and effective for the spotlight to shine brightly on Rick Piltz and EPA, where the rubber meets the road."

He explained this decision more fully a few days later, in a private letter to the president of the Nation Institute, Hamilton Fish. "The deciding matters were (1) I do not want to be involved in something that anyone might interpret as being a reward for taking the positions that I have taken (I would not even want to choose a favorite charity for an award), and (2) I do not want to spend any more time away from science."

While he received much congratulation and thanks, his e-mail also produced new disheartening stories. One former EPA employee informed him that that agency was "now considered to be even more secretive than the Pentagon." Tom Knutson, the hurricane specialist at NOAA's Geophysical Fluid Dynamics Laboratory, wrote, "The current state of affairs seems to be improving (at least unofficially). . . . In practice we're now just keeping NOAA public affairs abreast of things, but not asking for their pre-approval before speaking to reporters. At this stage, we're not seeking to draw too much attention to this change in practice, as I gather it is not an official policy." Admiral Lautenbacher's halfhearted statement had not been enough, especially considering NOAA's subordinate position within Commerce.

Jerry Mahlman, the former GFDL director who had publicly rebutted the admiral's statement, may have contributed the wisest comment:

Hi Jim,

I concur with, and support, your decision to return back to a rational life within NASA. You, however, have learned that you have gained more clout within, and outside of, NASA than I suspect that you thought that you commanded. I, too, was surprised to learn how much "street credibility" that I still retain within NOAA. I think of this being a very quiet award for both of us. My congratulations to your tenacity, and your courage, even though you probably thought that your decision did not require such courage.

Perhaps more significantly, I deeply respect and fully understand your decision to not accept the GAP award. If I had been in the same position, I would have agonized quite a bit before I too would have had to turn it down, as well. Simply put, the both of us exerted significant pressure on "the system," simply because it is, and has been for some time, our job as visible Agency Lab Directors to speak up when things aren't going so well in our respective agencies. I am not getting any apologies from Lautenbacher, but did not expect any. It is his future behavior that matters. I actually think that he realizes how badly he screwed up. That is more than enough "award" for me, and I suspect so for you. In my opinion, whistleblower awards are very appropriate for the lower level, non-empowered, employee, who risks his/her very job in the whistleblowing process. Obviously, you and I have never truly been

persecuted by our Agency "superiors." The fact
that said "superiors" caved in almost instantly
tells me that such nonsense was not truly in
their hearts. I find it very satisfying that
they already have implicitly agreed that their
complicity was quite inappropriate. But, still,
we will likely keep our eyes on them, just for
protection of our colleagues and peers throughout
our organizations that we have devoted much of
our lives to. My deepest congratulations for your
very highly deserved, and warranted, "non award."

   With warm regards,

   Jerry Mahlman

"Wow, you hit a lot of nails right on the head," Jim answered. "With the benefit of hindsight, I wonder why it took me so long to reject the award. . . . In a sense, perhaps, we were all guilty of some complicity. I never submitted outrageous press releases to Public Affairs, because I knew that they would not fly. . . . I should have forced Public Affairs to make changes, thus gathering harder evidence—but it seems they got pretty well exposed anyhow.

"You are right; we have to keep our eyes on them."

At the end of March, Michael Griffin released the media policy that had been hammered out by the Tiger Team. A definite improvement over both the written and unwritten policies of the past, its guiding principle was a commitment "to a culture of openness with the media and public that values the free exchange of ideas, data, and information." NASA employees were now freely permitted to speak to the press and the public about their work, and while coordination with public affairs was still required, advance notice of interviews needed only be given "whenever possible." Employees could also express their personal views on subjects outside their "official area of expertise or responsibility," as long as they made it clear that they were not speaking for the agency.

A couple of details seemed to speak directly to the events of December and January. Editing by public affairs "shall not change scientific or technical data, or the meaning of programmatic content." "Journalists may have access to the NASA officials they seek to interview, provided those NASA officials agree to be interviewed."

The Government Accountability Project, which had reviewed the policy before it was released, listed a number of troubling aspects. Since clearance would still be required for press releases, news features, Web postings, and the like, which could therefore be delayed indefinitely, the policy seemed to institutionalize "prior restraint censorship"—a tactic Glenn Mahone and Dean Acosta had frequently employed. (Data releases and other "postings designed for technical or scientific interchange"—such as GISS's monthly and yearly temperature announcements, presumably—would not require clearance.) And it was unclear how an employee's right to express "personal views" balanced against the requirement that all information that had "the potential to generate significant media, or public interest or inquiry" had to be coordinated with public affairs prior to release.

In GAP's legal opinion, one entire section aimed at preventing "unauthorized release of sensitive but unclassified (SBU) information" blatantly violated the federal Whistleblower Protection Act. After all, sensitive but unclassified information is precisely what a whistleblower releases. And at NOAA, pretty much anything having to do with climate had been deemed sensitive. In an open letter to climate scientists, GAP's legal director, Tom Devine, stated, "Under this so-called reform, Dr. Hansen would still be in danger of 'dire consequences' for sharing his research, although that threat is what sparked the new policy in the first place. . . . The loopholes are not innocent mistakes or oversights. GAP extensively briefed the agency lawyer on these requirements, who insisted he understood them fully. NASA is intentionally defying the good government anti-secrecy laws."

When Jim was queried by *The New York Times,* he admitted to being "a bit disappointed" at these and other shortcomings, but he expressed optimism and declared the new policy a definite improvement. "Things have changed dramatically since this became a public issue," he said. "This has been a healthy exercise, and hopefully similar things will happen at other agencies that have had similar problems."

By e-mail, he told his boss, Franco Einaudi, that he had decided to make "a very positive statement to the *New York Times,* mainly because I realize that Mike Griffin, Ed Weiler and others worked hard with good intentions." His optimism notwithstanding, he was bothered by ambiguities in the new policy. "Ambiguity is not bad when you have good people in charge." But he pointed out that if this document were adopted at EPA, for instance, the administrators there could still find ways to silence and intimidate. He had hoped for something like a "Bill of Rights" that would provide "a model that might be adopted by other agencies."

Franco told Jim that he was "right on. . . . That will always be the reality in all organizations. I do not believe that laws protecting Jewish people would have prevented what happened in Germany and in Italy or that McCarthyism could have been prevented in this country by laws. . . . We need to remain vigilant, although that too may not be effective. If being vigilant means to bring to the attention of my superiors problems that have occurred over time, I did that in the past and failed miserably."

Jim, Franco, and the others in Earth science at NASA were only too aware that Griffin had not punished the main perpetrator, Dean Acosta, nor any of his accomplices higher up; and the civil servants in public affairs remained openly afraid of both Acosta and David Mould. Sure, they were taking their first baby steps, but they still felt that they were walking on thin ice. Even six months later, Leslie McCarthy would tell me, "These people are ruthless. We don't want to *see* what they're capable of."

About two months after the new media policy went into effect, Griffin's office would respond to the letter it had received in February from senators Collins and Lieberman. An "internal inquiry" had revealed just a single untoward incident: "One recent media request to interview Dr. James Hansen . . . was inappropriately declined. . . . In addition, several instances of inappropriate editing of scientific materials have been alleged. These allegations, if true, are unacceptable at NASA."

A statement by Lieberman's office characterized this response as an admission of wrongdoing, but the folks on the Ninth Floor don't seem to have seen it that way. I have already quoted Michael Griffin denying that censorship of any kind occurred at his agency. David Mould, who took part in the "internal inquiry," as a member of the Tiger Team, says, "Now whether [the NPR interview] was *deliberately* denied . . . I don't know. I hope it wasn't. But it certainly was inappropriately denied, no question about that." He chalks it all up to a regrettable misunderstanding.

About two weeks after headquarters sent its letter of noncontrition to the senators, Shana Dale announced the formation of a new Office of Communications Planning at the agency. It was to be led by none other than Robert Hopkins, who as communications director at OSTP had stepped in to defend Philip Cooney at the Council on Environmental Quality, and whom Gretchen Cook-Anderson suspects of being her bosses' White House contact for the secret editing of NASA press releases. In the interim, Hopkins had done a stint at EPA.

In the late fall of 2006, Congress asked NASA's inspector general, Robert Cobb, its supposed watchdog, to investigate the allegations of censorship at the agency. When one of Mr. Cobb's underlings called me, in January 2007, he said that they would be producing a report in a matter of weeks. (I gave him no names or information.) Seven months after his call, there is no sign of a report, at least outside the Ninth Floor. In any event, Mr. Cobb's investigation seems to have been incomplete. A few of the important people in the censorship story, including Gretchen, were never contacted, and those who were were discouraged from volunteering information about incidents of which the investigators were not already aware. Cobb is reputed to have cozy relations with the managers from whom he is supposed to be independent. According to an April 2007 story by the Associated Press, e-mails indicate that he used to meet regularly with Sean O'Keefe, play golf with him, and tip him off about pending audits. A long inquiry by the President's Council on Integrity and Efficiency, which investigates inspectors general, revealed that Cobb had quashed a report on the *Columbia* shuttle disaster that would have been embarrassing to the agency.

Gretchen writes that she "heard rumors about this guy" when she was at headquarters. "You knew you could not go to his office and have your matter kept confidential. I'd wanted to lodge [an equal opportunity act] complaint against Glenn Mahone and Dean Acosta because of their treatment of me after I was in Glenn's 'doghouse.' . . . I was told by a confidential source that if I were to approach the inspector general's office with any complaint that my matter would most likely not be held in confidence, since their office was 'in bed' with O'Keefe and Glenn Mahone, and that my pursuing anything could backfire on me. . . . I never took my complaint forward formally as a result." Indeed the integrity committee investigated charges that Cobb had retaliated against whistleblowers.

Cobb also extends NASA's bizarre set of connections to the Justice Department. Almost laughably, he was an ethics adviser to Alberto Gonzales when Gonzales was George Bush Jr.'s White House counsel. Gonzales was later elevated to attorney general, of course, and resigned under an extensive ethics cloud.

After the integrity committee issued its report in May 2007, three lawmakers, including Democratic congressman Bart Gordon of Tennessee, who had replaced Sherwood Boehlert as chairman of the House Science Committee, called for Robert Cobb's ouster. Michael Griffin defended him, recommending only that he undergo some "leadership training." In his response to the integrity committee's report, according to the Associated Press, Griffin wrote, "This has been a trying year for Mr. Cobb and I have been impressed with his continued focus on his professional obligations to the Congress and to the agency." He added that the report "does not contain evidence of a lack of integrity on the part of Mr. Cobb." Griffin seems to hold an exceedingly high standard for admissible evidence.

Dean Acosta would leave the agency for the private sector on January 2, 2007, a few weeks after NASA awarded a generous settlement to one of his former supervisees (not Gretchen), an African American woman, who had filed a lawsuit against Acosta and the agency under the Equal Employment Opportunity Act, charging racial and gender discrimination.

This was not the first such suit against Dean. An individual who was familiar with this case told me it was "part of a pattern."

In the press release announcing Acosta's departure (point of contact: David Mould), Griffin was quoted as saying, "Dean has done everything I have asked and more. He will be missed."

The folks at GISS got some chuckles out of that one.

Furthermore, although the media policy that Michael Griffin announced in March 2006 gave his scientists the clear right to *express* their message, back in February he had landed a stealthy blow on the ability of his Earth scientists to *produce* a message in the first place. It would take a few months for Jim Hansen to realize what Griffin had done.

Jay Zwally says that when he read Jim's promise to give up whistleblowing, he chuckled to himself and said, "I'll believe *that* when I see it." Well, he must have laughed out loud when *60 Minutes* broadcast its segment with Jim and Rick Piltz the following Sunday, March 19. (The Government Accountability Project announced the founding of Piltz's watchdog project on Monday morning.)

If *The New York Times* started the tidal wave, this broadcast provided the second shock. Correspondent Scott Pelley not only covered the censorship story, he also gave Jim the opportunity to present his scientific message: that the human influence now dwarfs all "natural" factors governing climate and that if we don't stabilize the exponential growth of our greenhouse emissions within ten years and put them on a declining path by mid-century, climate will pass a tipping point and the situation will move beyond our control. The most disastrous consequence would be the dramatic rise in sea level portended by the recent spate of scientific papers.

Pelley didn't just take Jim's word for it, though; he checked with other scientists, and he went right to the top to find someone to speak on their behalf: Ralph Cicerone, president of the National Academy of Sciences and an esteemed atmospheric chemist who helped discover the ozone hole. Pelley noted that Cicerone "said the same thing every leading scientist told *60 Minutes*."

"Climate change is really happening."

"So, what *is* causing the changes?"

"Well, the greenhouse gases: carbon dioxide and methane and chlorofluorocarbons and a couple of others, which are all—the increases in their concentrations in the air are due to human activities. It's that simple."

When Pelley asked him to assess the importance of Jim's work, Cicerone replied, "I can't think of anybody who I would say is better than Hansen. You might argue that there's two or three others as good, but nobody better."

About six months later, I asked Cicerone if he might name those two or three others.

"In fact, I'm not sure I'd put anyone above Jim."

Goddard director Ed Weiler describes Jim's statements as "innocuous." "He did a great job on the show." When he is reminded that Jim started right off by saying he was being censored, Weiler responds, "Well, he was."

This broadcast stirred up a lot of emotion, owing perhaps to the powerful combination of television as a medium and this particular show's substantive reporting method. This was when the long knives came out. Cybercast News Service (CNSNews.com) published the first in a series of hit pieces on Jim the following Thursday, twisting statements from his e-mail on political inclinations to paint him as a partisan Democrat, much as George Deutsch had attempted over the radio. Deutsch would then pass his December 15 point paper to CNS, and this would provide the basis for the second article in the series, mentioned previously, which characterized Jim as a "loose cannon" and revealed the discussions at headquarters about firing him. The series would be written by Marc Morano, a former producer for Rush Limbaugh, who had been one of the first "journalists" to report on the Swift Boat Veterans for Truth campaign that dubiously questioned John Kerry's service in Vietnam. Morano had engaged in his most recent effort along the same lines only two months before he had turned his attention to Jim, when he had questioned whether Pennsylvania congressman John Murtha, who had begun calling for a withdrawal from Iraq, had truly earned his two Purple Hearts.

On the Sunday morning after the *60 Minutes* spot, a yelling match took place on ABC's *This Week* with George Stephanopoulos, pitting conservative columnist George Will against Fareed Zakaria, editor of *Newsweek International,* and Katrina vanden Heuvel, editor of *The Nation.* Will, who characterized the renewed interest in global warming as a creation of the liberal media, sealed his argument by reading from a decades-old article in the well-known scientific journal *Time* magazine that predicted an imminent ice age. So much for primary sources.

A couple of weeks later, conservative pundit and Fox News talking head Robert Novak did some Swift Boating of his own in his newspaper column. (Novak is perhaps most famous for his outing of covert CIA operative Valerie Plame Wilson, an action that laid the ground for the eventual perjury convictions of Dick Cheney's chief of staff, I. Lewis "Scooter" Libby.)

Novak employed a time-honored technique among global warming deniers (and Swift Boaters in general), which is to make false information seem true simply by repeating it so much that it takes on a life of its own. He didn't go to much trouble. None of his sources were primary; it seems that he found most of his "facts" in Morano's articles; and his central scientific assertion was so demonstrably false that it is hard to understand how the fact-checkers at his publisher, the *Chicago Sun-Times,* could have let the column through. Novak repeated a fraudulent claim he had found in a science fiction novel, no less, which had in turn been lifted from fraudulent congressional testimony by one of the most venerable of the global warming deniers.

In his 2004 climate thriller, *State of Fear,* novelist Michael Crichton had claimed that a prediction Jim had made in his legendary 1988 congressional testimony had been "wrong by 300 percent." A statement in a novel would not generally attract serious attention, but Crichton had insisted that the technical aspects of his book were accurate; and he had advertised this claim with academic-looking footnotes and a bibliography, which, for the rare reader who bothered to examine them, demonstrated that he looked exclusively to the deniers for scientific insight and misrepresented the conclusions of real scientists as it suited his purpose. Although his contrarian hero was a professor at the Massachusetts Institute of Technology, the institute did not seem to take this as a compliment. A review of the book in MIT's national magazine, *Technology Review,* began, "Michael Crichton has written that rarest of books, an intellectually dishonest novel."

Surreally, in the fall of 2005, Oklahoma senator James Inhofe, who was then chairman of the Senate Committee on Environment and Public Works, had asked Crichton to provide expert testimony on climate science at one of his committee's hearings. (Inhofe had already earned his place in history with a 2003 speech on the Senate floor in which he had declared that global warming was "the greatest hoax ever perpetrated on the American people." He would be so impressed by Marc Morano's work at CNS in the wake of the *60 Minutes* spot that in June 2006 he would hire Morano as communications director for his committee.)

It also seems that Crichton is the only expert George W. Bush himself has personally consulted on the climate issue. In a refreshingly candid manifestation of the faith the president placed in fiction rather than fact, the two held a private meeting at the White House in 2005, arranged by Karl Rove, during which they reportedly "talked for an hour and were in near-total agreement" on climate "science."

The truth is that in the article in the *Journal of Geophysical Research* that formed the basis for Jim's 1988 testimony and in the oral and written testimony itself, he presented three scenarios for future greenhouse emissions and their effect upon global temperatures. One he described as being "on the high side of reality"; a second on the low side, since it assumed "a more drastic curtailment of emissions than has generally been imagined"; and a third, between the two (business-as-usual), that he characterized as "most plausible." Dr. Crichton (an M.D.) simply ignored the second and third scenarios and presented the scenario that Jim had labeled implausibly high as his "prediction."

Crichton also chose to ignore the fact that with eighteen additional years of warming under our belts, Jim's business-as-usual scenario was proving to be spot-on.

Novak, incidentally, had no business not knowing this, for Jim had published a full discussion of the matter on his Web site just before Crichton had testified to Inhofe's committee. And when *State of Fear* had come out, he had told *The New York Times,* "Crichton has taken what is actually a triumph of climate science prediction and pretended that it is a failure." Yet Novak reported that Jim had "stepped back from his earlier predictions." Where did he get that one?

Jim was not acting like a lawyer, however. He was holding to the Feynman admonition and exhaustively reviewing the weaknesses in his own analysis. In his Web posting he pointed out that the remarkable success of his prediction had come partly by accident. The small, random climate variations in the real world over the previous eighteen years had matched up well with those in the computer model he had used to make his prediction; back in 1988 his estimate for climate sensitivity, the change in temperature that will result from a doubling of carbon dioxide, was slightly high; and, almost uncannily, he had chosen 1995 as the year for a random volcanic eruption that was roughly the same magnitude and led to roughly the same amount of temporary cooling as the actual eruption, in 1991, of Pinatubo in the Philippines. He had purposefully left volcanic activity out of the scenario Crichton had used for his particular purposes, because that scenario was meant to represent an upper bound.

Jim would not have troubled to check on his so-called prediction had this false controversy not come about. He pointed out that the inherent randomness of climate meant that it was still too early to know whether the business-as-usual forecast he had made eighteen years earlier really did match the real world (although it was possible to rule out Crichton's favorite "upper bound" scenario). It would take a few more years of data collection to tease the temperature increase he had actually predicted from random noise. In the end, incidentally, Jim believes his 1988 business-as-usual forecast will come in on the high side, mainly because his high estimate of climate sensitivity will ultimately dominate certain offsetting factors he neglected twenty years ago.

He has been improving his climate models all that time, of course, so he can now test them against actual temperatures, plugging in measured greenhouse and volcanic emissions rather than the guesses he used in 1988. His current models match the rising course of our planet's temperature quite precisely.

Although the deniers still tend to use Crichton's novel as the definitive scientific reference for Jim's "mistake," they are actually giving the novelist more credit than he deserves. He was parroting the 1998 congressional testimony of Patrick Michaels, who is one of the more vociferous global warming deniers and is somewhat less subtle than Crichton. In preparing for his testimony, Michaels took the graph Jim had presented ten years earlier and simply erased the two scenarios that disproved his false point.

Michaels is the official climatologist for the state of Virginia. He got plenty of mileage out of this obscure credential until the fall of 2006, when Virginia's governor, Timothy Kaine, asked him to make it clear that he is not speaking for the state when he voices his contrarian views. This came shortly after the revelation that Michaels had requested and received more than $100,000 the previous year from a consortium of Western coal utilities. This was nothing new, actually. Such had been his main source of funding since about the time Jim first brought global warming to public attention with the testimony Michaels later distorted.

But this Swift Boat capsized in the tidal shift of public opinion that Jim and his censors on the Ninth Floor had helped initiate. Nearly all mainstream reporters now joined Bill Blakemore in refusing to be spun. In the first week of April, *Time* magazine dedicated a special issue to global warming, featuring on its cover the "tipping point" phrase that Jim had first affixed to the issue in his Keeling talk.

And in May, *Vanity Fair* released the "green issue" that the folks in NASA public affairs had discussed as far back as December. Among numerous articles on global warming and other environmental matters, interspersed with photographs of Oscar parties and the standard freight of semipornographic ads and celebrity shoots, were utterly sensationalized aerial touch-ups of Washington, D.C., and New York City, flooded by twenty- and eighty-foot seas. Thanks to the censorship, once again, the story on Jim had evolved since its conception. He was nominated to the magazine's Hall of Fame, "because the heat is on, and he refuses to be put on ice." The set designer for Jim's photo shoot seems to have been a bit unclear on the concept, however, as he confused global warming with the hole in the ozone layer (of which there is only one, please remember). When Leslie McCarthy had received a sketch in advance, she had told them, "That's not what he does." Jim had ignored her e-mail on the subject, as he will, so he was "a little unhappy" when he showed up at the studio. It was far too late. He was photographed fully clothed, thank you very much, in an elegant, tweedy suit, standing in what seemed to be a schoolroom, holding the hole-punch with which he had evidently punched hundreds of "ozone" holes in the map of the world that hung on the wall behind him, the punch-outs scattered like confetti on the floor. The accompanying text, on the other hand, was excellent.

The media juggernaut ran on. In news outlets around the world, large and small, Jim's name became synonymous not only with the dangers of global warming but also with the Bush administration's pervasive mugging of science, which continued to be unveiled.

Both Jim and Kerry Emanuel were named to *Time* magazine's list of the most influential people of 2006, the *Time* 100. In his brief profile of Jim, Al Gore wrote, "His message is beginning to sink in. The world's premier climate modeler has helped push Americans to their own tipping point—to the realization that global temperatures are rising dramatically, that the consequences are grave and that there are solutions available that can reverse those planet-altering trends. He not only speaks truth to power—over and over again—but he also has succeeded in making concepts such as 'dangerous anthropogenic interference' understandable to a world that will be tragically affected by it if we do not change our energy-consumption habits.

"When the history of the climate crisis is written, Hansen will be seen as the scientist with the most powerful and consistent voice calling for intelligent action to preserve our planet's environment."

Gore made the list as well. The slide show that Jim had critiqued in January had been filmed for a movie, of course, and the buzz had begun with its premiere at the Sundance Film Festival in January. It was scheduled for release in late May. As *Time* reported in its profile of Gore, the trailer alone had been receiving ovations at movie theaters in Los Angeles.

Jim wasn't sure that he wanted to attend Time Warner's black-tie gala at the Waldorf-Astoria. He'd never really heard of his fellow honorees, the Dixie Chicks, who would be performing. But he had once regretted not taking Anniek to an award ceremony where John Denver had performed, so she went with him. They had a good time and they loved the music, although Anniek found occasion to forbear her husband's "inordinate obsessions" once again, as he had some business he wanted to discuss with another honoree, Secretary of State Condoleezza Rice.

Here is the e-mail he sent to Ralph Cicerone and Kerry Emanuel two days after the party:

```
Date: May 10, 2006 5:30 PM
Subject: George


Ralph, Kerry,


I had hoped to speak with Condoleezza Rice at
Time-Warner on Monday, but she disappeared quickly.
I wanted to suggest that she make time for hearing
an update on the state of understanding of climate
change, which is different than when we talked to
her five years ago, with the notion that she may
convince George to do something to change his
legacy on the matter. I did talk with John McCain,
who said that it would not have mattered, that he
(McCain) has been trying to convince George for
six years, that George has ruined his legacy on
```

this topic, and that the only one who could
influence him to change his position is Laura.
That being the case, I suppose it confirms that
communicating with the public is the one best
hope for progress.

Jim

Perhaps he was working with radical innocence again, attempting to
take the administration at its word. He points out that in the president's
Rose Garden speech back in 2001, Bush had said that as the evidence
changed, his policy on global warming would change with it. "So I
wanted to tell [Rice] that the evidence had really changed a lot since I had
spoken to the panel that she was on with the vice president . . . and ask if
we couldn't discuss that, with the thought that she might be the person
who would be able to influence George Bush. . . . I had the impression
that the State Department and the people that have to deal with the rest
of the world would not mind doing something about the climate, since
they're getting beaten over the head by the rest of the world. . . . But as it
turned out, she just came in and then disappeared; she was there very
briefly. That's what I was then talking to McCain about . . . and his response was 'Oh, you didn't miss anything. . . .'"

Communication with the public shifted into high gear two weeks
later, when Gore's movie, *An Inconvenient Truth,* was finally released.
And of all the scientists the former vice president might have chosen to
join him in a panel discussion at New York City's Town Hall the day after the movie opened, he chose Jim. He was given a few minutes to speak,
and his scientific points became the touchstone for Gore and everyone else
in the evening's discussion. The movie would go on to win an Oscar.

So, as Jim returned to science, Gore stepped to center stage. The amazing thing is, though, that even amidst the tumult of the six months we
have now covered, Jim had accomplished quite a bit of science. In fact, he
had entered one of the most creative years of what had already been an
exceptionally long and creative scientific career.

Chapter 8

The Veil of Venus

IN JANUARY 1967, an excited and exhausted twenty-five-year-old from Iowa arrived in the big city after a long, nonstop drive. He had little in the way of possessions besides the letter that told him his temporary address, the Paris Hotel on West End Avenue at Ninety-sixth Street, about a mile's walk from GISS. "Paris Hotel was supposedly a house of ill-repute," Jim recalls. "I never noticed anything, but I'm not very observant."

What he did notice right away was that he had found himself in a remarkable research environment. The institute was run at that time by Robert Jastrow, the man who had founded it six years earlier, a brilliant and feisty individual who had made a fundamental contribution to nuclear physics in the early fifties during a short stint under Robert Oppenheimer at the Institute for Advanced Study in Princeton. Jastrow had then taken an interest in astrophysics and the nation's nascent space program. He was invited to lead the theoretical division at Goddard Space Flight Center within a month of NASA's inception in 1958. Three years after that, he convinced the agency's top management to form a new institute in the neighborhood of Columbia University (where he had earned both his bachelor's and doctoral degrees), according to what is now known as the GISS formula. Jim would describe this formula in 2005, in a tribute to Jastrow on the occasion of his eightieth birthday: "Key ingredients: a small permanent research staff, an academic environment, post-docs and students, ability of staff to teach courses for student recruitment and work with university faculty and researchers, and public outreach to make results of NASA research understandable and available to the public."

Jim was an unusually self-directed postdoc, who never really sought out a mentor in his new surroundings. "I had the notion that radiation theory was very useful for remote sensing, as well as for understanding a planet's temperature, and I sort of had tunnel vision on trying to develop computer programs that would be useful for interesting problems, such as understanding the Venus clouds," he recalls. The main way he met the other scientists at GISS was by bumping into them at the computer as they "read in" the decks of punch cards that were used for programming in those early days of computing. GISS owned one of the only two IBM 360/95s that were ever built (the other was at Goddard), and for a short time they were the fastest machines in the world.

He had already developed the habit of working most of his waking hours. "In the middle of the evening," he recalls, "John Potter and Howard Cheyney [two other postdocs] and I would sometimes go to V&T, an Italian restaurant still on Amsterdam Avenue, for dinner, usually pizza, tossed salad, and a glass of beer—they had about the best thick-crusted pizza in New York and good cheesecake—or we would just go across the street from GISS to the Moon Palace, unfortunately now defunct. [This Chinese restaurant would figure prominently in the history of climate science.] I usually worked very late, but I quickly learned that walking back to the Paris Hotel down dark West End Avenue at one A.M. while thinking about something else was not such a good idea. One night, all of a sudden, in the middle of a block, one young guy appeared on my right, one on the left, and one in front of me. Then one flashed a knife and asked for my billfold. I said, 'Okay, okay, I'm not looking, but please leave my billfold,' and covered my eyes with one hand. Nice guys: they dropped the billfold on the street. The funny part of the story is that two days later, I remembered that my laundry ticket was among the bills. I went to the laundry, but somebody had already picked up my shirts. I hope they fit."

The senior scientists were as collegial as the postdocs. Only a month or so after Jim arrived, Patrick Thaddeus, a prominent astrophysicist on the staff, who shared Jim's interest in Venus, found that he had a scheduling conflict and asked Jim to present his paper in his stead at a scientific conference at Arizona's Kitt Peak Observatory. Once there, Jim found himself rubbing shoulders with some of the scientists whose papers he had devoured in graduate school, including Carl Sagan, who was then an assistant professor at Harvard, and Sagan's student Jim Pollack, who would later move to NASA's Ames Research Center in California and would collaborate with Sagan until the latter's death from cancer some three decades later. Pollack and Jim would become good friends and publish a few papers together over the years.

Jim had corresponded with Sagan from Kyoto while he was writing his Ph.D. thesis, and Sagan had graciously responded with a detailed letter. "He was a very nice guy," Jim observes. "I mean, he didn't throw away the student's letter." Jim's "original proposition" involving dust in the Venusian atmosphere had not yet been disproven, nor had Sagan's competing proposition of a strong greenhouse effect been proven, so they and Pollack engaged in an affable discussion over lunch in Arizona on the relative merits of the two ideas. (Jim had surprised his thesis adviser, Matsushima, by naming him coauthor on the article he had just submitted to *Astrophysical Journal* based on his thesis work.) "Carl asked me if I really believed that Venus was kept warm by the dusty atmosphere," Jim recalls, "and I said, well, it was easier to explain with the greenhouse effect, but somebody had already suggested that."

He would cross paths with Sagan off and on over the years, and he continues to admire Sagan's ability to communicate science to the public. "We're actually missing him now in this global warming thing," he says.

Jim's remarkable productivity was evident from the start. During his two-year postdoc at GISS he churned out roughly half a dozen papers on light scattering from hazy planetary atmospheres, following the line of thought, generally speaking, that had been initiated by the measurements he, Andy Lacis, and Professor Matsushima had made in the frigid Iowa cornfield in 1963.

A French astronomer named Bernard Lyot had invented an instrument capable of making extraordinarily precise measurements of the polarization of light and had thus revealed the remarkable angular dependence in the polarization of the sunlight scattered by the so-called veil of Venus, the clouds that shroud the entire planet. Jim had a hunch that he could use Lyot's detailed information to find out exactly what the clouds were made of. Were they dust, as he had proposed in his thesis? Or were they ice crystals—an idea that had been proposed by his friendly rivals Sagan and Pollack?

He began using the 360/95 to analyze Lyot's data, based on the simplified and approximate light scattering formulas he had employed in his thesis. As coincidence had it, one of the world's leading authorities on light scattering, Hendrik Christoffel van de Hulst from the Leiden Observatory in the Netherlands, was taking a sabbatical at GISS when Jim arrived, and he made Jim aware of a theoretical "doubling method" that promised to provide nearly an exact solution for the scattering from the Venusian veil. As Jim's postdoc neared its end, he successfully applied to the National Science Foundation to study with van de Hulst in Leiden the following year. But he had so impressed Patrick Thaddeus and another senior staff member, Ichtiaque Rasool, that they convinced Bob Jastrow not to let him slip away. He was offered a permanent position at GISS, while Jastrow, who had done a postdoc at Leiden himself, permitted him to go to Holland anyway. Lucky thing.

Exhibiting his characteristic naïveté (that is to say, willful ignorance of all things bureaucratic), Jim remained in Leiden only as long as it took him to work out van de Hulst's doubling method and give it a few tests on the smaller and slower computer at the observatory—about six months. Progress was fast, he says, because he learned so much from Joop Hovenier, a brilliant student who had been studying under van de Hulst for several years. In this short time, Jim also managed to visit Budapest just after Soviet tanks rolled into the main square (he remembers gun-toting Soviet soldiers lining the streets) and meet his future wife, Anniek Dekkers.

She was teaching high school and living in a house with a bunch of other young women in the old town of Leiden, just down the street from Pieterskerk, the medieval church where the Pilgrims who founded Plymouth Colony had worshipped before sailing to the New World, and not far from a bridge across a canal that led to the *Sterrewacht,* or observatory.

Anniek led quite a social life. "We don't do boyfriends, girlfriends," she says in Dutch-inflected English. "We have friends, and we meet at all times, day and night; and it was really just one big bunch of togetherness, so it was great." One evening, listening to one of her male friends play the saxophone in a jazz jam session at a café in the old town, Anniek happened to tell a woman who shared Jim's office that she was planning to take a sailing course in a week or two. This mutual friend knew that Jim also had an interest in sailing—he had bought a small boat called a Sunfish upon arriving in New York. In any event, she asked Anniek if she might tell this American in her office where and how to go sailing in Holland. Anniek didn't have time at first, but when the woman asked her again sometime later, she agreed to walk down the street and help this American fellow out.

"I'm a very serviceable person. . . . I like to make people's lives easier and comfortable, and that's the way I like to live, too, comfortably; and it doesn't mean a ton of money, it just means comfortable.

"I went over at nine thirty in the evening. Nine thirty seems to be the magical time in my life. . . . And this Jim, who came down the stairs, I noticed he was very white. I thought, 'Oh, this is what Americans look like?' In fact, I had not really met many Americans after high school. See, at that time I was twenty-six years old. After high school, before I went to college, I had lived one year in England. I liked to, you know, speak the language.

"So I thought, 'Oh my God, he's so pale; he's so white, so pasty. This guy really needs to go out.' So I said, 'Well, your idea for sailing is really good, but you should really take some time out and do it for quite a while; you need some color on your face.' And he smiled; he broke out in a smile, and I really liked that smile. . . .

"He was actually very handsome, but it did not show until he smiled. Yes, he had a shock of—unbelievable now—but a shock of chestnut brown hair, a really beautiful dark brown. It was very, very beautiful; and with his green eyes . . . but his skin was so white. So we talked about sailing, and he said, 'Oh, can I go with you?'

"So I said, 'No, really not, because the course is filled.'"

She seems to remember his being taken aback at this refusal. Her theory (denied by Jim) is that as the first boy in his family after four girls, he was used to special treatment. In any event, he was "very disappointed."

Although this first encounter took place only about a month before Jim was to return to the States, they managed to see each other a few more times before he left. "We would meet after the computer shut off, which was nine thirty in the evening," she remembers. "I worked hard, too, because I was teaching high school and I had a very busy social life, so I didn't even realize that that's what was happening—it was the best time for me, too—but I didn't realize this was his life."

She took him to the airport. They wrote. (She had no phone.) And when he visited over Christmas, he suggested that they take a vacation together, which is almost unheard of for Jim. ("He doesn't vacation well," notes Leslie McCarthy.) Anniek's memory of his word choice is telling. " 'I'm willing to take a week's vacation,' he said. 'What do you want to do, go to the Caribbean or go to my sister in Chicago?' I said, 'Oh, let's go see your sister.' I thought, 'Well, let's see a little bit more of this family.' And I met his sister, and she's quite amazing." Indeed, Jim's sisters all seem to be great storytellers.

He and Anniek were married in 1971, about two years after they met.

Nowadays, he usually comes across as a happy and astoundingly energetic man, but Anniek remembers him as being rather gloomy that evening at nine thirty when she met him on the Leiden stairway, mostly because he worked all the time. He admitted this to her as well.

"So he said after he started living with me, after we were married, that his life became happier and he became more optimistic. That's what he has always said."

One can certainly understand why.

After meeting one of the more soothing and accommodating individuals one might ever wish to meet, Jim ran head-on into rather the opposite as soon as he returned to New York. The famously short-tempered

Bob Jastrow became annoyed simply because Jim asked a few too many questions in their first meeting and docked his pay for a couple of months. ("I could see on the secretary's face that I had made a boo-boo," Jim remembers.)

Jastrow also assigned him to a project he wasn't especially interested in, but this did not prevent him from doing what he'd returned from Leiden specifically to do: load his new computer program onto the 360/95 and see if he could produce a polarization curve that matched Lyot's observations. The cards for Jim's program now filled two boxes, each about two feet long. He had to feed the "decks" into the machine every time he wanted to run it, and he would do this late at night when he could have as much computer time as he wanted. It didn't take long to find a match to Lyot's data, and he learned a valuable lesson in doing so.

The "rainbows" and "glories" in the scattered sunlight from Venus told him that the planet's veil was made up of tiny spherical particles in a surprisingly narrow size range, which meant that they were probably water droplets and not crystals of ice. Jim's formulas also revealed how the refractive index of these droplets varied with the color, or wavelength, of light, and this told him that they probably consisted of a solution of about 75 percent sulfuric acid. Droplets of just this sort exist in Earth's stratosphere, as a result of volcanic activity—in fact, their parasol effect cools the planet. It seemed to make sense.

But when he went to the reigning expert on atmospheric chemistry, a fellow named John Lewis at MIT, he was told, "That's impossible on Venus." So, in the paper he published in *Science* in 1971 (his first in that august journal), he gave only the physical characteristics of the droplets with no suggestion as to their composition.

By coincidence, Jim Pollack was looking into Earth's stratosphere at the same time. He encouraged another scientist to publish some lab results on the optical properties of sulfuric acid droplets, and this led an astronomer named Andy Young at Texas A&M to guess that Pollack might be thinking that the droplets on Venus were made up of sulfuric acid—when Pollack was thinking nothing of the sort. Young looked further into the matter, realized the droplets on Venus must be sulfuric acid, and swiftly published this result. "So," says Jim, "I provided him with ninety percent of his information but I did not reap the scientific benefits. It's much more interesting not just to do some detailed calculation in the middle of a problem but to look at the broader implications of the data."

As is common in a young scientist, Jim did not realize quite how much he knew, nor how well equipped he was to look at a wide range of problems. He thought he knew only the details of a specific problem on a faraway planet, when, in fact, his rigorous study of the interaction of light and planetary atmospheres had broader implications than he ever imagined. The greenhouse effect also happens to arise from the interaction of radiation with the atmosphere.

The planetary science community had become involved in weather (as distinct from climate) modeling in the late 1960s, as part of an international effort to improve weather prediction that John F. Kennedy had kicked off with a speech to the United Nations in 1961. The Global Atmospheric Research Program finally came into being in 1967. NASA got involved, based on the obvious but as yet unproven assumption that daily satellite observations would improve the reliability of weather forecasts, and GISS began developing a computerized weather model. Jim's contribution was to work on sunlight's heating of the atmosphere.

In 1973, Ichtiaque Rasool decided to leave GISS for headquarters—mainly out of frustration with Jastrow, who habitually made people wait on the couch outside his office for upwards of an hour before giving them five minutes of his time. Rasool passed his research grant on to Jim, and Jim hired Andy Lacis straight from his doctoral work at the University of Iowa. The two friends began working together on a solar radiation model for Earth, while Andy's able presence gave Jim the freedom to pursue his primary interest in Venus. At around that time, NASA announced the first Pioneer Venus mission, and Jim floated a proposal to fly a small "polarimeter" on the satellite—an instrument to measure polarization—inspired by the design of Lyot. The proposal was successful, but the satellite would not fly until 1978. This gave Jim a few years to work on other things—and, as it turned out, change course entirely.

*   *   *

Oddly enough, one of the greatest stimuli to modern research into Earth's climate—and into the impact of human activity on our atmosphere in general—was the development of supersonic aircraft, so-called SSTs, which are designed to fly in the stratosphere faster than the speed of sound. When the idea was first proposed in the early seventies, environmentalists feared that water vapor from the aircraft might deplete stratospheric ozone, and these fears attracted wide media and public interest. An international study group concluded that water vapor posed no threat and the SST would have little effect on the ozone layer; but a physical chemist at the University of California at Berkeley named Harold Johnston questioned the broader conclusion by suggesting—accurately, as it turned out—that the nitrogen compounds given off by the SST's propulsion system probably *would* destroy stratospheric ozone. This led the U.S. Department of Transportation to fund the Climatic Impact Assessment Program, a three-year, $21 million study of the environmental impact of SSTs. The study concluded that the aircraft probably would have a deleterious effect on the ozone layer, and the United States decided against building one. Paradoxically, the nation went ahead at the same time with the space shuttle, which has a stronger per flight effect on the ozone layer, since its solid rocket boosters inject hydrogen chloride directly into the stratosphere as it flies through it. On the other hand, the shuttle doesn't fly all that often. Of course, the British and the French went ahead and collaborated on the supersonic Concorde anyway, and the Concorde flew for almost three decades until it was discontinued for economic reasons in 2003.

One by-product of this broad research effort was the landmark, not to mention Nobel Prize–winning, 1974 discovery by Sherwood Rowland and his student Mario Molina at the University of California at Irvine that chlorofluorocarbons, or freons, pose a grave threat to the ozone layer. These synthetic chemicals were widely used at the time as coolants in air conditioners and refrigerators, and as propellants in spray cans.

Many of the leading players in the development of research priorities for the Climatic Impact Assessment Program were planetary scientists, and once that forest fire had been put out, they decided the country ought to put together some sort of cohesive program in basic atmospheric research so as to be prepared for the next. They decided to base the program at NASA, which they saw as the most science-driven of the big project-oriented agencies.

At NASA headquarters in 1975, Jim proposed to this brain trust (which included his former colleague Rasool) that GISS develop a comprehensive climate model from its existing weather model. A climate model looks at the entire planet on time scales of months to years to decades, while a weather model looks at smaller regions in more detail on time scales of hours to days. Jim intended to focus mainly on the effects of ozone and to make the model general enough so that it could be applied to the study of other planets, such as Mars and Venus. The brain trust was impressed, but they turned him down the first time around. He got funding the following year.

He believed a robust climate model would need to comprise three main elements: radiation, dynamics (basically, the forces that drive weather systems), and atmospheric chemistry. Since GISS was weak in the last area, he cast about for a chemist. The three most outstanding candidates were all working with Professor Michael McElroy at Harvard, and among them a postdoc named Yuk Ling Yung was considered the "most moveable." When Jim invited Yung to GISS for a day of interviews, he arranged that they meet Bob Jastrow for dinner at the Moon Palace.

"I primed Dr. Jastrow that this guy was really important. I wanted to get this thing to work," he says. "I needed a chemist, a really good chemist, and then we could have the best model in the world, because we had the expertise in these other areas. Unfortunately, Dr. Jastrow stood us up. We went to the Moon Palace and waited and waited. Dr. Jastrow went to play racquetball instead, which is the way Dr. Jastrow was."

Yung elected to remain at Harvard and collaborate with Jim from there. He eventually moved to Caltech, where, among many valuable contributions, he conducted the study about the threat that the hydrogen economy poses to the stratosphere, which would be shuffled under the rug by Dana Perino and her friends at the Council on Environmental Quality in 2003.

Yung's early collaboration with Jim not only turned Jim's mind in the direction of the greenhouse effect, it also provided the ground for the alternative scenario that Jim would present to Dick Cheney's climate change working group a quarter of a century later.

The sun delivers energy to its circling planets mainly in the form of visible and ultraviolet light, at short wavelengths. The surfaces of the planets absorb this light, heat up, and emit the absorbed energy back to space in the form of thermal or infrared radiation, which is simply light with a longer wavelength. We can't see infrared light, because our eyes have evolved to detect the much more plentiful sunlight. The hotter the surface of any planet, the more energy it will emit, and it will seek the temperature that balances the flows of the incoming short-wave and outgoing long-wave energy. This is the principle of radiation balance.

A straightforward calculation shows that an object with Earth's reflectivity, at our average distance from the sun, will seek a surface temperature of about zero degrees Fahrenheit. The so-called greenhouse effect of our atmosphere raises the temperature almost sixty degrees and makes possible life as we know it.

Greenhouse gases constitute less than one-tenth of 1 percent of the atmosphere, which is made up mostly of oxygen, nitrogen, argon, and hydrogen. The reason we can see the sun so clearly is that both the greenhouse and the nongreenhouse gases are transparent to visible light—in other words, they allow the sun's energy to pass through to the surface. The reason we don't freeze to death is that the trace greenhouse gases absorb the infrared energy going back out. They reemit this absorbed energy in all directions: roughly half continues out, and half is sent back toward the surface. This effectively adds to the inflow and subtracts from the outflow; each layer of the atmosphere acts as a sort of blanket over the layer just below it; and temperatures are warmer lower down and warmest at the surface.

From space, Earth would appear to be radiating at the rightful temperature of about zero degrees Fahrenheit, but a close look would reveal that the radiation originates at a mean altitude of about 20,000 feet, almost four miles from the surface, where the temperature has dropped by the requisite sixty degrees. The rate at which temperature drops with increasing altitude is known as the lapse rate: about three degrees Fahrenheit per 1,000 feet. In other words, if you have ever hiked up a mountain and felt it get colder as you climbed higher, you were *experiencing* the greenhouse effect. It is quite strong.

None of this is controversial. As I have mentioned, the first rigorous treatment of the effect of the two most important greenhouse gases, water vapor and carbon dioxide, was undertaken by Svante Arrhenius in 1896. Not only did he accurately calculate the total rise of sixty degrees, his estimate of what is now known as climate sensitivity—the rise in temperature that would accompany a doubling of the level of carbon dioxide that existed in his day (the so-called preindustrial level)—was within a factor of two of the value that is widely accepted today.

So, the importance of carbon dioxide was well understood by the time Yuk Yung met Jim Hansen in 1976. The recent interest in ozone had also revealed that, molecule for molecule, the freons were the most powerful greenhouse gases known (an excellent reason, besides their damaging effect on the ozone layer, to phase them out). Yung's crucial contribution was to realize that other greenhouse gases were worth considering: methane, ozone itself, nitrous oxide, ammonia, and other nitrogen compounds that play roles in industrial agriculture—all of which Jim would eventually include in his alternative scenario.

Jim and Andy Lacis worked on solar radiation; a student named Wei-Chung Wang worked on the infrared, greenhouse component; and together they worked up a "simple," so-called one-dimensional, radiation/convection model for Earth's climate. Yung provided the chemist's perspective on the non-CO_2 greenhouse gases, and this group published a paper in *Science* in which they suggested that these gases should be monitored along with carbon dioxide, since they also stood a good chance of increasing with human activity and might turn out to be just as important. (Dave Keeling had been monitoring carbon dioxide on the summit of Mauna Loa for almost two decades by then.)

Thus Jim's very first publication on the greenhouse effect, in 1976, came with a policy recommendation.

He frequently refers to a sort of epiphany he had around that time. Almost twenty years later, he would write about it in an article in *Scientific American* that was fashioned from his Time Bomb talk.

> A paradox in the notion of human-made global warming became strikingly apparent to me one summer afternoon in 1976 on Jones Beach, Long Island. Arriving at midday, my wife, son and I found a spot near the water to avoid the scorching hot sand. As the sun sank in the late afternoon, a brisk wind from the ocean whipped up whitecaps. My son and I had goose bumps as we ran along the foamy shoreline and watched the churning waves.
>
> That same summer Andy Lacis and I, along with other colleagues . . . had estimated the effects of greenhouse gases on climate. . . .
>
> Our group had calculated that these human-made gases were heating the earth's surface at a rate of almost two watts per square meter. A miniature Christmas tree bulb dissipates about one watt, mostly in the form of heat. So it was as if humans had placed two of these tiny bulbs over every square meter of the earth's surface, burning night and day. The paradox that this result presented was the contrast between the awesome forces of nature and the tiny lightbulbs. Surely their feeble heating could not command the wind and waves or smooth our goose bumps. Even their imperceptible heating of the ocean surface must be quickly dissipated to great depths, so it must take many years, perhaps centuries, for the ultimate surface warming to be achieved. . . .

Jim was intrigued by this paradox. One might say that he has dedicated his life to the task of resolving it.

He had entered the field at an odd moment, because for a few years in the
early seventies, a small and somewhat confused group of scientists har-
bored the mistaken impression that we might be headed for an ice age.
Their confusion was based on a primitive understanding of the parasol
effect and what turned out to be a second mistaken impression that the
planet had been cooling ever since the 1930s, the scorching decade of the
Dust Bowl.

Ichtiaque Rasool and his student Stephen Schneider had helped initiate this craze in 1971 with a paper in *Science* in which they inferred from
a primitive computer model developed by Schneider that the increasing
dustiness of the atmosphere stood not only to offset greenhouse warming
but might even "be sufficient to trigger an ice age." The notion was that
the massive clouds of particulate matter we were spewing into the air—
directly from tailpipes and smokestacks, and indirectly through slash-
and-burn agriculture, overgrazing, the destruction of the planet's forest
cover, and so on, which were exposing vast tracts of dried-out and eroded
soil to the air—had produced a tremendous parasol effect. This had supposedly caused the alleged cooling and might soon trigger a more drastic
drop in temperature.

Far from a majority of informed scientists shared this view, but the
media found it stimulating, and this, along with terrible droughts in Africa and the Soviet Union, and a major El Niño in 1972, brought the dark
possibility of climate disruption to the evening news. This released a spate
of doomsday books and the first television special ever dedicated to climate change, which was produced by the respected science writer Nigel
Calder. Calder also issued a book, *The Weather Machine,* in which he suggested that a full-fledged ice age might "start next summer, or at any rate
during the next hundred years."

Thirty years later, George Will would refer to this momentary and
minor delusion, which had been shared even in the 1970s by a just small

fraction of the relevant science community, on George Stephanopoulos's talk show, one week after Jim Hansen and Rick Piltz would appear on *60 Minutes*.

It is not commonly known that shortly after his paper went to press, Stephen Schneider discovered a mathematical error in his computer program that had amplified the cooling power of the aerosols relative to the warming effect of the greenhouse. In 1975, he published a second paper in *Science*, predicting that the greenhouse effect would overtake the parasol effect "soon after 1980." This proved more or less true, and Schneider has since become one of the most visible and outspoken seers of the greenhouse danger.

He was not the only one to become anxious right around then. In 1977, a committee chosen by the National Academy of Sciences issued a report concluding that if greenhouse emissions continued to grow at their present rate, temperatures could rise by as many as eleven degrees Fahrenheit by the middle of the twenty-first century—more than the difference between now and the depths of the last ice age. These results were announced in the middle of the hottest July in the United States since the Dust Bowl, and the press charged off in a new direction with hardly a backward glance.

The new level of consternation prompted geophysicist Frank Press, science adviser to Jimmy Carter, to ask the Academy for an opinion on the credibility of the computer models. The Academy made a superb choice to lead this investigation in the person of Jule Charney, a meteorologist from MIT. Charney had been involved in the earliest attempts to simulate weather with John von Neumann in the 1950s, and that seminal project had given rise to NOAA's Geophysical Fluid Dynamics Laboratory, among other things. Thus, he had an insider's view of the world's first three-dimensional climate simulation, or global circulation model, which had been developed at GFDL by Syukuro "Suki" Manabe. To an outsider, Manabe's would have seemed the only game in town; however, Charney had also acted as a scientific consultant to GISS when GISS was developing its weather model. He was privy to the existence of the new kid on the block, Jim Hansen.

The basic idea behind a global circulation model, or GCM, is to divide the atmosphere up into small boxes and design rules based on as realistic a set of physical laws as possible to describe how the air in the boxes will behave. A parcel of air will generally rise as it warms, fall as it cools, and circulate horizontally owing to the spinning of the planet, the reflected heat or rising evaporation from land and ocean, and the influence of neighboring parcels. One can also start the system in a specific state and impose a progressive change—carbon dioxide rising at such and such a rate, for example, or stratospheric ozone falling—and watch the system evolve with time. The most important outputs are changes in temperature and precipitation.

Since the ocean is a crucial player, climatologists have now developed "coupled atmosphere-ocean models." The topology and reflectivity of the planetary surface also come into play. As temperature and rainfall patterns change, for instance, so does vegetation, which affects reflectivity. And as sea levels rise, reflective coastal lands are replaced by dark, sunlight-absorbing water. Then there are other changes to the biosphere, which add or subtract carbon dioxide or methane from the air. All of these details have been included in one or another of the latest GCMs; and, in fact, there is no limit to the level of detail one might dream up. What brings the dreamer back to earth is the fantastic amount of computing time involved. These things generally use the fastest and largest computers around.

In 1979, the latest results from Manabe and Ronald Stouffer (previously mentioned in connection with censorship at NOAA) put Arrhenius's central measure, climate sensitivity, at 2°C for a doubling of carbon dioxide. Jim's GISS model, as yet unpublished and untempered by peer review, came up with 4°C. Although these models weren't as sophisticated as those we have today, the Charney panel nevertheless concluded that their predictions—and those of the one-dimensional radiation/convection models of the time—were believable. The panel was probably correct. They estimated that climate sensitivity was most likely about 3°C, with a range of plus or minus 1.5°C. Amazingly, their estimate of the most likely value, 3°C, still holds almost thirty years later; only the range has changed, and it has gotten smaller. The estimate is now based on an astounding amount of climatic data from the real world in addition to computer models. Jim, Andy Lacis, and their colleagues at GISS presently put the uncertainty at about half a degree Celsius.

The Charney panel also took the liberty of reflecting upon the societal consequences of proceeding with what Jim might call business-as-usual. Even at the low end of climate sensitivity they foresaw serious consequences, and at the high end they saw a planet transformed. "A wait-and-see policy may mean waiting until it is too late," they wrote.

As Jim delved into the changing climate of his home planet, his fascination with Earth began to eclipse his fascination with Venus. In 1978, after the Pioneer satellite was launched but before it reached Venus, he relinquished his position as principal investigator on the polarimeter experiment in favor of Larry Travis, whom he had hired from James Van Allen's physics and astronomy department five years earlier. (Like Jim, Larry learned a quick lesson about his new cultural surroundings when we arrived in the city. He commuted to GISS at first and parked his leased car on the street. After a few days, the front hood was removed. "Welcome to New York," writes Jim. "In those days you didn't leave a new car parked on the street on the Upper West Side. He decided to get a nearby apartment, so he could walk to work.")

Jim was coming into his own. As he kept one eye partially on Venus, he dedicated most of his eighty-hour workweek to assembling and managing a team with the complementary expertise necessary to develop a global circulation model. He also turned his attention to the matter of keeping the model honest with data from the real world. "I've always liked to put about equal emphasis on observations and modeling . . . ," he says. "Even now I argue that the record of the history of the earth is much more useful in . . . giving us an understanding of what [the human] impact is going to be . . . than models per se." He hired meteorologist David Rind at this time, "the most effective person at GISS in spurring model development and applications, and . . . our most active researcher in the crucial area of evaluating model performance relative to observation," as he later wrote. (Rind would have his run-in with the censors at headquarters as he rehearsed for a press conference about retreating sea ice in 2003.)

In 1979, Jim's group began to assemble a global database of temperature readings from thousands of weather stations, ships, and satellites reaching back to the late 1800s. (The ships and satellites were actually added later, to cover the oceans.) As we know, this work would eventuate, among other much more important things, in a certain shit storm at NASA headquarters in December 2005.

The notion that Earth had been cooling for the past few decades had been introduced on a suitably cold day in 1961 by a meteorologist from the U.S. Weather Bureau named J. Murray Mitchell. It didn't attract much attention until the early seventies, when the global cooling craze took hold, but by that time it had very much taken on the weight of received wisdom.

When Jim and his colleagues looked closely at Mitchell's data, however, they realized that it had come entirely from the northern hemisphere—in fact, only part of the northern hemisphere: from twenty degrees latitude northward, where the overwhelming majority of weather stations are located. Employing sound statistical methods and sensible physics to bring the southern hemisphere into the picture, they discovered that Mitchell's cooling trend was basically imaginary. Temperatures had indeed dropped in his particular northern latitudes from 1940 until sometime in the mid-sixties; but since 1880, the start of the instrumental era, they had steadily risen both at low northern latitudes and in the southern hemisphere. Furthermore, the north was now warming as well. The average temperature of the entire planet had dropped slightly as the northern latitudes had cooled, but it had begun to rise again in the mid-1960s.

* * *

All the pieces were now in place. In 1981, Jim, Andy Lacis, David Rind, and four others published the first example of the sort of comprehensive analysis that has now become their trademark. This epochal paper, in *Science,* is reminiscent of an early work by a young artist. The brushstrokes are finer and less detailed than they would later become in more fully realized work, but everything is there. The science is somewhat simplistic by today's standards, but the numbers are mostly accurate; and the uncertainties—all of which are less uncertain now—are clearly elucidated. This paper also marks the beginning of a string of accurate predictions by Jim and his colleagues that remains essentially unbroken to this day. It is surprising and sobering to read it a quarter of a century after it was written, not only for its prescience, but also because it raises the same difficult issues we face today, which now loom twenty-five years larger because we have done nothing to address them but talk.

The very first GISS analysis of temperature was just one component. It was noteworthy enough that they dispelled the myth of the cooling spell, but they also accounted for most of the details in the jagged curve depicting the inexorable rise of global temperature over the previous century, using their simple, one-dimensional computer model. They checked this model against their global circulation model, but the latter would not be revealed in the peer-reviewed literature until 1983, after eight years of gestation. That they didn't really need the GCM shows just how straightforward the greenhouse problem really is. They also demonstrated their mastery of the subject by tossing out accurate calculations of the cold temperature of Mars, which has an almost nonexistent greenhouse effect, and the blazing temperature of Venus, where the effect has run away.

On Earth, they looked only at the greenhouse effect of carbon dioxide, though they did point out that the abundances of the "trace" non-CO_2 gases that Yuk Yung had brought to their attention had now been measured and were also increasing. (In another paper released during this productive year, Jim, Andy, and a different complement of authors would demonstrate that the total greenhouse effect of the trace gases was then more than half the strength of carbon dioxide's.)

By now, Jim and Andy had also completed their study of the parasol cooling effect of the Mount Agung eruption, which they had first investigated as grad students. As it turned out, the huge drop in temperature caused by this single eruption went a long way toward explaining the misconceived cooling trend. They could track the ups and downs (mostly ups) of Earth's temperature very well over the course of the twentieth century simply by feeding measured levels of volcanic aerosols and carbon dioxide into their computer model along with hypothetical variations in solar output. (They guessed, more or less accurately in retrospect, that the greenhouse effect of the non-CO_2 gases and the parasol effect of manmade aerosols were partially canceling each other out.)

They also looked at the future. In a "slow growth" scenario that was essentially business-as-usual, they predicted "a high probability of warming in the 1980s," and that "warming should emerge from the noise level of natural variability by the end of the century"—both of which later proved true.

Venturing into the policy arena, they noted that the burning of all available oil and natural gas would probably "increase CO_2 abundance by [less than] 50 percent of the preindustrial amount," while there was virtually no limit to the damage that could be done by coal. They therefore suggested that the "key fuel choice is between coal and alternatives that do not increase atmospheric CO_2."

Today, a chorus has joined Jim in pointing out the danger of continuing to indulge our insatiable energy hunger with the first and dirtiest of the industrial fossil fuels.

This was a long paper for *Science*—ten pages, and Jim took two years to write it—but he actually had a lot more to say. He submitted four drafts before it was accepted, because the editors kept asking him to trim it back. He tells me that he had to remove one figure that he has only started to use again regularly as of 2006. It's a bar graph that parses out the amount of carbon dioxide that would be released if we were to burn every last bit of each of the different fossil fuels, and it shows that we can't afford to burn much at all besides the oil and gas. This graph has become relevant again because the price of oil is peaking, as it was in the late seventies, and so-called synfuels, synthetic oil and gas derived from coal, shale oil, and tar sands, may soon seem economical. (The buzzword today is *coal gasification*.) These synthetic sources take a double whack at the greenhouse, for carbon dioxide is emitted both as they are made and as they are burned as fuel. Unfortunately, Congress is considering this bad idea again after twenty-five years.

The GISS team even looked at sea level (although one of the few assertions Jim might now retract from this paper is that "continental ice sheets require thousands of years to respond"). "Potential effects on climate in the twenty-first century include the creation of drought-prone regions in North America and central Asia as part of a shifting of climatic zones, erosion of the West Antarctic Ice Sheet with a consequent worldwide rise in sea level, and opening of the fabled Northwest Passage." (This last seems to have been accomplished, incidentally.)

"The global warming projected for the next century is of almost unprecedented magnitude. . . . [W]e estimate it to be [about] 2.5°C for a scenario with slow energy growth and a mixture of non-fossil and fossil fuels." Jim and his colleagues predicted that this change would send temperatures above not only the highest levels of the past 10,000 years, since the dawn of civilization, but also above those of the Eemian interglacial, 130,000 years ago, so that Earth "would approach the warmth of the Mesozoic, the age of the dinosaurs."

Amazingly, Jim's projections for global warming according to business-as-usual in the twenty-first century are little different today than they were almost thirty years ago.

Bob Jastrow wasn't particularly aware of this work. He was more interested in the results that were beginning to stream in from Pioneer Venus. Shortly before Jim submitted the paper, Jastrow asked him to join him for lunch at the Moon Palace with Walter Sullivan, the science reporter for *The New York Times*. The idea was to talk about Venus, and they did; but the lunch also served to introduce Sullivan and Jim. Not long afterward, Jim shared the *Science* paper with Sullivan, one week before it would be published. (Jim has called this his "original sin.") The reporter and his editors immediately recognized the importance of the paper, and Sullivan's story, "Study Finds Warming Trend That Could Raise Sea Levels," brought the greenhouse effect to the front page of *The New York Times* for the very first time. A week later, an editorial concluded, "The greenhouse effect is still too uncertain to warrant total alteration of energy policy. But this latest study offers fair warning; that such a change may yet be required is no longer unimaginable." A similar editorial appeared in *The Washington Post.*

During the Carter administration, the science pundits had begun to shift carbon dioxide studies from NASA to the Department of Energy. Thus, as Carter's presidency came to an end, Jim found himself in a vulnerable position. He was reaching the end of a three-year grant from NASA to pursue his climate work, and the understanding was that the grant would be renewed by DOE. He received oral and written assurances to this effect.

Ronald Reagan took office in January 1981, and Jim's paper made headlines in August. The response was swift.

Reagan's new program manager for the carbon dioxide program, a certain Fred Koomanoff, reneged on his predecessor's written assurance to fund Jim's research. His budget was cut by $230,000, and he was forced to lay off five people. (Anniek was not entirely displeased, as he cut back to a forty-hour workweek for a while and took up coaching their kids' basketball and Little League baseball teams.) Koomanoff did let Jim go through the formality of making a presentation in Washington before cutting him off, but Jim believes he had already made up his mind. And to reiterate his dim view of Jim's work, Koomanoff also warned a group at Penn State, as Jim recalls, that they would lose funding if they based any of their work on GISS's global circulation model. Koomanoff preferred Manabe's model at GFDL, owing to its lower sensitivity.

This was an eventful year. It is worth noting that it set a global temperature record, as had the previous year. In fact, twenty years later, the IPCC's third assessment report would note that the human signature on climate change first became discernible sometime between 1975 and 1980. Mountain glaciers, which are among the most sensitive indicators, began a drastic worldwide retreat just then.

And, near the end of the year, Bob Jastrow retired from NASA, somewhat early, in order to focus on teaching. He'd been drawing salaries from both Columbia and Dartmouth for a minor amount of teaching while he was a full-time NASA employee. This wasn't quite kosher, and after an investigation by the NASA inspector general, it seems that he was asked to make a choice. He taught at Dartmouth for about a decade, then became manager of the Mount Wilson Observatory in California.

Jastrow is known as a mesmerizing speaker. He has often expounded upon space science and astronomy on television, and he has published a number of bestselling books about the universe. (Jim recalls that he was "terribly jealous of Carl Sagan's success.") Some of the statements in Jastrow's books seem to promote the present-day version of creationism known as intelligent design. Although he refers to himself as an agnostic on the issue, he gives coy interviews on the subject and his statements *are* bandied about by intelligent design advocates.

In 1984, Jastrow would help found the George C. Marshall Institute, a right-wing think tank whose first raison d'être was to promote Ronald Reagan's Strategic Defense, or "Star Wars," Initiative. As we shall see, Marshall's second crusade would involve global warming.

His departure provided a new opportunity to explore the recurring question as to whether or not GISS ought to be absorbed into Goddard Space Flight Center. But when Jim and Patrick Thaddeus were called down to Greenbelt, they made it clear that they, personally, would not move; if it came to that, they would seek academic appointments elsewhere. "Anyway," says Jim, "we argued that this was a very cost-effective organization here, and we said that either one of us would be willing to lead it. We left it up to them to decide; and why they picked me I don't know, maybe because Earth science was coming into prominence as opposed to astrophysics—I don't know." In any event, when Jim took the reins, he focused GISS's research on climate science. Thaddeus remained at the institute until 1986, then moved to Harvard University.

Jim eventually picked up some funding from the Environmental Protection Agency (not one of Mr. Reagan's favorites) and returned to an eighty-hour week. Through the eighties, his group deepened and expanded upon the questions they had raised in their landmark study at the beginning of the decade, revisiting old and examining new aspects of the problem with an increasingly powerful magnifying glass. Even the working scientists in the field today—many of whom were around back then—seem mostly unaware (or perhaps unwilling to admit) how many crucial insights and discoveries have originated at GISS.

In March 1982, for example, Jim and two colleagues published a study of sea level trends. This study, like their temperature analyses, was grounded in observation: tide gauge measurements from more than seven hundred stations around the world. Sea level is harder to measure than one might imagine. Shifts in ocean currents and winds sometimes change local levels; in some places, such as the Mississippi River Delta, the land itself is subsiding into the sea; and in others it is rising or falling owing to tectonic activity or the deposition of river silt. Jim and his colleagues estimated—accurately according to today's thinking—that the mean global level had risen about twelve centimeters (five inches) in the previous century. This was not exactly a new discovery, although their analysis was the most comprehensive and precise at that stage in the game. What *was* new was the revelation that the trend in sea level had "a high correlation with the trend of global surface temperature," and that, therefore, "a large part of [it could] be accounted for in terms of the thermal expansion of the upper layers of the ocean." Mainstream science now agrees that thermal expansion, caused by human-induced global warming, accounts for most of the rise in sea level that took place in the twentieth century.

Since at least the time of his epiphany at Jones Beach, Jim had been aware of the role that the oceans must play in delaying the planet's response to a change in greenhouse forcing. The thermal expansion he had now measured was an obvious sign that most of the energy streaming in with the industrial greenhouse buildup was being stored in the oceans, which change temperature slowly, owing to their enormous capacity to store heat. A large section of the seminal 1981 paper had been directed at this question, and one of the shortcomings mentioned in the paper itself had been the need to "tune" the response time of the oceans in order to match the theoretical curve from GISS's simple computer model to the rising curve of temperature.

Part of Jim's motivation to look more closely at this question arose from a series of attacks, led mainly by the Department of Energy, on the 1981 study, on the Charney Report, and on a second report that came to roughly the same conclusions, produced under the leadership of Joseph Smagorinsky, whose pedigree was as fine as Charney's. In the 1950s, Smagorinsky had led the team, of which Charney was a member, that had developed the worlds' first global circulation model under the guidance of John von Neumann—the model that had evolved into Manabe's at the Geophysical Fluid Dynamics Laboratory. It is a sign of the impact of Jim's study that it ranked as high in the minds of the skeptics as two studies by the National Academy.

There were many legitimate skeptics back then, and it is important to distinguish skepticism from contrarianism and bullheaded denial. As Jim has recently written:

> Skepticism, an inherent aspect of scientific inquiry, should be carefully distinguished from contrarianism. Skepticism, and the objective weighing of evidence, are essential for scientific success. Skepticism about the existence of global warming and the principal role of human-made greenhouse gases has diminished as empirical evidence and our understanding have advanced. However, many aspects of global warming need to be understood better, including the best ways to minimize climate change and its consequences. Legitimate skepticism will always have an important role to play.
>
> However, hard-core global warming contrarians have an agenda other than scientific truth. Their target is the public.

Their goal is to create an impression that global warming or its causes are uncertain. Debating a contrarian leaves an impression with today's public of an argument among theorists. Sophistical contrarians do not need to win the scientific debate to advance their cause.

The lead skeptic in the early days of the Reagan administration seems to have been Michael MacCracken at DOE's Lawrence Livermore National Laboratory. At a DOE-sponsored meeting that took place at a resort in West Virginia in 1982 or '83, MacCracken spent about an hour criticizing the 1981 GISS paper. (Koomanoff cited this talk specifically when he cut Jim's funding.) MacCracken followed his speech with a letter to *Science.* Then, Jim's mentor, Ichtiaque Rasool, got into the act with a letter to *Climatic Change* that went a little overboard, questioning Jim's integrity by suggesting that he "emphasized the worst case to get the attention of decision makers who control funding." Jim had indeed received attention from the people who controlled the purse strings, but it hadn't gone quite the way Rasool had imagined. Then, in 1983, MacCracken took the lead in yet another National Academy study (requested by the familiar White House Office of Science and Technology Policy), which placed climate sensitivity at the low end of the Charney range. "Overall, we find in the CO_2 issue reason for concern, but not panic," MacCracken's panel reassuringly concluded.

The very fact that Jim got funding from EPA indicates that President Reagan had nowhere near the unitary control—nor, most likely, desire for that control—that was exercised later by George W. Bush. Indeed, Jim helped EPA completely upstage MacCracken with a report of its own, released just three days later, suggesting not only that "substantial increases in global warming may occur sooner than most of us would like to believe," but that these increases might change "habitability in many geographic regions" and lead to potentially "catastrophic" results within decades.

Jim remembers that when he read what he calls the "Academy/DOE" report, he "realized that MacCracken had made a terrible approximation/fundamental mistake.

"In trying to improve upon the Charney estimate of climate sensitivity, he assumed that the response time of the ocean was fifteen years. That might seem like a reasonable number if you are picking a number; . . . however, he was at least implicitly assuming that the response time does not depend on climate sensitivity. That is a bad assumption and led him to the erroneous conclusion that climate sensitivity was probably less than Charney estimated, thus the climate change problem was less serious."

Basically, whether he was aware of it or not, MacCracken was assuming that the atmosphere had responded more or less instantaneously to the greenhouse changes of the twentieth century, so that the rise in temperature of less than one degree centigrade that had so far occurred gave a good measure of sensitivity. If the response took longer than MacCracken's guess of fifteen years, however, there was a substantial amount of what Jim calls "unrealized warming," or warming that was still "in the pipeline"—we hadn't felt it yet—and climate sensitivity was therefore higher.

MacCracken's confusion arose from what is admittedly the most confusing aspect of climate science: so-called feedback. If the lapse rate of the atmosphere is held fixed, along with the many other features that gradually come into play, from the biosphere, the planetary surface, and so forth, the simple change in temperature that would restore radiation balance after a doubling of carbon dioxide would lie somewhere between 1.2 and 1.3°C (about 2°F). This calculation can be done on the back of an envelope. One way to think about it is to realize that the added carbon dioxide makes the atmosphere more opaque to infrared light, so the mean level from which the infrared can now escape to space rises by almost 700 feet. That altitude now adjusts to the radiation-balancing temperature of 0°F, and with no change in the lapse rate, the planetary surface, which is now farther below, must rise in temperature.

But the actual sensitivity is about 3°C, more than twice the static value. That factor—about 2.4, actually—arises from feedbacks. And feedbacks are inherently slow to unfold, because they are a secondary effect of the change in temperature that is initially caused by a change in greenhouse forcing; they are not a direct effect of the forcing itself. The melting of highly reflective arctic sea ice would be an example of a feedback, as would changes in forest cover. One of the more important feedbacks discovered in recent years involves the melting of permafrost in Alaska, northern Canada, and Siberia. Plants that have been frozen for hundreds of thousands of years are now supplementing the manmade greenhouse effect as they decompose and send prodigious quantities of carbon dioxide and methane into the air. This is a sobering prospect, for arctic tundra harbors more than 500 billion tons of carbon, about twenty times the amount that fossil fuel burning emits in a year and more than twice the amount in all the rainforests on the planet.

Perhaps the most important feedback, which Svante Arrhenius recognized more than a hundred years ago, involves water vapor. As the atmosphere warms, it takes on more vapor, for the same reason that the air is more humid in summer than in winter. And since water vapor is an even stronger greenhouse gas than carbon dioxide, this supplements the original warming, which adds more water vapor to the air, and the feedback loop continues.

What Jim realized that MacCracken did not was that response time depends upon the feedback factor, 2.4. He points out that even if the oceans were to distribute the sun's heat instantly, that is, if the temperature of the abyss kept pace with the temperature at the surface, the response time would increase linearly with the feedback factor, owing to the secondary dependence of feedback upon temperature. "Whether climate sensitivity is 1.5°C for doubled CO_2 or 3°C for doubled CO_2, the flux of heat into the ocean starts out the same in both cases, so it takes twice as long in the latter case for the ocean to reach equilibrium."

Global circulation models are a help here, for they explicitly model the spreading of ocean heat as well as the most important feedbacks, such as sea ice; whereas in one-dimensional radiation models these processes are specified; they are not allowed to run their individual courses as temperatures rise.

At a symposium in 1984, Jim used a more realistic, slower model of oceanic heat flow to demonstrate numerically with the GISS GCM that the response time is actually longer than in the simple linear case: it goes as the square of the feedback factor. "This makes a huge difference, entirely vitiating MacCracken's conclusion," he says. Since this new result was based on a computer model, however, it remained open to question; so in 1985, he and the core members of his GISS group came out with an elegant paper in *Science,* slightly more than two pages in length, in which they confirmed this result analytically using a simple physics-based argument. With Charney's climate sensitivity of 3°C, they got a response time of between fifty and one hundred years. Thus, they suggested, "most of the expected warming attributable to trace gases added to the atmosphere by man probably has not yet occurred. This yet to be realized warming calls into question a policy of 'wait and see' regarding the issue of how to deal with increasing carbon dioxide and other trace gases." Jim considers the paper from the 1984 symposium, along with the clarification in *Science* a year later, to be among his most important papers. He believes they may be the ones that are cited most frequently in other scientists' work.

Incidentally, as Michael MacCracken's insight gradually deepened, he demonstrated that he was motivated by authentic skepticism rather than denial by recognizing the danger of global warming and joining the battle to do something about it.

Jim laconically observes that the discovery spurred by MacCracken's interest "was pretty important, because this lag effect obviously complicates the task of decision-makers." Indeed, a group from Yale has recently cited the "substantial (and uncertain) time lag between cause and effect" as a main reason why global warming may represent the "perfect problem"—in the same sense as the "perfect storm."

The frequency with which the White House and Congress were making requests of the National Academy is one indication of the level of interest in the early eighties, and Jim had become identified with the issue through his 1981 paper. His dawning realization that we were getting ahead of ourselves—and maybe even our children and grandchildren—in our heating of the planet increased his motivation to speak to the decision-makers himself.

He credits Rafe Pomerance, who was with the World Resources Institute at the time, for his effective behind-the-scenes work in taking the issue public. Al Gore also walked onto the scene around then and held hearings all through the decade, first as a U.S. congressman and then as a senator. Gore had received a superb education in greenhouse science as a student at Harvard in the 1960s from Roger Revelle, a giant in the field and a mentor to Charles David Keeling among other things. But these hearings did not gain much notice; and with Reagan in the Oval Office, there was no progress on policy.

Jim testified at several of the hearings, and as he became more comfortable speaking in public, his confidence in the science was building as well. As the decade wore on, for example, a prediction from his 1981 paper seemed to be coming true. Remember the one about "a high probability of warming in the 1980s"? That basically meant that the end of the decade should prove warmer than the beginning. Well, after the record-setting years of 1980 and '81—and even with the 1982 eruption of Mexico's El Chichón, which put the brakes on for a couple of years — temperatures continued to climb. Nineteen eighty-three surpassed 1980 as the second-warmest year on record; then '87 beat out '83, although it was assisted by an El Niño. The trend was pointing upward.

After yet another ineffectual hearing in November 1987, Jim suggested to Pomerance and the staffer who had arranged the hearing that future such events really ought to take place in summer, when it was hot. Senator Tim Wirth of Colorado, chairman of the Committee on Energy and Natural Resources, agreed; and as Jim later remarked, "Apparently he is a brilliant weather forecaster, because he scheduled a hearing for June twenty-third, 1988, which turned out to be one of the hottest days of the decade in the U.S., with a drought across much of the country."

Chapter 9

"A Logical, Well-Reasoned Conclusion"

THE SUMMER OF 1988 was another one of those moments when the planet seemed to be speaking up. Memorable waves of heat and drought settled on the continents of Eurasia and North America; farmers in the American Midwest experienced their worst growing season since the Dust Bowl; Southern cotton shriveled on the vine; barges by the thousands were stranded in the Mississippi River; Civil War vessels last seen as Confederate troops scuttled them on their retreat from Vicksburg rose above the surface of a Mississippi tributary named the Big Muddy; and the West experienced the worst forest fires in its recorded history—more than six million acres burned. Almost half the forests in Yellowstone National Park turned from deep, fulsome green to smoky and skeletal black. President Reagan found it necessary to sign a $4 billion farm relief bill.

In the days before Tim Wirth's June hearing, Jim realized that he had some strong medicine to deliver to the Senate, mainly as a result of a new study employing the GISS global circulation model that had just been accepted by the *Journal of Geophysical Research*.

What made the GISS model unique was its use of some fine mathematical physics to reduce the amount of computation involved, so that it worked about ten times faster than the other GCMs. This mathematics, developed in the 1950s by Akio Arakawa at UCLA, permitted the use of a coarser grid: the boxes of air could be larger than those in Manabe's model, for example. Arakawa had consulted on the early GISS weather model, from which Jim and his group had derived their GCM, and he had also consulted on the GCM itself sometime later. This elegant work played a role, by the way, in delaying the model's acceptance by the scientific community, as it took some time for the peer reviewers of the first, 1983 paper on the GISS model to be convinced that a coarse grid would be adequate. Jim took potshots about this for many years.

But the increased speed paid off in two ways. For one, it allowed the GISS group to make do with the minimal funding they'd been receiving since the advent of Fred Koomanoff in 1981: their model ran perfectly well on their mid-seventies-vintage Amdahl computer. More important, even with their old computer, they could watch global warming evolve with time. Even so, it took more than a year to run the simulations for this study.

Up to this point, global circulation models had been used only to model equilibrium: double carbon dioxide or some other factor, and see what you get. But Jim's new study in the *Journal of Geophysical Research* used real-world measurements of the changing atmosphere since 1958—when Dave Keeling had begun measuring carbon dioxide on top of Mauna Loa—to make retroactive predictions of changes in temperature. Volcanic eruptions and the other trace gases were included as well. The GISS model tracked the rising course of measured temperature rather well, along with the occasional dip owing to a volcano, and this served as validation.

Then, as Pat Michaels and Michael Crichton know (or should know) perfectly well, Jim considered three future scenarios: the one on the "high side of reality," the one on the low side, and the one he considered "most plausible," which has since proven quite accurate.

He would attach this detailed, twenty-four-page study to his written Senate testimony. There was more, such as the observation that global warming should first appear in central Asia, which was experiencing a severe drought that very summer, and in "ocean areas near Antarctica and the north pole, where sea ice provides a positive feedback." Consider the 2002 collapse of the Larsen B ice shelf and the 2005 press release about arctic sea ice that would occasion some frustration for

Waleed Abdalati. The paper also predicted continued warming in the 1990s and that the man on the street would probably start noticing something unusual about the weather by the turn of the millennium. The former prediction certainly came true. And residents of Europe who endured the summer of 2003, when 15,000 people died in Paris as a result of an unprecedented August heat spell, most likely confirm the second.

The day before the hearing, Jim called Rafe Pomerance to let him know that he was planning "to make a pretty strong statement." Pomerance and Senator Wirth notified the news media, and Wirth and his staff also set the stage by leaving the windows of the hearing room open all that sweltering night to ensure that the air conditioners would be working extra hard during the hearing the next day.

As is his wont, Jim began working on his written testimony that same evening, "trying to listen to the Yankee game at the same time"; and he was still writing away the next morning during a meeting at NASA headquarters run by Ichtiaque Rasool, who was trying to set up an agency-wide research program on climate. At one point during the meeting, Rasool remarked that no respectable scientist would make the statement that the present warming could be identified with the greenhouse effect. Jim looked up from his writing and said, "I don't know if he's respectable or not, but I know someone who is just about to make that statement."

He left the meeting at lunchtime and took a cab—in 101-degree heat—to Capitol Hill. When he stepped into the hearing room, a staffer intercepted him and directed him to Senator Wirth, who asked if it would be all right to rearrange the order of the hearing so Jim would speak first. Wirth knew he was going to make a strong statement, Jim recalls, "and he wanted the media to be sure to get it." Jim agreed.

He says that he spoke for only five minutes, and he vividly recalls his testimony, for he has repeated it hundreds of times. He made three main points: first, that he was "99 percent confident" that Earth was getting warmer and it was not a chance fluctuation; second, that the warming was sufficiently large to "ascribe with a high degree of confidence to the greenhouse effect"; and third, that his group's "computer climate simulations" showed that the manmade greenhouse effect was already strong enough to increase the frequency of extreme events such as summer heat waves and droughts in the United States, especially in the Southeast and Midwest. He pointed out that the 1980s had already seen the four warmest years of the century and that the first five months of 1988 had been warmer than any comparable period since 1880. He also racked up another accurate prediction: that the present year would set a new global temperature record.

In the questioning that followed, one senator, hoping to evoke a juicy quote for the headlines, asked if the greenhouse effect had caused the present drought. Jim replied that the greenhouse only alters probabilities; no specific drought could be linked to it directly. This led to endless confusion. The senators kept trying to lure the experts—Manabe was one—into linking that specific drought to the greenhouse effect, but none would bite. Nevertheless, sometime later, a question on the game show *Jeopardy!* indicated that Jim had made a direct connection; and a number of scientists would promulgate this misunderstanding as well—mostly in the context of criticizing Jim.

Surrounded by reporters after the hearing, Jim made his now legendary remark that it was time to stop waffling and admit that the greenhouse effect was here and affecting our climate now. This sound bite was not spontaneous, by the way; he'd formulated it at some point during the ball game the previous evening or the meeting at headquarters that morning. *The New York Times* singled it out as its "Quotation of the Day" the next morning.

In any event, this and Jim's terse testimony, delivered in his balanced Midwestern monotone to a group of sweating senators as the entire nation swooned from the heat, flashed across television screens and made newspaper headlines around the world. And to prefigure the shit storm that would unfold after his simple release of some temperature data about seventeen years later, the Reagan White House quickly placed calls to NASA headquarters to express their great displeasure. Jim heard rumors that he might lose his job and that GISS itself might be threatened.

He was asked to testify to the House of Representatives two weeks later.

"I just Xeroxed the testimony I presented to the Senate," he recalls. "I decided"—he laughs and stops. "I had a lot of phone calls and pressures, including political pressures, you know. 'Do you really mean this or that?' . . . So if I changed anything"—he laughs again. "So I decided to use exactly the same words for the second testimony."

The quake that Jim set off in the space of about five minutes before the Senate wasn't the only factor in the flood of ultimately doomed legislation that inundated Congress that fall (pressure from Europe had forced Reagan to join in the formation of the IPCC the previous spring), but many saw it as the most important factor. As well, this was an election year, and George Bush Sr.'s reluctant decision to travel to Rio de Janeiro in 1992 to participate in the Framework Convention on Climate Change is often traced to this moment. In Rio, Bush the father would sign the treaty that led to the Kyoto Protocol, which Bush the son would subsequently dismiss.

But while Congress and the public were electrified, the scientific community went ballistic, mainly at the bold confidence of Jim's assertions. When he showed the nerve to attend a climate workshop that fall, it devolved into what one observer called a "get-Jim-Hansen session."

This was a difficult time in his life. Anniek had been diagnosed with breast cancer, and that summer Jim's father died. Awakening frequently in the middle of the night, he began to read literature for the first time. ("I didn't come from an intellectual background. My father was basically a sharecropper.") He gravitated to stories of heroes who flouted convention or were persecuted for standing up for their beliefs. Two favorites were *Pride and Prejudice* and *The Grapes of Wrath*. He particularly identified with the politicized Okie Tom Joad. He says, however, that perhaps his favorite of all was George Eliot's *Middlemarch,* "mainly for her incredible mastery of English." But there was a topical interest as well. He describes the book as "a story, among other things, of great expectations going sour, because of compromised principles."

*   *   *

He carried on. In May of the following year, Bush the elder's first in office, he agreed to testify to Al Gore's Senate Subcommittee on Science, Technology and Space.

"I really didn't want to continue this," he says, "but I decided it was good to do it once more because of the misinterpretations of the 1988 testimony. I wanted to clarify something. I had focused on droughts because there was a heat wave and drought that summer, but I now realized that I should have emphasized more generally the effects of global warming on the hydrologic cycle: the fact that you could also expect more frequent heavy rainfall and floods—hundred-year floods might occur three times a century instead of once a century." This was the flip side of the expected increase in droughts and heat waves. Both the GCMs and some new physics-based theoretical work (courtesy of Kerry Emanuel) predicted more intense storms and hurricanes on the one hand and droughts on the other, as the oceans and atmosphere gained energy and the latter took on water vapor, too.

Jim was also dismayed at the evident inability of nearly all reporters, some lawmakers, and a wide swath of the public to grasp the notion of randomness. The media had so garbled the message he had tried to deliver the previous year—juxtaposing his waffling quote with images of the drought, for example—that he realized "that many people would misunderstand it the next time the temperature in a given season was colder than normal, in which case the attention drawn to the greenhouse effect may have done more harm than good.

"So I made up a set of large colored dice. The dice for the 1951 to 1980 period, which I used to define 'normal' climate, had two red, two white, and two blue sides, representing unusually warm, average, and unusually cool seasons, respectively. The second dice represented our model calculations of how greenhouse warming should alter these probabilities in the 1990s. It had four red sides, one white, and one blue. The point I wanted to make was that even though climate fluctuates chaotically, greenhouse warming should load the climate dice enough for the informed layman to notice an increase in the frequency of warmer than normal seasons." He used these dice in television appearances for about a year.

In the weeks leading up to Gore's hearing, NASA's office of legislative affairs passed Jim's written testimony up to the White House Office of Management and Budget for review. OMB proceeded to change the text, and the main point in particular, that the greenhouse effect was changing climate. The approved version stated that the cause was unknown.

Jim had been enduring this sort of censorship for several years, actually. In 1986, under Reagan, OMB had deleted a few recommendations from a piece of his Senate testimony; and before another hearing in 1987 they had edited every section, making it seem that no one knew anything about greenhouse science. In the second instance, Jim had asked and been allowed to testify as a private citizen, using his unaltered testimony.

Now he felt that he'd had enough.

"After a couple of iterations, I decided, 'Shoot, I'll just let them leave it the way they want it, but I'm going to tell Al Gore.'"

He sent Gore a fax, prompting him to ask specific questions during the hearing, so that he could clarify the differences between his actual opinions and the text he had been forced to submit.

"Senator Gore was very interested in that," he remembers, "and called me at home that evening and asked if it was all right if he reported this to *The New York Times,* realizing that it would probably get me in some trouble." When Jim assented, Gore quickly notified the *Times* and other news outlets. "In fact," Jim says, "the article in the *Times* came out the day of the testimony. I was still preparing my testimony on the airplane, so I didn't notice that it was a front-page article."

In disavowing his own written testimony in person before the committee, he produced what have probably been the most spectacular headlines of his career. It was the lead story on all the major television networks that night.

Like father, like son. The parallels are remarkable.

George Bush Sr. had also pledged to do something about global warming when he was running for office. In fact, that particular false promise marked one of the rhetorical crescendos of his campaign. "Those who think we are powerless to do anything about the greenhouse effect forget about the 'White House effect.' As president, I intend to do something about it," he had declared in August 1988, about two months after Jim's momentum-shifting testimony. At the same time, the candidate promised to convene an international conference on the environment, which ultimately led to Rio.

Only months into his first year in office, the father was pressured by Europe to lead on the issue—as the son would be on his first trip to the Continent in the wake of his recalcitrant Rose Garden speech. Even Margaret Thatcher was calling for action.

The battle lines in the two Bush cabinets were also nearly identical. The first time around, Secretary of State James Baker and EPA Administrator William Reilly favored action; whereas OMB and the Department of Energy opposed—not to mention the pugnacious White House chief of staff, John Sununu.

The one difference seems to be that the father at least admitted to censorship, although he, too, resorted to scapegoating. His spokesman, Marlin Fitzwater, blamed the episode on a nameless OMB bureaucrat "five levels down from the top." But the administration had been set back on its heels: the first international meeting on the greenhouse issue that was ever held in Washington took place about a year later, and it was widely seen as an attempt to blunt the criticism from this first Bush muzzling attempt.

The day of Jim's testimony was a long one. After working single-mindedly enough on the morning flight to Washington to miss his own name on the front page of the *Times,* he quickly delivered his message and tried to escape, but Gore had set up a press conference outside the hearing room. Jim declined to participate, "but when I walked out the door, there was no way to escape," he remembers. "There were reporters there, and the cameras were there, and Al Gore, of course, wanted the opportunity. So there we were, whether I liked it or not; and it was on the evening news, of course. But I got on the plane and came back. My girls softball team had a game that evening."

He arrived home in time to catch his son, Erik, pitching for his high school freshman baseball team, then went and coached a game for his daughter Kiki's softball team. (Anniek says, "Sports was a very big thing in our kids' lives when they were growing up. Actually, I think it was appreciated more to be good in sports than in academics.") Jim must have missed his many appearances on the news that evening, because during Erik's game he changed the oil in his car as it sat in the parking lot by the ball field; and when Kiki's game was over, he drove into the night to face his detractors at a Workshop on Greenhouse-Gas-Induced Climatic Change that was already under way in Amherst, Massachusetts.

In the eleven months since his first earthshaking testimony, the minds of the scientists had begun to change. Although Richard Kerr, a news reporter for *Science,* summarized the workshop in an article entitled "Hansen vs. the World on the Greenhouse Threat," the text demonstrates that "the World" did not actually disagree all that much with Jim's science. In fact, they probably hadn't disagreed all that much the previous year. His critics objected mostly to the nonscientific way he was telling his story. Some quibbled with his precise wording; others disagreed on sophisticated technical points—small matters that took nothing from his main argument. A journalist observed later in *The New York Times Magazine,* "It's not his science that gets Jim Hansen in trouble—it's his style. Hansen has all the moves of a hustler but none of the guile. Backed by a body of exhaustive and universally respected research, he routinely flouts his profession's tacit restrictions on categorical and unauthorized statements while maintaining the pacific innocence of a curious child."

Radical innocence again?

Atmospheric scientist Michael Oppenheimer of the Environmental Defense Fund had something of an outside perspective on the scientific infighting. "Other scientists had been saying stuff like this in the bathroom at seminars, but he had the guts to say it in public," he observed. (This was the man who had said shortly after Jim's 1988 testimony that he had "never seen an environmental issue mature so quickly, shifting from science to the policy realm almost overnight.")

At the workshop in Amherst, one statistician told Kerr, "This kind of giving the result and not telling the whole story, that's what I'm criticizing"; while a GCM expert confided, "If there were a secret ballot at this meeting . . . most people would say the greenhouse warming is probably there."

Through it all, Jim did not once accuse his colleagues of pettiness. In the more than thirty years that he has been working on the greenhouse issue, he has been the object of endless scorn and personal attack, yet he has never responded in kind. He has stuck to the Feynman admonition, focusing resolutely on observable facts and science and going out of his way to point out the shortcomings and uncertainties in his own arguments. When I first met him in 2000, twelve years after this most difficult passage in his life, he honestly seemed to bear no grudge. "Mostly it was legitimate disagreement or concern that the statements were stronger than they should have been," he said evenly. "The scientific method does require that you continually question the conclusions that you draw and put caveats on the conclusions—but that can be misleading to the public. It seems to me that when we talk to the public we have to try to give such a summary. And it's not easy for most scientists to do—and not easy for me."

In the main, Jim's critics were honest scientists being legitimately skeptical. The potshots they aimed (and Kerr heard many at this meeting) simply demonstrate that scientists are as human as anyone else. "When we're at this level of signal-to-noise, anyone can disagree with me. I don't argue with that," Jim told Kerr. However, nearly all the folks at that conference will now accept the statements Jim was making at that time. Indeed, as I have already pointed out, the IPCC would note in 2001 that the human signature of climate change rose out of the noise sometime in the late 1970s.

If one looks closely at who said what and then considers each individual's training and background, one can nearly always identify the particular blind spot that led each to his individual conclusion. The statistician objects to Jim's "99 percent" confidence. The modeler defends his own model result. Interestingly, the man with his eye on what is basically the bottom line, Tom Wigley, leader of the British group that tabulates global temperatures, comes to Jim's support.

I submit that the widespread skepticism that Jim Hansen faced in the late 1980s arose from the fact that no other scientist came close to having the insight into the global climate system that he did. And that situation still remains. While the mainstream is now mostly with him, he still receives plenty of potshots, pretty much for the same old reason. His insight derives not only from a perspective unrivaled in its panoramic breadth, but also, and more importantly, from his deep understanding of the physics—an understanding engendered by his intellectual brilliance, first of all, and by his incredible work ethic, his honesty, and the fine training he received in James Van Allen's department in Iowa.

As he told Kerr in 1989, "The one thing that has the greatest impact on my thinking is the increase in atmospheric carbon dioxide from 280 parts per million in the nineteenth century to its present 350 parts per million. It's just inconceivable that that is not affecting our climate. There's no model that would not say it's affecting it right now. It's just a logical, well-reasoned conclusion."

Almost twenty years later, he says, "The bottom line of Dick Kerr's article was, 'If Hansen is right, it will be a case of physical intuition winning over—over something.' He's right, in that of course it's your intuition once you think you understand the problem. You can't rigorously prove *everything*. That's what the community is objecting to: you can't rigorously prove something, but you understand the problem well enough to make a statement with a very high degree of confidence.

"You can reach a point where you think you understand the system well enough to make some statement, and when I do that I realize that I'm never going to get the community to make that same statement with an equal degree of certainty, just because so many of the people in the community are looking at a piece of the problem and they're not willing to accept that someone else may have looked at other parts of it. Since they only understand this part of it, they don't want to make an assessment of the whole thing, and they object if somebody does."

Science by democratic consensus, I point out.

"Yes. It doesn't work. Right. That's not the way science works."

This is another reason that global warming represents the perfect problem. Science, with a capital *S*, has not been a great help because the community as a whole is astonishingly conservative (and also because not all scientists, being human, are good scientists). It is commonly agreed, for example, that the community finally caught up with Jim's 1988 insights about seven years later, in 1995, when the IPCC issued its second assessment, stating that "the balance of evidence suggests that there is a discernible human influence on global climate." One could argue, however, that the community didn't really catch up with him for nineteen years, until 2007, when the fourth IPCC assessment asserted with "very high confidence that the globally averaged net effect of human activities since 1750 has been one of warming." And if you really wanted to press the point, you could argue that the community still hasn't caught up with Jim's understanding of twenty years ago, for the 2007 panel specifically points out that "very high confidence" means 90 percent certainty. There was some discussion of using the phrase *virtually certain,* which would have been equivalent to Jim's 99 percent, but that didn't happen.

In the years that it has taken the IPCC to reach 90 percent certainty, the atmospheric level of carbon dioxide has risen about 30 parts per million. It recently passed 380 parts per million. It continues to climb at the rate of between one and two parts per million per year. Thus we are on track to pass the doubling point, 560 parts per million, near the end of this century. And the tipping point, most likely, will come a good deal before the doubling point.

Shortly after Jim returned from Amherst that May, he received a phone call—in the evening, at home—from Senator John Heinz III of Pennsylvania, a Republican, who told him that he had spent some time defending him to White House chief of staff John Sununu. Heinz also read him the letter he had written to Sununu, defending Jim's statements as reasonable and asserting that it was certainly within his rights to say them. Evidently, Jim had been lucky to escape with his job. (In the Statement of Political

Inclinations that he would release in 2006 in the wake of the second Bush muzzling attempt, he would admit that Heinz's intervention may have played a role in his deep respect for the man and in his hope that he would eventually run for president.)

Jim also received pressure in the other direction, although it was significantly less threatening. When Al Gore had learned that Jim and his GISS colleagues had produced a short film clip about rising temperatures, Gore had asked him to soup up the discussion of droughts a bit more than Jim felt he could justify based on the data. His refusal led to their first interpersonal tensions.

While Jim had hoped that his attempt at clarification before the Senate might focus the discussion on the science, it seemed that it had not. "Photographs of me holding a one-watt Christmas tree bulb appeared in a few newspapers, but with no discussion of what I was trying to explain," he wrote. "Instead, the focus was on politics. *Newsweek* juxtaposed photos of John Sununu and me as apparent antagonists."

Somewhere in there, he decided to leave the stage and focus on science.

He says, "The media circus in 1988 and '89 brought a lot of attention to the problem, but then successfully communicating the story via the media is very difficult, and I didn't feel I was particularly good at that, nor do I enjoy it all. I didn't feel that it was my job to try to draw attention to it anymore. Rather I thought that I could contribute scientifically. That, I think, is more my strength."

He sent his dice to Carl Sagan with the suggestion that "he try to make the story clearer."

Then, near the end of 1989, the deniers got into the act, led by none other than Jim's former boss Bob Jastrow, who suddenly manifested as an expert on solar variability. Under cover of the George C. Marshall Institute that he had helped found, Jastrow and two other elder statesmen of science, Frederick Seitz, president emeritus of Rockefeller University and past president of the National Academy of Sciences, and William Nierenberg, director emeritus of the Scripps Institution of Oceanography, issued a slim, unrefereed report asserting that no one knew enough to say anything definitive about climate and ascribing most of the fluctuations in temperature of the past century to changes in solar activity (so, evidently, they knew a little something, but no one else did). They even suggested that greenhouse warming would be a good thing, as without it the decrease in solar activity that they forecast for the twenty-first century portended a mini ice age.

"A report that essentially wishes away greenhouse warming is said to be having a major influence on White House policy," read a news article in *Science*. Nierenberg had been called in to brief White House officials, and Sununu was said to be "quite taken" with the report. "It has been widely reported that Sununu tried to block EPA head Reilly from attending an international meeting on climate change at The Hague in early November," the article continued. "At that meeting, the United States refused to commit itself to cutting emissions of carbon dioxide."

So it took George Bush Sr. about eight months longer to decide to do nothing than it would take his son, twelve years later. George Jr. would capitulate to the machinations of his vice president in the middle of March.

In fact, Jim and a few other scientists had been acknowledging the paucity of data about solar variability for years. On the other hand, what they did know indicated that its effect was probably about ten times smaller than the manmade greenhouse effect—and, furthermore, that sunlight was probably *gaining* in intensity, rather than diminishing. Even John Eddy, the solar physicist whom Jastrow had been pestering with weekend phone calls as he had been composing his report, labeled its solar arguments "preposterous."

But the game had begun. Richard Lindzen of MIT, a man who leans heavily upon his various credentials, which include election to the National Academy at a young age for his work in atmospheric circulation, coauthored a letter to President Bush supporting the paper by the Marshall Institute—and simultaneously took aim at the GCMs by proposing a second preposterous notion regarding water vapor.

It is often difficult for the ordinary mortal to follow Dr. Lindzen's complex logic and locution, but he was basically saying that changes in water vapor would lead to a negative feedback: the upper troposphere would dry as the atmosphere warmed; this would counteract the effect of the manmade greenhouse gases and act to stabilize temperatures.

I once attempted to interview Dr. Lindzen, but he fended me off. Journalist Ross Gelbspan had better luck, managing to meet with him for two hours in 1995. "In contrast to his often tortured scientific pronouncements," Gelbspan wrote, "I found his social and political expressions to be lucid, succinct, and unambiguous. Indeed, I found him to be one of the most ideologically extreme individuals I have ever interviewed." Lindzen has compared the rise of the environmental movement to the rise of the Nazi party in Weimer Germany. A cigarette smoker, he has also been known to deny that there is a connection between smoking and cancer. He is still kicking the dead horse of his water vapor theory, although virtually no legitimate scientists found it conceivable in 1989, and fewer believe it today. A test of his notion would arise naturally in mid-1991.

Jim never wasted much time on it. He casually pointed out that the planet performs an experiment that disproves it every year. As anyone whose skin has gotten sticky in summer would suspect, and as Arrhenius deduced more than a century ago, every layer of the troposphere takes on water vapor in summer and dries in winter. This is a positive feedback; it's as simple as that.

When Lindzen first brought his convoluted theory public, many took note of the seemingly spiritual aspect of his belief. He admitted that he had no data to back it up, and he spoke of water in quasi-religious terms. In a draft of his first journal article on the subject, he wrote, "The most likely area to search for severe problems [with the GCMs] is in the interaction of climate with water (in all its phases). The remarkable thermodynamic properties of water almost certainly lead to its acting as nature's thermostat." He also observed that if this particular alchemical substance did not meet his magical needs, something else must. Seven years later he would appeal to a belief in a benign, or even divine, principle of balance in testimony before the Senate Committee on Environment and Public Works: "In some ways, we are driven to a philosophical consideration: namely, do we think that a long-lived natural system, like the earth, acts to amplify any perturbations, or is it more likely that it will act to counter-act such perturbations? It appears that we are currently committed to the former rather vindictive view of nature."

With generous help from the fossil fuel industry, the Marshall Institute orchestrated probably the single most effective disinformation campaign that has been aimed at global warming. Between 1998 and 2005, according to a 2007 report by the Union of Concerned Scientists, the institute received $630,000 from ExxonMobil. In 2004, the oil giant's funding represented about 21 percent of the institute's total expenses. Lindzen has sat on Marshall's science advisory board. The institute has published his diatribes as well as books by Pat Michaels, whose distortion of Jim's 1988 testimony would prove useful to Michael Crichton. Sallie Baliunas, author of the backdoor journal article questioning a primary conclusion of the 2001 IPCC assessment, of which Philip Cooney would become so enamored that he would brag about it to Dick Cheney's office, would join Marshall's board of directors; and she and her coauthor, Willie Soon, would publish copious similar balderdash disguised as "sound science" under the institute's auspices.

In short, the first time Jim Hansen put global warming on the table, oil and coal interests swiftly succeeded in sweeping it off.

According to an annual report from the early nineties by the Western Fuels Association, a large coal-mining and electric-power-generating cooperative with facilities in the Midwest and Mountain states, "When [the global warming] controversy first erupted at the peak of summer in 1988, Western Fuels Association decided it was important to take a stand. . . . Scientists were found who are skeptical about much of what seemed generally accepted about the potential for climate change. Among them were [Pat] Michaels, Robert Balling of Arizona State University, and S. Fred Singer of the University of Virginia. . . . Western Fuels approached Pat Michaels about writing a quarterly publication designed to provide its readers with critical insight concerning the global climatic change and greenhouse effect controversy. . . . Western Fuels agreed to finance publication and distribution of *World Climate Review* magazine [with Michaels as editor]."

Western Fuels also spent $250,000 to produce a video named *The*

Greening of Planet Earth, which claimed that global warming would be a good thing, because it would increase agricultural output—a claim that was dubious at the time and has now been more or less completely discounted. According to Ross Gelbspan, "Insiders at the [first] Bush White House said it was Chief of Staff John Sununu's favorite movie—he showed it that often."

Beginning in 1988, mainly in the United States, coal companies for the most part, oil companies as well, launched an enormous public relations campaign to "reposition global warming as theory rather than fact." This was the stated goal of a campaign launched by the Information Council on the Environment (ICE), which was the creation of a second consortium of coal and utility companies. Gelbspan observes that an ICE campaign launched in 1991 was

> according to strategy documents that were later exposed in the press, . . . aimed specifically at "older, less educated men" and "young lower-income women." The geographic targets of the campaign included areas where electricity came from coal and districts whose congressmen served on the House Energy Committee.
>
> The effectiveness of the campaign can be seen in the results of two *Newsweek* polls, conducted in 1991 and 1996. In 1991, 35 percent of the people polled said they believed that global warming was a serious problem. By 1996 the number had dropped to 22 percent.

Dr. Michaels continues to enjoy a close relationship with Western Fuels. His *World Climate Review* has now morphed into the *World Climate Report,* published by the Greening Earth Society (GES), which was founded by Western Fuels on Earth Day 1998. In fact, according to the Union of Concerned Scientists, "GES and Western Fuels are essentially the same organization. Both used to be located at the same office suite in Arlington, Virginia"—although one could not possibly tell this by looking at the GES Web site or its publications.

The central tactic of these deniers is perfectly captured in a sinister maxim recently uncovered in an internal memorandum of the Brown & Williamson Tobacco Corporation, circulated in 1969, just as this and other tobacco companies embarked upon their wildly successful public relations campaign to undermine the proven link between smoking and cancer. "Doubt is our product, since it is the best means of competing with the 'body of fact' that exists in the mind of the general public."

The parallel is not coincidental. The title of the 2007 Union of Concerned Scientists report is "Smoke, Mirrors, and Hot Air: How Exxon-Mobil Uses Big Tobacco's Tactics to Manufacture Uncertainty in Climate Science." Consider the career of Frederick Seitz, one of Jastrow's coauthors on the original sacred text of the deniers, the 1989 Marshall Institute report. (Seitz has also served as chairman of the board of Marshall.) During the 1970s and '80s, as he drew a salary as president emeritus of Rockefeller University, Seitz was also paid almost $600,000 by the R. J. Reynolds Tobacco Company to distribute about $45 million for medical research into *anything but* the health effects of cigarette smoking. This, yes, perfectly legitimate research was used as window dressing to demonstrate the company's purported interest in public health, as it simultaneously ran cover for its deadly product and served to muddy the scientific waters surrounding it.

In an exposé of Seitz that appeared in the same 2006 "green issue" of *Vanity Fair* that featured a surreal photograph of Jim Hansen snipping "ozone holes" in a map of Earth, reporter Mark Hertsgaard quoted Stanton Glantz, "a professor of medicine at the University of California, San Francisco, and a lead author of *The Cigarette Papers* (1996), which exposed the inner workings of . . . Brown & Williamson." "Looking at stress, at genetics, at lifestyle issues let Reynolds claim it was funding real research," Glantz told Hertsgaard. "But then it could cloud the issue by saying, 'Well, what about this other possible causal factor?' It's like coming up with fifty-seven other reasons for Hurricane Katrina rather than global warming."

Representative Henry Waxman, who chaired the 2007 hearing at which Jim sat between George Deutsch and Philip Cooney, also chaired hearings in 1994 at which "tobacco executives unanimously declared under oath that cigarettes were not addictive," wrote Hertsgaard. Now, Waxman told him, "not only are we seeing the same tactics the tobacco industry used, we're seeing some of the same groups. For example, the Advancement of Sound Science Coalition was created to debunk the dangers of secondhand smoking before it moved on to global warming."

The Advancement of Sound Science Coalition (TASSC) was originally set up in 1993 by a global public relations firm named APCO with funding from Philip Morris. Its formula of employing rogue scientists, grandly financed by industry, to challenge the mainstream view of the dangers of secondhand smoke proved so effective that the coalition widened its scope. The fossil fuel industry eventually awarded TASSC a leading role in its campaign to sabotage the Clinton administration's attempt to sign on to the Kyoto Protocol.

The tobacco experience does not bode well for a solution to global warming. That industry succeeded in postponing meaningful action on smoking for more than three decades, at the cost of hundreds of thousands of lives per year. The good scientists (that is, the smart, rather than the morally superior ones) knew the truth about smoking and cancer about forty years before the government did anything about it. Yes, the scientific community was "virtually certain" that smoking caused cancer by the time the government came around. But it was also certainly too late.

Furthermore, the legal remedies that were finally meted out on Big Tobacco may be an irritation, but they are hardly a constraint. In 2006, an enthusiastic Morningstar investment report on the Altria Group, which is the holding company of Philip Morris, began, "It's beginning to look as if the only thing that can bring Altria to its knees is kryptonite." The company remained among the most profitable in the world. Philip Morris had collected $63 billion in sales the previous year, while spending a comparatively minor $5 billion on legal fees and settlement costs. The financial analyst took positive note of the fact that governments everywhere have a vested interest in the sale of tobacco products, owing to the tax revenues they generate. Philip Morris had spent almost half of its $63 billion on excise taxes, and "governments tack their own sales taxes on the company's products at retail, which produces even more tax revenue for their coffers."

In many ways, fossil fuel burning is to the biosphere as cigarette smoking is to the human body. Oil, gas, and coal companies are commensurately larger; they have been generating record profits in recent years; and they connect at a more fundamental and much more lucrative level to government bureaucracies and militaries. Even as George W. Bush was admitting that the United States was addicted to oil in his State of the Union address in January 2006, to choose a picturesque example, his administration was exhibiting what might be seen as addictive behavior in its obsessive and incompetent censoring of Jim Hansen and his fellow climatologists at NASA and elsewhere. That was about seventeen years after mainstream science knew enough about the dangers of global warming to justify some level of positive action.

One can understand why Jim Hansen might have sought refuge in science back in 1989. He didn't clam up totally, though; in fact, he lightened up a bit.

In April 1990, NASA held a conference on the Climate Impact of Solar Variability at Goddard Space Flight Center in Greenbelt. This must have been a reaction to the Marshall Institute's disinformation campaign.

Jim opened his presentation by admitting that he'd gotten a little worried the previous day as he'd been putting his viewgraphs together: they "seemed pretty dull." But after thinking about them for a while, however, he had realized that they led to a remarkable conclusion. He promised his audience that if they stuck it out to the end of his talk, they might find this conclusion interesting. "I can't guarantee that I will convince you . . . ," he said. "But I'm pretty sure that it is right. In fact, if you disagree with it, I would be happy to make a friendly little wager—one which much of the community apparently believes to be very improbable, so perhaps it's a good chance for you to take my money."

He has often said that even the deniers have helped spur the true scientists in his field to do better work. (It goes without saying that legitimate skepticism always helps.) In this case, Jastrow's preposterous claims about the sun had prompted Jim to review the available data. This showed that solar variability was not an insignificant player, but that Jastrow's suggestion that the sun might lose enough intensity over the coming century to offset global warming, while not "strictly impossible," seemed highly unlikely.

Satellite observations stretching back to 1978—only about ten years—had recently shown that the sun brightens and dims periodically, with a beat of about eleven years and a total difference in brightness of about 0.1 percent, which works out to about one-tenth the amount of energy that is presently directed at the surface by the manmade greenhouse blanket. The solar cycle had bottomed out in about 1985 and was now on the upswing—in other words, it was adding to anthropogenic warming. Jim's group had added the solar cycle to their global circulation model and then rerun the business-as-usual scenario that he had presented to the Senate in 1988. This brought him to his "remarkable conclusion."

"We are likely to set a modern global temperature record in the next one to three years, measurably exceeding the already high levels of the 1980s," he predicted. Then he offered his friendly wager to all takers: $100 that at least one of the three years from 1990 to '92 would be the hottest of the previous century. He set a stringent standard for success: the year had to set a record in all three major long-term temperature studies that were then under way: the GISS analysis, the British analysis, and a method that employed NOAA weather balloons to measure temperatures in the mid- to upper troposphere.

He had hoped to offer the bet to Richard Lindzen the previous December, when the two had been scheduled to participate in the same discussion panel at the annual AGU meeting, but the discussion had been squeezed out of the schedule. Here in Greenbelt, he was hoping Bob Jastrow might bite; and the two did engage in some friendly sparring, but Jastrow refrained on account of the approaching solar maximum. This was "interesting, since he has long argued that the Earth is already heading into an ice age," Jim pointed out in the write-up to his talk. "Also, the satellite data do not indicate a greater irradiance this solar cycle than in the previous one."

As it turned out, another of the more vocal skeptic-*cum*-deniers of the time, Hugh Ellsaesser of DOE's Lawrence Livermore National Laboratory, was the only person to take Jim up on his bet, and Ellsaesser lost at the first opportunity. Nineteen ninety set a record in all three data sets. The deniers all groused that it was a fluke, of course; and sure Jim had been lucky, but he argued that he'd placed a responsible bet: his precise understanding of the physics had told him the odds were greatly in his favor.

He hasn't made a public bet since. As he would tell journalist Bill McKibben a few years later, Anniek "thought it was a bad example for young people, like Pete Rose."

He says that he became "even more enthusiastic about science" after he stepped out of the limelight at the end of the eighties, thanks both to the newfound peace and quiet and to a qualitative change in the way he worked: he pulled back from managing the whole GISS team on big projects and began focusing on specific problems with a few close colleagues. The major pieces had been put in place, after all, both in the team's understanding of the climate system and in the systems they had developed to study it. The picture they had first outlined quite accurately in 1981 had gained much depth and detail in the intervening decade. There would be a few important new insights in the nineties, but this was mainly a time to work on new details, improve precision, and add color and texture to the canvas.

Their progress was perhaps best exemplified by a superb review article on the relative roles of the sun, dust, and greenhouse gases that Jim and Andy Lacis wrote for *Nature* in 1990. Not only did it give a perspective on the previous decade and a half of work; it tendered, yet again, prophetic indications of the years to come. Here Jim and Andy first used the phrase "climate time-bomb" in connection with the ocean-based delay, for example, although they were not yet aware of the potential explosiveness of the polar ice sheets. Their most important insight was to recognize that the greatest unknown at that time—far more important than the sun—was cooling by manmade aerosols.

Having demonstrated their firm grasp of natural, that is, volcanic aerosols, in previous work, the two pointed out that there still wasn't much solid data on the so-called human volcano: the atmospheric haze stirred up by industrial mankind that had led the small group of climatologists to predict in the 1970s (with far more sincerity but about the same level of inaccuracy as Jastrow and his friends at the Marshall Institute) the possibility of an imminent ice age. The human volcano has three main components: sulfates, which are emitted mainly by fossil fuel burning, especially coal-burning power plants; organic aerosols, including black carbon soot, which arise from the burning of biomass such as wood and dung as well as fossil fuels; and, third, straightforward dust that is entrained by surface winds in deserts or semiarid lands, especially when their vegetative cover is destroyed and they are subject to erosion. The cooling effect of aerosols is amplified by the fact that these particles provide tiny surfaces on which water vapor may condense into droplets. They thus seed the air to produce a type of cloud that tends not to produce rain, because the droplets are too small. Such clouds sometimes reflect even more sunlight back into space than the aerosols that produce them.

In spite of the overall uncertainty in the magnitude of the human volcano, Jim and Andy concluded that its direct impact overall was "clearly one of cooling"; and they estimated, based on the limited information available at the time, that this counterbalancing human effect might be about half as strong as anthropogenic greenhouse forcing.

They ended with a so-called *gedanken* or "thought" experiment—a form of thoughtful amusement that has a long history in the culture of physics. Einstein concocted a few famous gedanken experiments in the course of his decades-long debate about the philosophical underpinnings of quantum mechanics.

They pointed out that fossil fuel burning, which had so far caused about half the anthropogenic greenhouse effect (the other half coming from freons, methane, and so on), had also released sulfates, which cooled both through their own parasol effect and increased cloud cover. According to the knowledge of the time, the carbon dioxide from the burning would stay in the air for about a century, while the sulfates would remain for only a few days.

Since they were not sure exactly how much the anthropogenic cooling effect was offsetting the greenhouse effect to which it was intimately tied, Jim and Andy considered two cases, representing the upper and lower bounds of their uncertainty. Case I, the upper bound, assumed that the cooling effect was about half as strong as the total greenhouse effect; in other words, it exactly offset the greenhouse effect of its associated carbon dioxide. This led to a paradoxical conclusion. "If fossil-fuel use were stabilized (or reduced)," they wrote, "warming would accelerate, because the short-lived anthropogenic aerosols would stabilize (or decrease) but CO_2 would continue to increase. CO_2-induced warming is eliminated in Case I only by continued exponential increase of fossil-fuel use. But that would be a Faustian bargain, because fossil fuels would run out, whereupon a huge CO_2-induced warming would begin."

Their Case II assumed that the overall cooling effect of anthropogenic aerosols was negligible compared to the greenhouse effect of anthropogenic carbon dioxide. Then, "any reduction in the use of fossil fuels reduces the growth of CO_2 warming in a straightforward way."

This gedanken experiment lay the ground for the alternative scenario that Jim would present to Dick Cheney eleven years later, of course; and you will recall that, by that time, Jim knew that the real world matched up pretty well with Case I. Thus the cooling effect of the traditional forms of air pollution that are connected to fossil fuel use, most importantly the sulfate aerosols that cause acid rain, mask the greenhouse effect that is produced in the same burning process. If we were to stop using fossil fuels today, the aerosol mask would quickly drop from the sky, and, owing to the longer atmospheric lifetime of carbon dioxide, anthropogenic warming would swiftly double in strength. But the aerosols have many bad side effects; we cannot afford to let them continue to grow exponentially. This is why the talk that Jim gave in Iowa just before the presidential election in 2004 was named "Dangerous Anthropogenic Interference: A Discussion of Humanity's Faustian Climate Bargain and the Payments Coming Due."

Present thinking holds that one-third of the carbon dioxide emitted today will still be in the air 100 years from now, and almost a quarter will remain after 500 years. As Jim would write in 2007, "We take 500 years as a practical definition of forever because it is long enough for large responses from both the ocean and ice sheets. Resulting climate changes would be, from humanity's perspective, irreversible."

There is another implication to all this that I, personally, find rather astounding. Aerosol-induced cloud cover is especially pronounced over the continental United States, as a result of its pervasive industrialization. That means the sky was noticeably clearer and more blue above my hometown in Massachusetts back in the mid-1800s, say, or in revolutionary times, or before Europeans arrived on this continent, than it is today.

Just three weeks after he published the article with Andy, Jim published a second review article, also in *Nature,* with four French scientists from the Vostok collaboration, which was then about halfway through one of the more extraordinary and fruitful projects in scientific history: an attempt to drill an ice core to the base of the more than two-mile-thick East Antarctic ice sheet at Russia's Vostok station, which holds the record for the lowest temperature ever recorded, -129°F or -89°C, on the dark, midwinter day of July 21, 1983.

An ice core is something like a tree-ring core. A hollow drill, a meter, or three feet, long and a few inches in diameter, cuts its way down into an ice sheet or some other type of glacier, one meter at a time, retrieving tubular segments of ice that are hauled to the surface, extracted from the drill, and stored for later analysis. As the drill works its way slowly (very slowly) into the ice, it provides samples of the annual layers of snow—ice below the firn depth—hopefully all the way to the glacier's base.

The Russians began drilling their first core at Vostok in the 1970s. In 1985, after recovering about 2,200 core segments—more than two kilometers, or one and a third miles, of ice—they encountered technical difficulties that forced them to stop. They collaborated with the French on the analysis of this core, and the results were published in three exquisite papers that appeared consecutively in a single issue of *Nature* in 1987.

An extraordinary amount of information can be extracted from an ice core. The isotopic composition of the ice itself provides a measure of the temperature of the air at the time the ice fell as snow, for example, and the air bubbles that were trapped as the snow was compressed first into firn and then into ice serve as samples of the atmosphere from some time *after* the snow fell. The reason for the delay is that the air in the firn mixes with the air above it during the years—sometimes centuries—that it takes for the firn to solidify. Estimates of this delay time enable climatologists to match each layer of air bubbles with the layer of ice, somewhere below it, that matches up with it in time.

The 1987 papers demonstrated that the ice at the bottom of this first Vostok core was 160,000 years old; it reached further back in time than the beginning of the most recent, 100,000-year, ice age cycle. (Remember that the last time it was about as warm as it is today was during the Eemian interglacial, about 130,000 years ago.) More importantly, perhaps, the carbon dioxide in the air bubbles at Vostok and the temperature derived from the isotopes tracked each other closely over the entire 160,000-year record. Additionally, the greenhouse effect calculated from the changes in carbon dioxide was about the right magnitude to explain the temperature swings. Thus, simultaneous measurements from the same record demonstrated that the greenhouse effect of carbon dioxide has been one of the main governors of temperature on geological timescales.

This is not to say that changes in carbon dioxide *caused* the ice ages. It had been shown in the mid-seventies that the great advances and retreats of polar ice have been paced by periodic changes in our orbit about the sun. Changes in the eccentricity of the orbit underlie the main 100,000-year cycle that has held sway for the past million years or so, while changes in the tilt of Earth's rotational axis and in the season when we are closest to the sun, that is, the precession of the equinoxes, underlie other, shorter and less momentous ice age cycles. These orbital changes do not affect the total amount of sunlight coming in; they affect only its seasonal and latitudinal distribution. And the direct solar effects are surprisingly small—about ten times smaller than the anthropogenic greenhouse effect. Thus the carbon dioxide changes at Vostok actually lag the first small changes in temperature that were instigated by orbital change: greenhouse changes were in fact a natural feedback, as were the other changes detailed below. However, the greenhouse changes and the subsequent feedbacks *they* caused ultimately determined the magnitude of the temperature swings.

Jim had realized for years that so-called paleoclimate data such as Vostok's could provide an experimental measure of climate sensitivity—and, therefore, a real-world check on the validity of the global circulation models. He had presented his first attempt at doing this at the symposium in 1984, where he had also introduced the notion of ocean-based delay. The idea was to compare conditions 18,000 years ago, at the height (or depth) of the most recent ice age, with the conditions of today. If he could determine the difference in temperature and the differences in the most important forcings, he had pretty much everything he needed to estimate climate sensitivity.

He had based his 1984 estimate on a comprehensive synthesis of ice age conditions that had been conducted in the mid-seventies by a collaboration known as CLIMAP (Climate: Long-Range Investigation, Mapping, and Prediction). The CLIMAP data weren't precise enough to constrain the GCMs all that much, but they did basically agree with them: Jim came up with an empirical range of between 2.5 and 5°C for doubled carbon dioxide, which represented a slight shift in the upward direction from the range Jule Charney had given in 1979.

By 1990, when Jim began collaborating with the Vostok scientists, they had analyzed the methane and the levels of dust and other aerosols in their ice core in addition to the carbon dioxide. Methane, like carbon dioxide, rose and fell with temperature, whereas dust tended to go the other way. This made sense: as methane and carbon dioxide levels fell and the air cooled, it would have lost water vapor through feedback and become drier and more dusty.

Jim and his French colleagues inferred the size of the reflective polar ice sheets (which also gave them sea level) from a deep sea–bed record: a much shorter, sort of muddy version of an ice core. We won't go into the details of that.

Taken all around, they now had nearly a complete picture of the extent to which all the important forcing agents had changed since the so-called last glacial maximum, 18,000 years ago, when the planet was colder by about 4.5°C, or 8°F. This empirical evidence told them that a doubling of carbon dioxide (or an equivalent change in forcing resulting from an increase in any combination of greenhouse gases) would change global temperatures by between 3 and 4°C. There was less uncertainty in this estimate of sensitivity than in the one from 1984, but it still came in on the high side of the Charney range, which was centered on 3°C.

The beauty of this approach was that it accounted implicitly for most climate feedbacks (but *not* changes in the polar ice sheets, since those were imposed by the empirical data; this is an important point that Jim would revisit). And since it essentially agreed with the GCMs, it confirmed the validity of their treatment of feedback. This analysis also added confidence to the estimate of the "feedback factor" that Jim had made in 1984. The direct greenhouse effect accounted for only two of the more than four degrees of difference between now and the last glacial maximum— the rest came from feedbacks—so the empirical feedback factor lay somewhere between two and three, as Jim had previously calculated. This also meant that the ocean-based delay time that depends on that factor was somewhere around 100 years.

Jim often alludes to the misplaced emphasis that the contrarians or deniers place upon computer models—mainly as a diversionary tactic, it seems. Richard Lindzen, for instance, begins most of his arguments by criticizing some aspect of the GCMs (and one in particular: that they don't take account of his specious and apparently divine balancing principle). But Vostok and innumerable other pieces of evidence from the real world deliver the same message as the GCMs, while standing entirely separate from them.

Jim continues to follow the train of thought that he and the French members of the Vostok collaboration were pursuing in 1990. After a second failed attempt to reach the basal ice beneath their station, the collaboration would finally succeed in 1998, 3,623 meters, or 2.25 miles, down. Jim's magisterial analysis of the vast amount of climatic detail provided by this third Vostok ice core would be the centerpiece of the Keeling talk that would get him in trouble at the end of 2005; and he would finally succeed in publishing it in 2007, almost twenty-five years after he first turned his attention to the paleoclimate record. This empirical analysis is probably the most convincing and sobering evidence there is of the very real danger of continuing to indulge our business-as-usual energy habit.

But it is probably fair to say that the superb piece of work that Jim and the Vostok scientists produced in 1990 *proved* that global warming was a clear and present danger that long ago. Since then it has mainly been a matter of dotting the *i*'s and crossing the *t*'s. And watching it happen.

However, the next major act in the climatic drama turned out to be a cooling spell, initiated by the largest volcanic eruption of the twentieth century, Mount Pinatubo in the Philippines, which exploded at 8:51 A.M. on the morning of June 12, 1991, and eventually sent about 20 million tons of sulfur dioxide as high as sixteen miles into the stratosphere. Stratospheric sunlight transformed Pinatubo's dust column into just the sort of water droplets filled with sulfuric acid that Jim had studied on Venus almost twenty years earlier, and stratospheric winds then distributed this reflective shield around the globe.

In September, when NASA called representatives from various agencies to a meeting to present preliminary measurements of the optical effect of the volcano's aerosol cloud, Jim realized that this "provided a nice chance, again, to test our understanding." He, Andy Lacis, Reto Ruedy, and Makiko Sato, all from GISS, decided to add the eruption to their global circulation model and make a prediction. In a paper submitted before the end of the year, they suggested that the eruption had occurred too late to prevent 1991 from rivaling the temperature record that had been set the previous year, but that "intense aerosol cooling" would "maximize late in 1992," a minimum in temperature would be reached then or early the following year, and there would be "a return to record warm levels in the later 1990s."

It should come as no surprise that all of this came true. Global temperature dipped by almost half a degree Celsius (1°F) by late 1992 and recovered enough by 1995 for that year to tie and perhaps beat the record of 1990. Record heat for 1995 was all the more noteworthy as the solar cycle hit a minimum around then, and it was also a low year for ozone levels. Nineteen ninety-eight would set a clear record as well.

The GISS GCM predicted the time course of the temperature dip quite well, but Jim is quick to point out that it overestimated its magnitude by 10 or 20 percent. I have tended to emphasize the accuracy of his predictions and calculations, but he tends to focus on the errors, because that's how he learns. "Being a good scientist doesn't mean being right all the time," he says. "If you are, you are probably not making the propositions and taking the risks that you should in order to make fundamental contributions."

Speaking of which, Pinatubo went a long way toward proving that water vapor feedback is positive and, therefore, that Richard Lindzen's spiritual faith in the munificence of water "in all its phases" is almost certainly misplaced. Measurements would show that Pinatubo's cooling caused every level of the troposphere to dry, which it would do if the feedback were positive. Humidity would increase with warmth and decrease with cooling. In 2002, a group from the Geophysical Fluid Dynamics Laboratory would publish a full study of the volcano's drying effect—as well as the amplification, via feedback, of the drying on the cold spell. Anthony Del Genio of GISS would name his accompanying news article "The Dust Settles on Water Vapor Feedback."

In the nineties, the GISS group zeroed in on various sources of error and uncertainty. They worked on the physics behind their global circulation model, so that by the end of the decade, it had a sensitivity of about 3°C (2.7°C to be precise), in agreement with the real world according to Vostok. (They weren't "tuning" the model to match Vostok; improvements to its physics brought it into alignment with the real world.) They developed a simplified model geography that they named Wonderland, which preserved the essential features of Earth but permitted their GCM to run even faster, so that they could probe deeper physics. They gained access to a supercomputer at Goddard Space Flight Center and began running simulations for periods as long as a thousand years. This helped them develop a comprehensive understanding of all the important changes in forcing that industrial mankind had put in place since 1850: greenhouse emissions, aerosols, clouds (the least understood), and land use. They came to understand the primary significance of black carbon soot. They improved their understanding of natural changes in the sun and from volcanoes. And, finally, they put it all together in the optimistic alternative scenario that they revealed in the *Proceedings* of the National Academy of Sciences during the election year of 2000.

Jim has a favorite quote from Oscar Wilde: "When people agree with me, I always feel I must be wrong." And since his colleagues hadn't been disagreeing with him all that much since he'd dropped from view at the beginning of the decade, he might have felt some measure of gratification at the response to this new study. He was pilloried by a climate science community that had now accepted the dire warnings he had issued a decade earlier, for they now believed he was letting the fossil fuel industry off the hook. A news article in *Nature* quoted three scientists by name and one or two anonymously, all of whom were critical and some of whom landed surprisingly low and untruthful blows. The editors of the journal then edited Jim's response so heavily that he refused to let them publish it. Ironically, one of the critics they quoted was Michael MacCracken, who had experienced a dramatic change of heart since the early eighties, when he had criticized Jim's work from the other direction.

On the other hand, many lawmakers in both the House and the Senate joined Dick Cheney in twisting the alternative scenario into an argument for unbridled fossil fuel use. While Jim believed both sides were either misrepresenting or misinterpreting his work, he still hoped that the fact that everyone seemed to find something to like might provide a basis for compromise.

Never happened.

*   *   *

One of the occupations he had especially enjoyed during his break from politics was his work with the Institute on Climate and Planets. The educational outreach program that he had helped found in 1993 tended to dominate GISS every summer, when about fifty students and teachers from various high schools and colleges in the New York City area would crowd into the building on upper Broadway with the usual GISS staff to work on seven different research-related projects.

"A GISS scientist would head each team and try to define a problem that would be on a level that high school students and teachers could understand and where they could make some contribution," says Jim. "We would choose research projects that were of interest to ourselves rather than trying to find some separate problem for them to go work on."

The first project that he led focused on the Pinatubo eruption. In the summer of 2001, as I've mentioned, after his fruitless and admittedly naïve attempt to convince the vice president's climate working group that it might be worthwhile to do something meaningful about global warming, he asked his team of students to try their hand at doing what their political leaders would not. ("And who better to investigate this problem than just the people who will inherit the consequences of whatever plan is carried out?" Jim and two colleagues later wrote in an unpublished story about the team's work.) Their approach clearly indicates that he continued to place a high priority on carbon dioxide and fossil fuels.

At the meetings in Washington, he had been particularly impressed by the questions asked by Treasury Secretary Paul O'Neill and by the diplomatic quandary faced by Secretary of State Colin Powell as a result of the administration's go-it-alone intransigence on this issue. So he cast his challenge to the students in the form of a written request from a fictional secretary of state, whom he pictured in his mind as a combination of Powell and O'Neill. The secretary "was puzzled by the secretary of energy," Jim explains. "Clearly, in the cabinet-level group, the 'other side' was led by the secretary of energy. The energy department, as is their wont, showed business-as-usual projections for U.S. energy requirements in which growth continued at a couple of percent per year. With no change in the energy mix, that means CO_2 emissions will continue to rise." Indeed, DOE projected a whopping 15 percent rise over the next ten years.

Taking a cue from the interest that the vice president himself had expressed in the alternative scenario (such as it was), Jim's fictional secretary asked the team to find a way to meet the nation's growing energy needs as forecast by the energy department, while keeping to the greenhouse requirements of the alternative scenario. The secretary did not mention the non-CO_2 greenhouse gases and soot, which comprise about half the scenario, because that side of the problem is more easily addressed. (By way of example, of course, his nonfictional counterparts would actually address methane emissions, albeit halfheartedly, a couple of years later.)

Jim encouraged the students to focus on facts and employ quantitative methods from science and economics, and he named them the A-team, after the alternative or A-scenario. "The A-team toiled assiduously for two summers," he writes, "never losing their enthusiasm or the sense that they were doing something important." The reason for their demise was that funding for the outreach program ended.

First they looked into energy use, both globally and nationally, and divided it into sectors, such as transportation versus industry, and subcategories, such as automobiles versus trucks or aircraft. This demonstrated that the United States was in a prime position to take the lead, since it consumed a quarter of the world's energy to provide for the needs (and luxuries) of only one-twentieth of the population. Put another way, the average American consumed five times the energy of the average global citizen. The team also pointed out that the United States as a nation consumed about one-third more energy than the European Union, and that as "Europe has more than a third again as many people as the United States, this means that energy use per person is nearly twice as much in the United States as in Europe, despite comparable standards of living. This gap in energy use has been widening, as the annual growth rate of energy use by the United States has been 1 percent per year since 1980, but only 0.5 percent per year in Europe."

Globally, energy consumption had been growing at about 1.7 percent per year for the past twenty years, while carbon dioxide emissions had been growing more slowly at 1.3 percent. The difference was explained by the widespread conversion from coal to natural gas that had taken place in the period, since gas emits much less carbon dioxide per unit of energy produced. The A-team drew attention, however, to the insidious nature of this seemingly modest yet still exponential rate of emissions growth: even 1.3 percent per year would almost double annual emissions by mid-century. They also pointed out that trends were very different in China and India, where consumption had been growing at 4 and 6 percent per year, respectively, and where most of the growth had been fueled by coal.

Jim had designed the alternative or A-scenario to cut emissions sufficiently to ensure no more than 1°C of additional warming above the global temperature of the year 2000—the limit for dangerous anthropogenic interference, according to his latest climate work. Leaving out the non-CO_2 gases and black carbon soot, this required a leveling off of carbon dioxide emissions by about 2015 and diminishing emissions thereafter.

The A-team's central conclusion was that "plausible increases in renewable energy sources during the next two decades, even with strong government support, could not halt the growth in CO_2 emissions." In other words, alternatives such as wind and solar power could not do the job alone. "A greater potential was found for energy efficiencies. Indeed, infusion of *available technologies* was found to be capable of halting growth of emissions for decades. With the help of increasing renewable energy use, the flattened and even declining CO_2 emissions of the A-scenario were judged as being possible and leading to a large reduction in requirements for oil imports" (emphasis mine).

In the years since the A-team did their work, their basic formula has become a mantra to those seeking a solution: efficiency in the short term, new technology in the long term. Efficiencies based on existing technologies will buy time for the development of new energy technologies, which must kick in by mid-century, when we must turn to the task of cutting global carbon dioxide emissions by somewhere around 70 percent. That number is flexible, as it depends upon what we do about the non-CO_2

greenhouse gases and soot. And renewables will help: we need a full court press.

The A-team identified the two greatest threats, both in the United States and globally, to be the building of new coal-burning power plants and the worldwide growth in emissions from private transportation. They saw transportation as being marginally more important, as it appeared to be the fastest-growing emissions sector. This owed both to the shift from automobiles to SUVs and light trucks in the United States in the 1990s—compounded and indeed promoted by the fact that SUVs and light trucks were not required to meet EPA mileage standards—and steady growth in the number of vehicles in the developing world.

Regarding power plants, Jim writes, "Efficiency of energy end-use in the near term is critical for the sake of avoiding new, long-lived CO_2-producing infrastructure. (Unfortunately, exactly the opposite aim fits coal producers best: if they can see more plants built, it will guarantee profits for the rest of their lives.)" The implementation of "green" residential and commercial building codes combined with energy-efficient lighting and appliances would be sufficient to hold electrical needs—and, therefore, the number of power plants—constant for decades.

The A-team chose to study vehicular emissions in depth, and they focused on the United States, not only because this was their charge from the fictional secretary, but also because, as the greatest emitter and a technological and political leader, the United States is in the best position to set a trend for the world to follow. They used hard data published by the Federal Reserve to determine automobile survival rates, for example, so that they could estimate the time it would take for innovations to penetrate the market; and they looked at reports by the National Research Council, the Department of Transportation, and the California Air Resources Board (CARB) to assess the costs and potential emissions rewards of different automotive technologies. (In 2004, CARB had approved a regulation that would require automakers to start selling vehicles with reduced greenhouse emissions by 2009. The only way to do this is to increase gas mileage, so they were effectively setting a de facto mileage standard. The automobile manufacturers swiftly filed suit—and Jim would eventually get involved, as we shall see.) The A-team also designed a Web-based tool to enable themselves or anyone else to calculate future emissions curves for different scenarios.

They found that even a "moderate action" scenario involving the gradual introduction of existing technologies, such as variable valve lift and timing and the simple five-speed transmission, could increase the average gas mileage of the U.S. car and light truck fleet by about 20 percent. Assuming plausible rates of market penetration, they found that these simple technologies would save 5.5 million barrels of oil per day by 2030, or, at $50 per barrel (a conservative price in retrospect), $100 billion per year. The corresponding drop in oil imports was so huge that they began calculating it in terms of ANWRs: the total recoverable oil reserves in the much contested and now iconic Arctic National Wildlife Refuge, as estimated by the U.S. Geological Survey. By 2050, the cumulative amount of saved oil would exceed seven ANWRs, and the cost savings would exceed $2 trillion.

Moderate action did not quite reach the alternative scenario, however; so they also introduced a "strong action" plan (more or less identical in outcome to the CARB regulation). This plan calls for the introduction of advanced hybrid vehicles achieving forty-five miles per gallon in real driving conditions by 2015 and hydrogen vehicles by 2030. Hydrogen seemed a plausible idea at that time. Nowadays it does not. Since the A-team assumed that the hydrogen vehicles themselves would be emission-free but that the method used to produce hydrogen would emit some carbon dioxide, it is probably reasonable to assume that some combination of technologies that meets their strong action plan can be developed in the next twenty years. Indeed California seems to be banking on it.

Strong action not only met the A-scenario; it would save 5.8 million barrels a day and $109 billion a year by 2030, and 8.4 ANWRs by 2050.

"It should not escape one's attention that such savings for the United States balance of payments and oil requirements would have positive implications for the national economic well being, as well as national security," Jim noted quietly. He didn't even mention the spectrum of environmental benefits that would accrue from the associated drop in coal mining, oil drilling, and natural gas recovery, as well as the transportation of all three (think oil spills)—nor the enormous benefit to human health of the reduction in air pollution.

A few years later, Jim would hire a summer student to take a similar look at energy usage in American homes. The student looked only at heating, air-conditioning, and water heating and addressed these issues only with simple improvements such as more efficient equipment and better insulation and windows. While his work was understandably superficial, he found that the A-scenario was achievable in this sector, too, and that the economic and strategic benefits were similarly mind-boggling.

Then, as the Bush administration proceeded to ignore such commonsense thinking and even began to censor it, one of Jim's most fundamental predictions gradually came true. The first glimmering occurred in 2000, when a team led by Sydney Levitus, director of NOAA's Ocean Climate Laboratory in Silver Spring, Maryland, demonstrated that all the world's oceans had been warming since the mid-1950s. There were oscillations; but the trend was clear, it was global, and it represented a tremendous amount of stored energy. Positive temperature changes were measured at depths of 3,000 meters, almost two miles down.

This relatively simple result had not been simple to get. It was deduced from about 5.1 million measurements, roughly 2 million of which had been basically lost for decades. Research ships and other vessels have routinely dropped temperature sensors into the water to obtain depth profiles for more than a century, but up until recently, each had its own way of recording the data. Sometimes it was simply handwritten on paper and filed away to gather mold. Levitus and his colleagues had taken seven years to assemble their database under the auspices of a UN project called Global Oceanographic Data Archaeology and Rescue. Anyhow, their simple proof that the oceans were getting warmer had implications that reverberated around the world.

The news services carried stories. So did *The New York Times*. And it created a big stir in the scientific community, since it seemed to confirm yet another crucial aspect of the GCMs. In the paper itself, which appeared in *Science,* Levitus and his coauthors cautioned that they could still not "partition the observed warming to an anthropogenic component or a component associated with natural variability. . . . However," they added, "our results support the findings of Hansen et al., who concluded that a planetary radiative disequilibrium . . . existed for the period 1979 to 1996 (with the Earth system gaining heat) and suggested that the 'excess heat must primarily be accumulating in the ocean.'" Levitus told the *Times* that he personally believed some of the warming was "due to greenhouse gases."

The "Hansen et al." to which he referred was an extensive modeling study that Jim's "Pinatubo group" had published in 1997. A few high school students appear on the author list. They had shown that the planet was in a state of radiative imbalance with the sun, owing mainly to anthropogenic greenhouse and aerosol changes and, in addition to demonstrating that the heat must be going into the oceans, had duplicated the observed rise of about 0.2°C in surface temperature over the previous fifteen years. "One implication of the disequilibrium," they wrote, "is an expectation of new record global temperatures in the next few years. The best opportunity for observational confirmation of the disequilibrium is measurement of ocean temperatures adequate to define heat storage."

The following year, 1998, would set a temperature record, of course.

So it was certainly appropriate for Levitus to mention this study. However, he and, in fact, most of the scientific community seemed unaware that Jim had first predicted that the oceans would absorb the earliest greenhouse heat in 1984 or thereabouts. Nor did the community seem to recognize the serious policy implications of the decades-long delay that this newly verified insight implied between cause and effect. As Jim told the *Times,* "In my opinion, the rate of ocean heat storage is the most fundamental number for our understanding of long-term climate change."

He agreed that the new result did not prove where the warming had come from. Levitus and his colleagues threw down the gauntlet in their paper by pointing out that this could only be done with a global circulation model and, furthermore, only with the sort of transient simulation to which GISS's nimble GCM was especially well suited. It would be necessary to simulate the evolution of the system over the past century or so. Jim did not race to pick up the gauntlet, however, as he had other things on his mind: the global warming time bomb and the potential collapse of the polar ice sheets, for example. Levitus picked up the gauntlet himself.

About a year later, his group and another from the Geophysical Fluid Dynamics Laboratory (a fellow NOAA entity) came close to duplicating the changes Levitus had observed in the oceans with one of GFDL's so-called coupled atmosphere-ocean models. But their aim was primarily physics. They reviewed further empirical data from mountain glaciers, sea ice, and the polar ice sheets—all of which had been melting—together with the atmosphere and the ocean, and showed that every component of "Earth's climate system" had been warming. This meant that the oceans, which were absorbing the most heat by far, could not have been borrowing this heat from another component that was cooling: there had to be an imbalance with the sun. "This suggests a possible human influence on the observed changes," they concluded, in understated scientific prose.

But the paper that followed this one in the same issue of *Science* pretty much sealed the deal. This was a report by a group from the Scripps Institution of Oceanography on simulations with an amazing GCM called the Parallel Climate Model (PCM), which had been jointly developed by about half a dozen major government laboratories. The "atmospheric component" came from the National Center for Atmospheric Research in Colorado, the "ocean component" came from Los Alamos National Laboratory in New Mexico, the sea ice component came from the Naval Postgraduate School in Monterey, California, and the whole thing ran in a so-called massively parallel computing environment. The PCM duplicated the Levitus ocean measurements in convincing detail, both in time and in space. It even came close to getting the "fingerprints" right: the geographic pattern of the way the heat had spread in all five major ocean basins. As the authors stated in their abstract, "The chances of either the anthropogenic or observed signals being produced by the PCM as a result of natural, internal forcing alone are less than 5 percent."

This was resounding proof even though there wasn't much new physics involved and the authors seemed to have succumbed to a common course hazard among computer modelers, which is to become so enamored of your simulation of reality that you lose sight of the real thing. All mention of the ocean-based delay and ramifications for policy or society were lost in the unseemly boasting about their admittedly remarkable GCM. In the closing paragraph they actually stated, "Perhaps the most important aspect of this work is that it establishes a strong constraint on the performance and veracity of anthropogenically forced climate models," and claimed that to their knowledge the PCM was the only model that could simultaneously match the observed climatic change both above and below the ocean surface. Their knowledge was partial.

In June 2005, Jim, Andy Lacis, and a few other GISS scientists, in collaboration with others from the Jet Propulsion Laboratory and Lawrence Berkeley National Laboratory, brought it all into focus with a pithy paper named "Earth's Energy Imbalance: Confirmation and Implications." This paper, which appeared six months before Jim's group would announce that the year had set another temperature record and initiate yet another round of censorship by a Republican White House, stands among the top five or so most influential publications of Jim's long and still ongoing career. Ralph Keeling alluded to it when he introduced Jim for his Keeling talk. Ralph's father, Charles David Keeling, had been discussing it with Ralph's brother Eric, just minutes before he died.

Since there had not been a major volcanic eruption since Pinatubo more than a decade earlier, since the radiation imbalance caused by human activity continued to grow, and since the excess energy must have been going into the oceans, this group decided to use the measured accumulation of oceanic heat to estimate the radiation imbalance. The rising heat content in the top 750 meters of the oceans, deduced from a new, more complete set of depth profile data, was compared with simulations by the latest, entirely updated GISS GCM, which incorporated an ocean. The simulated curves of rising heat content over the past decade, and its geographic fingerprint, matched their empirical counterparts well. Harkening back to Jim's epiphany on Jones Beach in 1976, this meant that the typical square meter of the planet's land and ocean surface was continuously absorbing about one watt more sunlight than it was re-emitting as heat. It was as if a vast array of small Christmas tree bulbs was sitting above the surface on a one-meter grid. As for the paradox that had intrigued Jim thirty years earlier, he and his colleagues here pointed out that if this seemingly modest imbalance had been maintained since the beginning of the present Holocene era, which began 10,000 years ago, it could have melted enough ice to raise sea levels more than 3,000 feet—if there were that much ice, which there isn't.

The surface will heat up until it rights balance, of course, and the magnitude of the imbalance implied that there was precisely 0.6°C, or 1°F, still "in the pipeline." So, even if we had stopped our many climate-altering activities in 2005, the planet would continue to warm for more than a century, until equilibrium is reached.

Jim and his coauthors drew attention to the "critical importance" of this thermal inertia for policy makers: "This delay provides an opportunity to reduce the magnitude of anthropogenic climate change before it is fully realized, if appropriate action is taken. On the other hand, if we wait for more overwhelming empirical evidence of climate change, the inertia implies that still greater climate change will be in store, which may be difficult or impossible to avoid."

In other words, we could cross a tipping point toward catastrophic climate change fifty or a hundred years before knowing that we've done so.

Recall that the alternative scenario, which had been designed to avoid such a tipping point, permitted only 1°C of warming above the temperature of the year 2000. Since the new study showed that 0.6°C was already in the pipeline, the margin was getting thin.

The authors discussed other implications, but since it turns out that Jim—unbeknownst even to himself, I think—happened to be entering one of the most creative phases of his life and would make yet another quantum leap in understanding over the next year or so, we will discuss the broader implications and the science behind them when we get there.

*   *   *

As we know, it was difficult to get climate-related press releases through the NASA system at that time. A pregnant and miserable Gretchen Cook-Anderson, recently relegated to the doghouse by her boss, Glenn Mahone, was still sending them all to the Ninth Floor for vetting by the White House. So Jim resorted to his new tactic of writing up a draft release and posting it on his Columbia Web site. This one was named "Earth's Energy Out of Balance: The Smoking Gun of Global Warming," and it dwelled extensively on implications. The "smoking gun" phrase and much else was left out of the release that Gretchen managed to pass through headquarters. (It went to press the day she left for Goddard.) But the scientific community and many outside it still appreciated the truth in the phrase and began using it and passing it around themselves. It's not as if the evidence had not been overwhelming before this time, but as Jim put it in his unedited release, "There can no longer be genuine doubt that human-made gases are the dominant cause of observed warming."

Considering the body of his life's work, which now reached back thirty years or more, this remark evinced unusual patience and forbearance. In point of fact, mainstream science had been certain enough about the danger of the manmade greenhouse build-up to justify action since sometime in the early 1990s, and all reasonable doubt had been put to rest with the IPCC report of 2001. What Jim was saying here was that the door had been shut altogether. As Mark Cane, an El Niño specialist who is one of the most thoughtful and intelligent people in this field, said to me in 2000, "If you were to ask me the way you might at a cocktail party, okay? You're going to make an investment or you're going to buy a house or you're going to decide to change careers—some big decision in life. You're not ninety-nine percent sure that it's a good idea and you do it anyway. We're surer than that. We surer about global warming than the threshold where most of us are ready to make a decision. . . . I think it's highly likely that the changes we're seeing already are due to global warming. It's the best explanation. . . . Is it one hundred percent certain? No. Of course not. Nothing is ever one hundred percent certain. But it's the most likely explanation of what we've observed already. You need a Rube Goldberg device to get you out of it."

Even in March 2006, when Jim was caught up in the censorship drama and seemed barely to have scraped away with his job, he was willing to admit that there had been a shred of doubt five years earlier, at the start of the Bush-Cheney presidency. But now he and his fellow climatologists had "made the science story much stronger than it was in 2000."

"Yet we have not been able to impact the U.S. position," he said. "And when you get to the further step, where not only do you have the information to make the story clear but you have this censorship, you know, that's when you really get angry. I think the only way to get action now is for the public to get angry, for the public to see the frustration and see what the problem is, see that we have political leaders who are under the thumb of special interests. That is really why we're not doing anything, because they're more interested in short-term profits than in the long-term health of the planet—and the long-term health, frankly, of the economy.

"No court of justice or court of international opinion will forgive us for what we're doing now, because now we know the problem and we're just pretending we don't understand it. We are going to be responsible, but it will be our children and grandchildren that have to pay."

Jim Hansen might finally have lost his patience. At about that time, he dropped some of his vaunted Midwestern equanimity. He was commencing to dive into his work, as both a scientist and an activist, with the fervor of a man whose hair is on fire.

As he did, he discovered a new reason for anger.

Chapter 10

"Me, Too"

In the first week of February 2006, at the height of the censorship controversy, Michael Griffin decided to stifle his agency's Earth scientists in a far more effective way, by quietly gutting their budget. It is difficult to know exactly who was responsible for the budget decision, since Griffin essentially handed it down from on high. It was certainly in keeping with the Bush administration's unitary disregard for openness and due process—not to mention the environment—but it is hard to know whether anyone at the White House was directly involved. Griffin claimed forthrightly that he had set the priorities.

He was faced with a dilemma, to be sure. NASA is perennially asked to do too much with too little, and budgets outside the Pentagon were extremely tight, owing to the hemorrhaging costs of the Iraq War. Lawmakers, especially those from districts with jobs and contracts that rely on the space shuttle, wanted to keep it flying for the next three or four years. The shuttle fleet would also be needed if the agency was to fulfill its commitment to complete the construction of the International Space Station by 2010. And especially after the *Columbia* disaster in 2003, which had grounded the fleet for two and a half years, the shuttle and space station programs were gobbling up billions of unbudgeted dollars. Then there was Mr. Bush's (or perhaps Mr. Cheney's) New Vision for Space Exploration, a program for which Griffin, an engineer, felt special enthusiasm. He was already deeply involved in the first step, which was to design the so-called Crew Exploration Vehicle (CEV), which would replace the space shuttle and later be used to construct a permanent base on the moon ("where twenty-four men have gone before," as *Nature* observed). The ostensible purpose of the moon base is to provide a training ground for the next adventure, to Mars.

According to the agency's present, notoriously low projections, "the vision" will cost $105 billion over the next ten years, by which time there still won't be a twenty-fifth set of U.S. footprints on the moon. It is ironic that this program was proposed by the first accountant ever to lead NASA, Cheney's friend Sean O'Keefe, as it is basically a budget buster. O'Keefe's notion was to pay as you go, and he lowballed the costs from the start. Its cost may very well be measured in trillions, and it is essentially an open-ended deal. It has a strategic and perhaps a military aspect as well. And, as it happens, Michael Griffin has worked on a similarly expensive and open-ended, clearly military program that was also based in space. In the late 1980s, he worked as the deputy of technology for Ronald Reagan's Strategic Defense Initiative, or Star Wars program, which was almost universally regarded as unfeasible by the nation's top scientists. Star Wars remains alive twenty years later in the form of the Missile Defense Agency. Feasibility still has not been shown, but the program continues to march along at a clip of almost $10 billion a year—a number that has more than doubled in the Bush-Cheney era. Furthermore, some of the large aerospace firms that have won contracts from the Missile Defense Agency are also working on "the vision"—for example, Lockheed Martin, which recently won an $8 billion contract to build the CEV, now named Orion. If "the vision" remains a high priority and a program that the United States insists upon carrying out alone, it threatens to eat the lunch of every other program at NASA for decades to come.

Well, after promising over the fall that he would take not "one thin dime" from science to address overruns in other areas, that is precisely what Griffin did in the budget he announced on February 6, 2006. True, the allotment for science would rise 1.5 percent in the coming year; however, increases over the next several years would lag behind not only inflation but increases everywhere else in the agency. Compared to the budgets O'Keefe had envisioned, science would lose about $3 billion over the next several years. And this came on top of the 5 percent cut O'Keefe had imposed in 2005. Under Griffin's plan, science funding at NASA would not return to its 2005 level until 2011. As an editorial in *Nature* noted at the time, "NASA is undergoing a historic shift in direction without consulting scientists or paying attention to their advice. Projects with great appeal to scientists and to the public—including the search for planets around other stars and the study of dark energy—are being abandoned so that NASA can return astronauts to the moon half a century after the Apollo landings."

It may be worth noting that many if not all of the agency's visible successes in recent years have come from its science effort. After all, Dick Cheney inserted himself into a video about the Mars rovers in advance of the 2004 election. Furthermore, ICESat, GRACE, and the other NASA satellites that are observing the polar ice sheets and numerous other features of our planet may be the most crucial scientific experiments that mankind is now conducting.

Since Griffin did not specifically mention Earth science at his budget press conference in February, it took his employees (and the lawmakers who fund his agency and supposedly authorize its programs) about a month to realize how good a trick he had pulled in that area. Here's an excerpt from an e-mail Jim sent to a wide list when he finally figured it out. It carried the title "Swift Boating, Stealth Budgeting, and the Theory of the Unitary Executive." (He rebutted the distortions of Michael Crichton and Pat Michaels as well.)

> Most people are aware that something bad happened to the NASA science budget this year, yet the severity of the cuts and their long-term implications are not universally recognized. In part this is because of a stealth budgeting maneuver of the administration. . . .
>
> When the administration announced its planned fiscal 2007 budget, NASA science was listed as having typical changes of 1 percent or so. However, the absolute numbers for Earth Science research actually had a staggering reduction of about 20 percent from the prior year budget. How

could that be accomplished? Simple enough—reduce the 2006 budget retroactively by 20 percent! One-third of the way into fiscal year 2006, NASA Earth Science was told to go figure out how to live with a 20 percent reduction of the current year's funds.

The NASA Earth Science budget is practically a "going out of business" budget. From the tax-payer's point of view it makes no sense at all. The remaining 80 percent of the budget is used mainly to support infrastructure (practically speaking, you cannot fire civil servants, buildings at large centers such as Goddard Space Flight Center will not be bull-dozed to the ground, and the grass at the centers must continue to be cut). But the budget cuts wipe off the books most planned new satellite missions (some may be kept on the "books," but only for a date so far in the future that no money needs to be spent now), and support for contractors, young scientists, and students disappears, with dire implications for future capabilities.

Funny thing, this is happening right at a time when NASA data are yielding spectacular and startling results. A pair of small satellites that measure the Earth's gravitational field with remarkable precision found that the mass of Greenland decreased by the equivalent of 50 cubic miles of ice in 2005 [a reference to the GRACE mission]. The area on Greenland with summer melting has increased 50 percent, the major ice streams on Greenland (portions of the ice sheet moving most rapidly toward the ocean and discharging icebergs) have doubled in speed, and the area in the Arctic Ocean with summer sea ice has decreased 20 percent in the last 25 years.

One way to avoid bad news: stop the measurements!

```
Only hitch: the first line of the NASA mission is
"to understand and protect our home planet." Maybe
that can be changed to ". . . protect special
interests' backside."
```

Then, in a responding e-mail, a fellow NASA scientist clued Jim in to a second aspect of Griffin's quiet maneuver.

```
Hi Jim-

Let me start by reaffirming my appreciation
for all you are doing to get the truth to the
American public about current Earth science,
NASA's programs, and the current budgetary and
political situation.
    I read with great interest the draft you sent
on Swift Boating, etc. I noted your quote re: the
first line of NASA's mission being: "to understand
and protect our home planet."
    I'm sorry to say that I discovered a couple of
months ago that this is no longer the case. In
the process of writing a proposal...I found NASA's
mission quoted as:
    To pioneer the future in space exploration,
scientific discovery, and aeronautics
research. . . .
```

To which Jim replied:

```
Wow—that is unbelievable, but only too
believable—I do not think it was an accident
that the change was made when the budget was
re-jiggered. I have mentioned that "understand
and protect" line in NASA's mission on NPR and
many other media in the past several months as
rationale for why NASA should be concerned about
climate change. Thanks. I need to chew on
```

```
this.... Stealth budgeting, indeed, and additional
slime.
```

Only when parts of this exchange were shared with *The New York Times* and the diminishing status of our home planet began making headlines did most NASA employees even realize that their agency had taken a major change of course. That goes for congressional lawmakers as well.

At the end of an article in *World Watch* that would evolve from his "Stealth Budgeting" e-mail, Jim would expand upon the notions of both unitary governance and "slime":

> The budgetary goings-on in Washington have been noted, e.g., in editorials of *The Boston Globe* ... decrying the near-termination of Earth measurements. Of course, the *Globe* might be considered "liberal media," so their editorials may not raise many eyebrows.
>
> But it is conservatives and moderates who should be most upset, and I consider myself a moderate conservative. When I was in school we learned that Congress controlled the purse strings; it is in the Constitution. But it does not really seem to work that way, not if the Bush administration can jerk the science budget the way they have, in the middle of a fiscal year no less. It seems more like David Baltimore's "Theory of the Unitary Executive" (the legal theory that the president can do pretty much whatever he wants) is being practiced successfully. My impression is that conservatives and moderates would prefer that the government work as described in the Constitution, and that they prefer to obtain their information on how the Earth is doing from real observations, not from convenient science fiction.
>
> Congress is putting up some resistance to the budget manipulation. The House restored a fraction of the fiscal year 2007 cuts to science and is attempting to restore planning for

some planetary missions. But the corrective changes are moderate. You may want to check your children's textbooks for the way the U.S. government works. If their books still say that Congress controls the purse strings, some updating is needed.

But may it be that this is all a bad dream? I will stand accused of being as wistful as the boy who cried out, "Joe, say it ain't so!" to the fallen Shoeless Joe Jackson of the 1919 Chicago Black Sox, yet I maintain the hope that NASA's dismissal of "home planet" is not a case of either shooting the messenger or a too-small growth of the total NASA budget, but simply an error of transcription. Those who have labored in the humid, murky environs of Washington are aware of the unappetizing forms of life that abound there. Perhaps the NASA playbook was left open late one day, and by chance the line "to understand and protect our home planet" was erased by the slimy belly of a slug crawling in the night.

Had Jim known exactly who had done the dirty deed, he might have chosen a different metaphor. A high insider at headquarters told me that Michael Griffin rewrote the mission statement and the agency's strategic plan basically on his own. A few months after Jim published his *World Watch* piece, he learned from Mary Cleave, the associate administrator (AA) for Science, that she had not been consulted. This was quite unusual. In fact, it might have been illegal. The "political" I have previously mentioned, who worked "on the Ninth Floor, behind the glass doors at NASA" during the Clinton years and claims to be a Mike Griffin supporter, expressed shock at the utter lack of consensus-building that preceded this historic change of course. "That one's very odd," this person said. "There's a law on the strategic plans of these government agencies. It's called the Government Performance and Results Act, GPRA. You have to have a strategic plan, and it gets graded, and everybody takes it very seriously. . . . When I was there, every AA in the agency had to sign off. Now they're claiming this low-level person just changed it, and I'm not just buying it."

I think we've heard this story before.

Griffin was also blithely ignoring an interim report issued the previous summer by the National Academies declaring that NASA budget cuts had placed "the vitality of Earth science and applications programs . . . at substantial risk," and warning that the nation's entire system of Earth observing satellites—comprising many in addition to ICESat and GRACE—was "at risk of collapse."

But the administrator had demonstrated his most glaring disregard for science in specific and draconian cuts to Research and Analysis. This is where the thinking is done, the intellectual work, what you might call the "real science," both within and without the agency. R&A provides grants to universities to fund seed projects and develop young scientists, for instance, the sort of program that had allowed Jim and Andy Lacis to attend graduate school in Iowa and had helped build the capability to reach the moon the first time around. Jay Zwally's analysis of the European satellite data from Greenland, which resulted in the press release that tested Griffin's Statement on Scientific Openness, also fell under R&A. Virtually every scientist, NASA or otherwise, who was asked to comment on the budget—before Sherwood Boehlert's House Science Committee and elsewhere—described this as its most troubling feature. The agency's Earth science advisory council virtually pled for R&A funds to be restored. "The large retroactive cut in [2006] will have devastating effects on the research community, especially young researchers, if it is not alleviated in [2007]. A one-time cut can be at least partially absorbed . . . but a long-term cut of that magnitude would have severe impacts on the lifeblood of the Earth science community, with strong negative implications for the ability of the community to meet national needs at a time when the importance of Earth science and global change issues are growing markedly."

On the other hand, Griffin may have been sending a more specific message: the entire budget of Jim's institute falls under R&A. (We've heard this story before, too.) The budget had dropped 20 percent. By 2007, Jim would be filing grants with private foundations just to keep GISS afloat. He had never resorted to this before, even under Ronald Reagan and Fred Koomanoff.

*   *   *

He'd been going at his usual full tilt on science back in December, when he'd been sidetracked by the censoring, so there was a backlog when he returned to a relatively normal routine in March. Some studies were nearly ready for journal submission; others were at earlier stages. Plus, Jim is always thinking, watching the climate story unfold, sitting alone in his apartment in the early morning, for example, perusing the maps of Earth's temperature that his group produces monthly, looking for patterns. He can't help but have an insight every once in a while—every few days, it seems. Some scientists live on this the way the rest of us live on food.

It was my privilege to sit with him at his breakfast table on a Saturday morning in March 2006, less than two weeks after he had sent out his "Back to Science" message, as he walked me through an early draft of a paper he was writing at the request of a meteorology journal—the first entirely new paper he would produce that year. The editors wanted him to respond in a credible scientific forum to the distortions of Michael Crichton.

In addition to misrepresenting Jim's 1988 "prediction," Crichton had spent a few pages of his book finding fault with the modern temperature analyses, arguing mainly that they were biased by the "heat island" effect of big cities. The heat island argument had been around for decades, Jim's group and the others that compile the records had long since corrected for the bias, and Crichton should have known as much. However, as with so many of the false claims of the deniers, this one persists. And it is easily dispensed with: Jim showed me maps indicating that the greatest warming in the past century has occurred in remote regions such as the Arctic and Siberia, and that the oceans have warmed, too, of course: the smoking gun. This is not to mention the worldwide retreat of mountain glaciers, which are not normally located in urban areas, and an uncountable number of other changes in the natural world.

Dealing with Crichton's nonsense may have been necessary, but it wasn't all that intriguing, and it wasn't exactly science. "So I try all along to make this paper interesting," Jim told me. "I go in two different directions. I go to the shorter time scale and the longer time scale. I think these things are more important."

His attention had recently been drawn to the so-called Pacific warm pool, the region in the vicinity of Indonesia that harbors the warmest water in the oceans. He had been checking in weekly on a graph on a NOAA Web site of subsurface water temperatures in the warm pool and scanning his own group's maps of sea surface temperatures at the same time. Then he had encountered a surprise: the face of La Niña on the maps from the previous six months.

La Niña is an intensification of the usual easterly wind and ocean currents along the equator, in which strengthened trade winds peel back more than the usual amount of sun-heated surface water in the east, by South America, and carry it west to the warm pool. This enhances the upwelling of cold water from the abyss to the ocean surface, off the coast of Peru. The cold tongue of water originating at the coast and lying right on the equator extends farther west than usual. By piling up warm water in the western Pacific (the ocean surface actually tilts), La Niña, in a sense, "loads the gun" for her brother, El Niño.

"So here's the last six months," Jim said. "You see this La Niña pattern in the Pacific? It looks very similar to September nine years earlier, which was followed by the largest El Niño of the century. So, in a sense, we're set up to have another El Niño."

He found the heat buildup below the surface to be even more convincing, although he couldn't show it to me that day because he didn't have an Internet connection in his apartment.

"Then, look at the last month," he said. "As soon as we got this data—the end of February, beginning of March—I thought, 'Oh, boy, we're going to get an El Niño this year,' because, see, it has warmed along the coast of South America by about one degree."

The trade winds were weakening: an El Niño was on the way. In this first draft of his new paper, Jim "suggested" that an El Niño was likely to originate later in the year and that it might possibly rival the previous two, record-setting occurrences, in 1998 and 1983. He knew this was a tricky business, however; none of the usual El Niño forecasting models was predicting one at that point, and they're not always right anyway. He quoted Mark Cane, who was the first person to predict these events with any kind of accuracy: "Every spring, Mother Nature rolls the dice" to see if an El Niño will turn up. It's always a guessing game.

Jim then mentioned a more important idea: that by adding energy to the tropical Pacific, heating up the warm pool, and heightening the temperature difference between east and west, global warming is, in effect, loading a larger gun for El Niño. The recent warming hasn't yet affected equatorial water temperatures in the vicinity of Peru, because most of that water wells up from depths that have not yet absorbed significant greenhouse heat. The warm pool has gained about one degree of warmth since 1870, while temperatures off the coast of Peru are unchanged. Jim suspects that this will tend to make El Niños stronger and more destructive but not necessarily more frequent, in the same way that ocean heat provides additional destructive energy for the sort of hurricane that destroyed New Orleans in 2005.

After a lot of hesitation and a few discussions with his GISS colleagues, especially Makiko Sato, Jim withdrew the first of these two thoughts from later drafts of the paper—the prediction that an El Niño might begin in the fall of 2006. He still gets worked up about that decision.

He writes of his concern that a "wrong prediction (which would be a perfectly good thing from a scientific perspective) would be very unfortunate at this time, given the need for rapid action to deal with global warming. It would give contrarians something to, inappropriately, point to as a reason to distrust my science. I recognized this possibility, so I reluctantly dropped the prediction from the paper. . . .

"The way I look at it, the great fun in science is that you get to reason about how things work, leading you to make predictions that test your understanding. The predictions that you make had better include some that are wrong or you are not pushing the envelope of scientific understanding. Some of the most extreme predictions, the most unlikely, are the most fun. When you make one of those, you had better identify it as such or you will look like an idiot later, but these cases still have merit, and indeed the scientific community gives you credit for them. They don't conclude, 'Boy, you were stupid,' they give you partial credit for having made people think about the underlying assumptions."

He sent the first draft out to some colleagues, including Mark Cane, and they criticized some of his ideas, of course. They were especially dubious about the prediction that he eventually withdrew, since none of the models agreed with it. But Jim says that only whetted his appetite to keep it in there; his real reason for taking it out was the one he mentioned above.

Guess what? There *was* an El Niño that fall, although it wasn't a strong one. Nevertheless, Jim stands by his assertion that global warming will probably increase the likelihood of stronger El Niños. They are *more* likely, but they are still exceedingly *unlikely*. After all, there have only been two super El Niños in the last century, and there had been none for almost a century before the one in 1983. "The real world did not produce a super El Niño [in 2006]," he says, "but that did not present significant evidence against my proposition."

This was the first time Jim had ventured a professional opinion on El Niño. His arguments were dead simple and make good sense, but it will take many years to determine whether they are correct, because El Niño visits so rarely.

His interest had originally been drawn to the western Pacific because of some new information from the long end of the timescale: a million-year record of sea surface temperatures recently mined from the muddy bottom of the warm pool, near Indonesia. Aside from storing a tremendous amount of heat, the warm pool also contributes a significant fraction of all the water vapor—the most powerful greenhouse gas—to the atmosphere. Surface temperatures there reflect average global temperatures better than they do in most regions; in fact, to a certain extent the warm pool controls the planet's temperature. "It is probably not an exaggeration to say 'as the Pacific goes, so goes the world,'" Jim wrote in the paper.

By splicing the seabed record together with a modern, instrumental temperature record from the same region, Jim showed that we presently seem to be crossing into the warmest period of the Holocene, the past 12,000 years, and that we are within about 1°C of the high points that have been reached only a few times in the past *million* years. The Holocene has been a congenial and relatively stable period in which sea level has remained essentially fixed. This has allowed human civilization to flourish and to build a vast infrastructure at the water's edge. But, as I have pointed out, during the Eemian interglacial 125,000 years ago, which is the most recent temperature high point of the past million years, sea levels were between thirteen and twenty feet higher than today's. And the last time temperatures were 3°C warmer than today, during the Middle Pliocene about 3 million years ago, the seas were between 50 and 115 feet higher.

This new data had changed Jim's perspective a bit, and if his concept of a tipping point is valid, a small change made a grave difference. He realized that we might be closer to a dangerous level of warming than he had thought even in December, when he gave his Keeling talk. His alternative scenario allows 1°C above the temperatures of 2000, remember, so it now seemed that even the alternative scenario might lead to a sea level rise of five to ten feet. Given the uncertainties (which cut both ways), we are at least uncomfortably close to the warmth of the Eemian; in fact, given the half a degree that is already in the pipeline, together with the thousands of long-lived coal-fired power plants that are already in place, we may be committed to exceeding it. If this is the case, our choice is not between no change and a significant change, but between a significant change and disaster: business-as-usual would easily give 3°C and a minimum of fifty feet.

Jim eventually submitted this paper to the *Proceedings* of the National Academy of Sciences, and it attracted worldwide attention when it came out—no doubt buoyed by the publicity boost he had received from his friends in headquarters public affairs. On a single day in September 2006, news stories appeared in the United States, Canada, New Zealand, Scotland, China, the Philippines, Turkey, Brunei, and even Cuba.

*   *   *

The censorship experience had added a couple of new dots to the ones Jim had connected in his Keeling talk: the need for activism and the need to take the message to the public. His new fame meant that he had a lot of opportunities for the latter—many people wanted pieces of his time—so he selected his appearances for maximum effect. This did not necessarily mean maximum exposure. In May 2006, he testified as an expert witness for the California Air Resources Board in the suit brought by the automobile manufacturers against CARB's new emissions regulation. (It was clear that he should appear as a private citizen in this instance, since his employer, the federal government, weighed in as a friend of the court on the opposing side.) That same month, he joined more than a dozen other climate scientists, including Sherwood Rowland and Mario Molina, Nobel laureates for their work in atmospheric ozone chemistry, in filing an amicus curiae brief in support of the plaintiffs in a case that would eventually be heard by the Supreme Court. It was filed by the Commonwealth of Massachusetts against the Environmental Protection Agency.

In the wake of George Bush's post-victory reversal, deciding not to classify carbon dioxide as a pollutant, EPA had formally complied by issuing a decision not to regulate automobile emissions, in 2003. Massachusetts had sued, arguing that the agency was required to regulate the gas under the Clean Air Act; and eleven other, mainly coastal states had eventually sided with Massachusetts. Eleven Midwestern and Mountain states, including Michigan, had sided with EPA. In 2005, a Washington, D.C., appeals court had decided in favor of EPA. Massachusetts was now asking the Supreme Court to take up the case, and the scientists were arguing that the agency had misinterpreted the science. In justifying its decision, EPA had placed much emphasis on a report that Bush himself had requested from the National Academy just as his vice president's climate change working group had been meeting in 2001. The very first line of the report states unequivocally, "Greenhouse gases are accumulating in Earth's atmosphere as a result of human activities, causing surface air temperatures and subsurface ocean temperatures to rise." However, much like Philip Cooney at the Council on Environmental Quality, EPA had cherry-picked from the report, emphasizing uncertainties and minimizing dangers. Jim had been a member of the panel that had written the report, and he had joined four other panel members, including Rowland, in the drafting of the amicus curiae.

Over the fall, Jim joined another automobile lawsuit in Vermont. And at the end of November, he participated in a quiet, by-invitation-only retreat at a plantation in Thomasville, Georgia, that brought together leading scientists and evangelical Christians hoping to put aside their differences about evolution, the age of the Earth, and so on and "search for common ground in the protection of the creation." (It is typical of Jim that when the organizers asked him in advance which sessions he would like to attend, his first choice was "Working Together.") The seeds of this effort had been planted years earlier by Sir John Houghton, the British atmospheric scientist and evangelical who was the lead author of the 2001 IPCC report on the scientific basis for global warming. Houghton had formed bonds with fellow Christians and scientists across the Atlantic; and shortly thereafter, a few U.S. environmentalists and scientists, most prominently E. O. Wilson of Harvard, had begun reaching out to evangelicals as well. This retreat was convened by Harvard's Center for Health and the Global Environment and the National Association of Evangelicals, which represents 45,000 churches.

Although the evangelical movement was by no means unified on this issue, a few prominent members participated in the retreat, including Joel Hunter, pastor of a "distributed" megachurch in Florida with a total congregation of 7,000, and the Reverend Richard Cizik, vice president for governmental affairs of the National Association of Evangelicals. A professor from Pat Robertson's Regent University participated as well. Representing science were Jim; E. O. Wilson; biologist and oceanographer Rita Colwell, director of the National Science Foundation from 1998 to 2004; author, ocean ecologist, and MacArthur Fellow Carl Safina; and others.

In January 2007, at the National Press Club in Washington, noting that they had "happily discovered far more concordance than any of us had expected," the twenty-eight retreat participants issued An Urgent Call to Action.

We clearly share a moral passion and sense of vocation to save the imperiled living world before our damages to it remake it as another kind of planet. . . .

We agree that our home, the Earth, which comes to us as that inexpressibly beautiful and mysterious gift that sustains our very lives, is seriously imperiled by human behavior. The harm is seen throughout the natural world, including a cascading set of problems such as climate change, habitat destruction, pollution, and species extinctions, as well as the spread of human infectious diseases, and other accelerating threats to the health of people and the well-being of societies. Each particular problem could be enumerated, but here it is enough to say that we are gradually destroying the sustaining community of life on which all living things on Earth depend. . . .

We declare that every sector of our nation's leadership— religious, scientific, business, political, and educational—must act now to work toward the fundamental change in values, lifestyles, and public policies required to address these worsening problems before it is too late. There is no excuse for further delays. Business as usual cannot continue yet one more day. . . .

At about this point in time, Jim began mentioning the Creation in his standard, Keeling-type talk.

He had actually added one of the dots mentioned above—and very close to E. O. Wilson's heart—the previous spring, when he had begun to understand the implications of business-as-usual for global biodiversity. (At the same time, he added a new bullet point to one of his slides: "Best Hope: Public Must Become Informed and Get Angry.") Recent studies had shown that plants and animals were migrating toward the poles at an average rate of about four miles per decade, but that that didn't seem fast enough, as changes in temperature were migrating at almost eight times that rate, thirty-five miles per decade. Estimates attributed the eventual extinction of 20 percent of all plant and animal species to habitat destruction and the other direct pressures mentioned in the Call to Action. This was disturbing enough, but when business-as-usual global warming was added to the picture, the estimates rose to 60 percent. Jim began to rank species extinction just below sea level rise on his list of the gravest concerns.

He wrote articles and editorials in the popular press. He gave his talk to diverse audiences, updating it almost weekly. He testified at congressional hearings. He spoke at universities; he attended forums and symposia; he spoke to obscure but relevant trade groups: a meeting in Dallas attended by 16,000 water quality specialists, the annual meetings of the Solar Energy Society and the National Association of Regulatory Utility Commissioners. He attended a conference on so-called peak oil and participated in a widely viewed webcast convened by Architecture 2030, a nonprofit dedicated to the transformation of the building sector "in a way that dramatically reduces or eliminates the need for fossil fuel." Yes, he won prizes and awards and appeared in a television special on the Discovery Channel, hosted by Tom Brokaw, but these were not the moves of an attention seeker.

And the planet continued to change. After hitting its record minimum in the fall of 2005, arctic sea ice grew to its smallest-ever maximum the following spring. While the minimum in the fall of 2006 was low, coming in second overall, it did not set a record. But 2007 shattered the record that had been set only two years earlier. There were 460,000 fewer square miles of arctic sea ice in late September 2007 than there had been in September 2005, about the area of Texas and California combined, a drop of more than 20 percent. Remarkably, 2007 broke the record in mid-August. The news was announced by Mark Serreze of the University of Colorado (a colleague of Waleed Abdalati's): "Today is a historic day. This is the least sea ice we've ever seen in the satellite record and we have another month left to go in the melt season this year."

Over the fall of 2006, a new wave of GRACE data rolled in: three news flashes on the state of affairs in Greenland. (Since it is a complex task to interpret GRACE's gravitational measurement, a number of different groups are working on it.) In August, a group from the University of Texas at Austin found that from 2002 to 2005 the island had been shedding ice into the sea at an average rate of about 217 billion tons per year, the equivalent of fifty-six cubic miles of water. In September, Velicogna and Wahr, who had reported on Antarctica in the spring, now delivered a more nuanced message from the top of the planet. Their overall result corresponded well with the one from Texas: an average loss of 225 gigatons per year from April 2002 through April 2006. But the title of their article was "Acceleration of Greenland Ice Mass Loss in Spring 2004." Prior to April of that year, the rate had been 95 gigatons per year; in the period from May 2004 through April 2006, it more than tripled to 311.

A group at Goddard Space Flight Center led by a brilliant young scientist named Scott Luthcke had applied their analytical talents to the GRACE data as well. They processed the raw information in an entirely different way from the other two groups, which gave their method much finer resolution. This meant that in contrast to the other two methods, theirs was not "contaminated" by changes that might have been taking place in the oceans and so on nearby. It also meant that they had less trouble with postglacial rebound (the "rising sponge" problem). Jay Zwally and Waleed Abdalati then realized that Luthcke's GRACE results had for the first time clearly shown a seasonal cycle and spatial pattern that was consistent with their understanding of how the ice actually changes. (The results showed, for instance, that the margins of the ice cap were gaining mass in winter, presumably from snow, and losing it in summer, presumably from melting.) This resulted in a study published in November that came up with only half the mass loss that the other two groups had estimated: 101 gigatons per year for the period 2003 through 2005. Nevertheless, this marked a significant change from the findings Zwally had reported earlier in the year on the basis of the European satellite data. Recall that that study found Greenland to be gaining mass from 1992 to 2002 at a rate of about 11 gigatons per year. Zwally subsequently revised this number downward to 4 gigatons per year. Either way, it now appeared that Greenland had shifted from a state of near balance at the end of the previous decade to significant loss in just a few years. Something big seemed to be happening. (Zwally is a painstaking fellow. After about fifteen years of work, he and his colleagues are about to publish their first mass balance estimates from ICESat; and he is confident enough in their Greenland result to allow me to mention it here: a loss of 80 gigatons per year for the period from 2003 to 2006, which jibes reasonably well with his and Luthcke's GRACE estimate.) And while their absolute numbers didn't agree with those of the other two groups, all three—as well as others I have not mentioned—agreed precisely on the degree of *change* over the previous few years. Whatever their starting point, they all found that Greenland was now losing about 110 gigatons *more* ice every year than it had been losing (or, in Zwally's view, gaining) at the turn of the millennium. Greenland had begun to tip. And there was little reason to expect that the lead foot of global warming would be lifted from the accelerator in coming years or even decades.

Another benefit of Luthcke's unique approach to GRACE is that its fine resolution allows him and his collaborators to look at Greenland's watersheds individually. This adds to the confidence one might place in their overall result. Their November study found that high elevations were gaining mass, low elevations were losing it, and, obviously, the losses were winning out. Moreover, the greatest losses were occurring in the same watersheds that had registered increases in the frequency of "icequakes" as well as faster flow rates under radar interferometry. This was the global warming signal Zwally had described in his press release in the spring, only now it was stronger—as he had predicted. "Our new results suggest that the processes of significant ice depletion at the margins, through melting and glacier acceleration, are beginning to dominate the interior growth as climate warming has continued," the November paper concluded.

Please note that all three of these studies were funded by just the sort of Research and Analysis grant that Michael Griffin had drastically and quietly cut earlier in the year. Thus, at the same time that he was ignoring the need to build new satellites to carry on with these critical missions after GRACE and ICESat die, he was limiting the ability even to take advantage of them while they are alive.

Not surprisingly, the administrator continued to ignore the advice of the country's leading scientific organizations, the National Academy and the American Association for the Advancement of Science (AAAS). The opening words of a 400-page report released in January 2007 by the Academy's National Research Council (NRC) struck a similar tone to the Urgent Call to Action that was released by evangelicals and scientists only one day earlier: "Understanding the complex, changing planet on which we live, how it supports life, and how human activities affect its ability to do so in the future is one of the greatest intellectual challenges facing humanity. It is also one of the most important challenges for society as it seeks to achieve prosperity, health, and sustainability."

Characterizing "the United States' extraordinary foundation of global observations" as being "at great risk," the NRC estimated that by the end of the decade "the number of operating missions will decrease dramatically and the number of operating sensors and instruments on NASA spacecraft, most of which are well past their nominal lifetimes, will decrease by some 40 percent." Moreover, the sensors of the future would generally be lower in quality than the ones they were replacing; and in important cases a gap between the death of one satellite and the launch of its successor would preempt the calibration of a new sensor against the one it was replacing—a basic requirement in the long-term observation of a changing system. And although the crisis centered mainly on NASA, NOAA was in trouble, too: important aspects of weather prediction were even in jeopardy.

Griffin's response, in the budget he announced the following month, was to take even more money from science. He froze the NASA science budget for the next several years, removing even the 1 percent increases he had doled out in 2006. Congress has attempted to redress this action by authorizing money specifically for Research and Analysis, for example, but as Jim had remarked the previous year, "The corrective changes are moderate."

In restrained but unambiguous language, both the NRC report and a special statement issued by the board of the AAAS the following April pointed out that the crippling of the nation's ability to observe our planet had resulted not just from tightening budgets, but also, as the board put it, from "an explicit redirection of NASA's priorities away from Earth observation and toward missions to the Moon and Mars." Noting the surreptitious change that had been made to the agency's mission statement, they observed that the "aim of better exploring the Moon and Mars has attractions, but we agree with the sentiment expressed by the former chairman of the House Science Committee, Representative Sherwood Boehlert (R-NY), who observed at a hearing on this topic in April 2005 that 'The planet that has to matter most to us is the one we live on.'" (Boehlert had decided to retire from the House of Representatives long before it switched to Democratic control in the fall of 2006. Unfortunately, his able staffers David Goldston and Johannes Loschnigg left with him.)

And shortly after the scientists and evangelicals and the NRC issued their separate calls to action, the IPCC, in its own way, issued another: the panel began rolling out its fourth assessment report in February. These assessments are released in three phases, the first on the scientific basis, the second on the effects, and the third on mitigation, that is, what can be done. The first is always the most anticipated, as it usually provides some emblematic statement of the current level of uncertainty (always decreasing), and this one lived up to this billing. Global warming was "unequivocal," the panel stated. It was "evident from observations of increases in global average air and ocean temperatures, widespread melting of snow and ice, and rising global mean sea level," and it had been measured on every continent except Antarctica. (GISS scientists Drew Shindell and Gavin Schmidt had a good idea why the frozen continent had not joined in, of course, as well as a strong hunch that it was getting ready to.) "Most of the observed increase in globally averaged temperatures since the mid-20th century is very likely due to the observed increase in anthropogenic greenhouse gas concentrations," the panel affirmed. They also noted that the atmosphere had taken on water vapor "since at least the 1980s," in contradiction of Richard Lindzen's faith-based theory, and that it was "likely" that typhoons and hurricanes would "become more intense" in the future.

The second report, released in April, delivered the clear message that the effects of global warming are already here and that scientists are increasingly confident in their predictions for the future. While a moderate warming might prove beneficial to some regions, it would prove stressful to most; and at about the level of one degree Celsius, the allowance in Jim's alternative scenario, virtually all regions would be adversely affected—the poorest regions of the developing world disastrously. The third report, which strayed the closest to policy and was therefore the most indirect and poorly written, nevertheless came as close as any report from a gun-shy UN body possibly could to a call to action. The panel agreed with Jim and the A-team that effective technology to limit greenhouse emissions is available now, that the potential benefits far outweigh the costs—in fact, as the A-team found, that in many cases mitigation would provide immediate economic and health benefits—and that there is no time to lose.

Though the tone of this assessment was uniformly grim, even before the first release in February some scientists were complaining that it wasn't grim enough. Astoundingly, given the cascading events unfolding with increasing regularity in both polar regions, this assessment seemed to paint a rosier picture of sea level rise than the previous assessment in 2001: it seemed to lower the worst-case estimate of the rise this century from three feet to two. I say "seemed" because it was a case of poor communication more than anything else. Basically, even though the panel understood that the current ice sheet models were woefully insufficient—leaving out Zwally's lubricating meltwater effect, the uncorking effect of melting ice shelves, and other things—they published numbers from the models anyway, because they had nothing else to go on. The underlying science in the report was okay, and the caveats were there if you looked for them, but clarity might better have been served had they left the estimate blank rather than provide a misplaced peg for people to hang their hats on. The vast majority of news outlets got the story completely wrong, and the deniers found at least one reason to crow amidst the overall grimness—not realizing, evidently, that even two feet of sea level rise would not be a good thing. As Waleed Abdalati says, "Climate change in general typically has winners and losers. Some dry places will get wetter, some wet places will get drier, some cold places will get warmer, and some warm places will get colder. Sea level has nothing but losers. There's no benefit to that, and there aren't many things on Earth that are quite like that, frankly."

Since drafts were circulated beforehand, many scientists realized in advance that it might play out this way. A few days before the report was released, Lonnie Thompson of Ohio State University, perhaps the leading expert on the worldwide retreat of mountain glaciers, observed to the Associated Press that the panel had ignored "the gorillas—Greenland and Antarctica." The same AP story reported that Michael MacCracken had "fired off a letter of protest over the omission."

Jim's approach was to join a group of experts with complementary expertise in appropriate specialties to publish a preemptive strike, online in *Science,* the day before the report was released. The lead author of this one-page "brevia" was Stefan Rahmstorf of Germany's Potsdam Institute for Climate Impact Research, who had recently employed a "semiempirical" method (which also ignored the Zwally and champagne cork effects) to estimate that the seas would rise between twenty inches and five feet by 2100. The new preemptive brevia simply compared previous IPCC projections with observations and showed that ever since the projections had begun in 1990, temperature changes have consistently landed near the upper bound of the panel's projections, and sea level rise has greatly exceeded them.

Understand that this entire argument was about the *rate* of sea level rise, not the total amount. The IPCC concurred with Jim that business-as-usual would probably lead to the highest temperatures since the Eemian interglacial, 125,000 years ago, when sea level was between four and six meters (thirteen and twenty feet) higher. No one was saying we wouldn't get there eventually; they just had different notions of how long it would take. But the question of speed was generally agreed to be more pertinent to society.

In March, as the flurry was dying down, Jim circulated an essay entitled "Scientific Reticence and Sea Level Rise," in which he argued that a cultural tradition of reticence was preventing his colleagues from communicating their true understanding of the dangers. "Scientific reticence may be a consequence of the scientific method," he wrote. "Success in science depends on objective skepticism. Caution, if not reticence, has its merits. However, in a case such as ice sheet instability and sea level rise, there is a danger in excessive caution. We may rue reticence, if it serves to lock in future disasters. . . .

As a physicist," he wrote, "I find it almost inconceivable that business-as-usual climate change would not yield a sea level change of the order of meters on the century timescale." And as far as he could tell from discussions with his colleagues, his view was not unusual. Yet there had been little open discussion of this dangerous possibility, even in scientific circles. It reminded him of his experience at the meeting in Amherst in 1989, which *Science* reporter Richard Kerr had summarized in his article "Hansen vs. the World on the Greenhouse Threat."

It may be a sign of an epochal shift in the culture of climate science that in June 2007, about eighteen years after he wrote that article, the same Richard Kerr chose to write another news article about Jim, contrasting those early days with the present. "Climate modeler James Hansen knows all about sounding the alarm," the story began. But this time around, Kerr found Jim "at the head of an informal movement." He seemed to be "out on a limb, again," but this time he had company. "No longer reticent, other scientists are going public about how bad things might get by the end of the century." Now, instead of whispering to Kerr in the halls, quite a few spoke openly, expressing concern on a par with Jim's. NASA glaciologist Bob Thomas, an expert on the ice sheets who disagrees strenuously with Jay Zwally's conservative mass balance estimates, told Kerr that scientists need to find a way to explore the extreme end of the possibilities "so we can communicate with the public without becoming scaremongers." Thomas felt that there had to be "a better way" than the IPCC approach of science by democratic consensus.

Jim was relying on far more than intuition in finding it "inconceivable" that business-as-usual would not yield a sea level rise of some meters this century. For in the year and more since the censorship episode, as he had been taking the news of our dangerous proximity to a tipping point to so many different audiences, he had been working furiously on hard science in the background. What he termed "crystallizing scientific data and analyses" had brought him to a new, more sobering level of realization about the extreme sensitivity of the climate system.

If one looks at the history of global warming science, one will find that as the science has improved, both the certainty and the magnitude of the danger have nearly always increased. Jim is not the only one to have been surprised in this way. The entire community has experienced a series of sobering realizations over the past fifty or sixty years.

This time, he had followed his usual two-pronged approach of looking at the real world on the one hand and modeling it on the other. There had been some frustration on the modeling end. In collaboration with more than forty other scientists, he had prepared a major new study with GISS's latest global circulation model by the time of his Keeling talk. This was the paper he burrowed away to work on after he returned from San Francisco on the red-eye. He had hoped to finish it by the end of 2005, but it took almost a year and a half to get it published, owing partly to distractions, partly to the extraordinary length and detail of the study—and possibly to scientific reticence, for the paper was entitled "Dangerous Human-Made Interference with Climate," and it attacked this "subjective" question head-on.

On the other hand, the delay may have been a good thing, since his work on the other side—looking at new paleoclimate data—added to his understanding and fed back to the modeling work. Meanwhile, all his traveling and communicating gave him a better view of the economic and political landscape and taught him more about the epochal transformation that is happening right now to so many aspects of our world. By the spring of 2007, Jim was bursting with things to say, working on six different papers at the same time, all of which referenced and built on one another. One was on scientific reticence; a second discussed the climatic implications of peak oil; a third, "The State of the Wild," focused on climate and biodiversity; and the final three were extensive and highly technical reports on paleoclimate and his latest GCM work. (The huge original paper had been split in two.) This tour de force explored his current worldview in extensive detail.

During one eventful week in late April, everything came together, and he and his group got the last few papers into the press. Actually, they just missed the Friday 5 P.M. deadline for one, so it went in Monday morning. That gave him two days to prepare his testimony for Massachusetts congressman Edward Markey's Select Committee on Energy Independence and Global Warming, which had recently come into being under the new Democratic leadership. This testimony, which Jim posted to his Columbia Web site, expresses the pith of his latest thinking.

He says he is most proud of the paleoclimate work. After all, he has always believed that the real world provides the proof, and the modeling is there mostly for support. The seabed core from the Pacific warm pool was just one of about six records, including a "stack" of globally distributed seabed cores comprising a composite record going back more than 5 million years, that he synthesized in a dense, twenty-six-page paper in the *Philosophical Transactions* of the Royal Society of London. As usual, he tossed out new insights left and right, including, for example, quite a plausible explanation as to why, something more than a million years ago, climate switched from a "41,000-year world," where it was dominated by the tilt of the planetary axis, to a "100,000-year world," where it was dominated by the eccentricity of the orbit. (Believe it or not, he explained that one to the congressmen and -women on Markey's committee.)

He put the third Vostok ice core, recovered in 1998, together with three records of sea level to show that the venerable Charney estimate for climate sensitivity—3°C for a doubling of carbon dioxide—seems right as far as it goes, but that it is almost certainly low. Jim tells me this is the most important message of his recent work.

Remember that the first Vostok ice core, which he had analyzed in 1990 with the French group, reached back 160,000 years. This third core reached back 420,000 years, so both are confined to the 100,000-year world. The bubbles in the ice from the third core yield records for three greenhouse gases: carbon dioxide, methane, and nitrous oxide. First, Jim showed that the calculated greenhouse forcing from these three gases

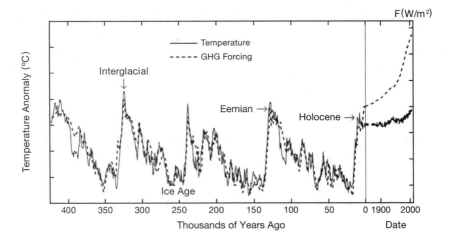

Greenhouse gas forcing in watts per square meter (W/m²) along with temperature fluctuations for the past 420,000 years. The data to the left of the vertical
line come from the third Vostok ice core. The GISS group uses the levels of
three greenhouse gases as recorded by air bubbles trapped in the ice to calculate forcing. Temperatures are inferred from the ratio of hydrogen isotopes in
the ice. The data to the right of the line come from in situ measurements of atmospheric greenhouse gases and from GISS temperature measurements. The
zero point of temperature corresponds to the average global temperature from
1880 to 1889. The zero point of forcing corresponds to its preindustrial value.
Owing to polar amplification, temperature fluctuations at Vostok are twice
those of the planet as a whole, so in order for the scales to match, the measured temperature anomaly has been multiplied by a factor of two to produce
the curve to the right of the line.

(keep in mind that this is a numerical calculation, not a GCM) tracks the
temperature at Vostok incredibly well.

The main section of this graph, with the compressed timescale, shows
Vostok temperatures and greenhouse forcing. Over the past 420,000 years—
during which all changes would have been "natural," presumably—the
temperature changes led the greenhouse changes by a few hundred years
or so, too short a time to distinguish in the graph. This is expected, since
the changes were instigated by orbital oscillations. These affected the distribution of incoming sunlight over seasons and latitudes and caused initial, small changes in temperature, which then led to walloping feedbacks.

During a warming, such as the one that began 130,000 years ago and led to the Eemian interglacial, the oceans, soils, and biosphere gave off greenhouse gases; and this boosted temperatures dramatically. Notice that the warmings took place much more rapidly than the coolings.

In the modern industrial age, on the right, the manmade greenhouse changes—which are, obviously, not the result of feedback—have led the temperature changes, owing to the delaying effect of the oceans. Temperature didn't change much at first, but it has picked up in the last thirty years. The temperature curve has now assumed the classic shape of exponential growth. Along with greenhouse forcing, it is getting steeper and steeper every year.

If the right-hand timescale were compressed to match the left, the greenhouse forcing of the industrial era would appear as a vertical "spike." It should be obvious that this constitutes a jolt to dwarf any this planet has received in the 420,000 years of the Vostok record. In fact, it is unprecedented in a few million years.

At the depth of an ice age—and you can see that there are four, roughly 100,000 years apart—the polar ice sheets would have reached maximum extent. They grow mostly in the Arctic, on the surfaces of North America and northern Europe, because there is no land besides Antarctica, which was covered with ice all through this period, to support them in the south. As the planet warmed, of course, polar sea ice and the northern ice sheets would have melted. This would have caused sea levels to rise, and at the same time dramatically lowered the reflectivity of the entire planet, leading to another powerful feedback. Thus, it is not surprising that sea level also tracks temperature and greenhouse gas levels.

The top graph on the next page shows a record of sea level derived from a core drilled in the bed of the Red Sea. The middle graph shows the changes in the planet's reflectivity that Jim calculates from this record of sea level, along with the greenhouse changes from Vostok. Notice that they track each other rather well. To calculate reflectivity, Jim makes reasonable assumptions about where and how much of the planet's surface would have been covered in ice. The bottom graph shows observed temperatures again, now with the temperatures he calculates, based purely on the measured

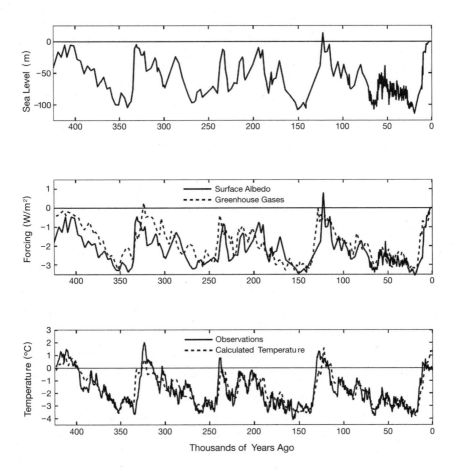

Top: Sea level for the past 420,000 years, from M. Siddall, E. J. Rohling, A. Almogi-Labin, Ch. Hemleben, D. Meischner, I. Schmelzer, and D. A. Smeed, 2003. Sea-level fluctuations during the last glacial cycle. *Nature* 423:853–58. Zero corresponds to the level of today.

Middle: Forcing in watts per square meter caused by changes in the Earth's surface albedo (reflectivity) as deduced from the sea levels in the top graph, along with the forcing calculated from greenhouse gas levels in the third Vostok ice core. In this and the bottom graph, zeros correspond to preindustrial values.

Bottom: Measured temperatures in the Vostok ice core along with calculated temperatures based on the measured forcings from the middle graph. Climate sensitivity, the only adjustable parameter in these calculations, is set to the Charney value of 3°C for a doubling of the preindustrial level of carbon dioxide.

greenhouse levels from Vostok and reflectivity calculated from measured sea levels, along with the Charney value for climate sensitivity, 3°C. Again, this is not a computer simulation, it is a numerical calculation.

To my mind, the close match between calculation (theory, if you like) and observation shows that Jim Hansen understands climate pretty well and doesn't need a global circulation model to do it. It also provides empirical evidence of the serious risk we are running by spiking our atmosphere with greenhouse gases.

Now Jim steps outside the box. He noted in 1990 that this empirical method of calculating climate sensitivity accounts for feedbacks implicitly and therefore validates the GCMs. But in the new Royal Society paper, he points out that the empirical method accounts only for what he calls "fast" or "Charney" feedbacks—changes in water vapor, aerosols, clouds, and sea ice—because greenhouse levels and the size of the polar ice sheets are specified in this calculation; they are in a sense the ground on which the calculation stands. Jim always knew that they were feedbacks—among the most powerful feedbacks—but he had assumed that they were so slow that they would not come into play for centuries or millennia. But the ice sheets are changing dramatically right now, melting arctic tundra is sending millions of tons of carbon dioxide and methane into the air every year, and, in another "slow" feedback that was unforeseen by Charney, forests are migrating toward the poles. As evergreens replace tundra and scrubland, the surface becomes much darker, because trees are in fact "designed" to capture light efficiently, for photosynthesis.

This means that the ground is now shifting: the slow feedbacks are already kicking in. The computer models are much more sluggish than the real world. And climate is significantly more sensitive than Jim believed even two years ago.

In his extensive review of the paleoclimate record, Jim found "no evidence of millennial lags between forcing and ice sheet response." But he *did* find ample evidence that significant portions of the ice sheets have disintegrated in a matter of centuries in the past. At the end of the most recent ice age about 14,000 years ago, for example, the seas rose between three and five meters per century for four centuries in a row. That's one meter, or three feet, every twenty years, and it adds up to a total rise of twenty meters or sixty-six feet.

If Richard Lindzen were interested in the truth of this matter, he might be disappointed to learn that the main culprit here is probably the substance in which he has placed so much faith: "water in all its phases."

As Jim writes in the abstract to the Royal Society paper (in rather incendiary prose for a staid, peer-reviewed journal), "One feedback, the 'albedo flip' property of ice/water, provides a powerful trigger mechanism. A climate forcing that 'flips' the albedo of a sufficient portion of an ice sheet can spark a cataclysm." He is saying that when the ice on the surface of a glacier begins to melt, the quick structural change in the material itself allows it to absorb as much as three times the incoming sunlight that it did before. This makes an enormous difference. "Albedo flip" has been the main driver of the global retreat of mountain glaciers that began to accelerate in the early eighties. They react much more quickly than the ice sheets because they're smaller.

As Jay Zwally knows, the meltwater produced by such a flip also softens the underlying ice, seeps through to the bed, and helps the whole thing slide into the sea. He has shown that it is precisely at the line where surface melting begins that the Greenland ice sheet has begun to move more rapidly. Others have shown that the area of summer melt in Greenland increased from 173,000 square miles in 1979 to 231,000 square miles more recently. And as the ice flips and melts and then slips and lurches toward the sea, its surface drops to lower and warmer altitudes, which is another positive feedback. This basic story line has already led to the disappearance of an entire 700-cubic-mile ice field in Glacier Bay, Alaska, which has contributed almost eight millimeters to sea level all by itself.

It all adds up to something Jim has been saying for years: that these sloppy, wet processes are inherently fast—or, as he says, "cataclysmic"—while the dry process of snow deposition that allows ice sheets to grow is very slow. This also explains one of the more basic pieces of paleoclimatic evidence: the asymmetry of the Vostok data, the fact that the warmings happened so much more rapidly than the coolings.

For some reason, most of the attention has focused on Greenland, when the gravest threat is most likely posed by West Antarctica. The West Antarctic ice sheet, similar in size to Greenland's, harbors the frozen equivalent of about five meters or sixteen feet of sea level rise; and everyone agrees that it is losing mass. One coastal region there, near the Amundsen Sea, has been called "the weak underbelly of Antarctica," because a few major ice streams, such as the Pine Island and Thwaites glaciers, converge to form the ice shelf there. In the event of catastrophic collapse it is even possible that the gargantuan East Antarctic ice sheet, which holds a terrifying 230 feet of sea level, could drain to this region through a gap located in an unfortunate spot in the Transantarctic Mountains.

It seems that up until now the main mechanism draining West Antarctica has been the gradual pulling loose of its champagne corks. Warming ocean water has been eating away at the bottom of the ice shelf in the vicinity of the weak underbelly and causing it to thin at the amazing rate of eighteen feet per year over the past decade. (The shelf is 200 to 300 feet thick.) As a result, the underwater grounding lines of the glacial plugs (or corks) are moving inland. But a team from the Jet Propulsion Laboratory and the University of Colorado, Boulder, has recently surprised the research community by announcing that they detected widespread melting on the *surface* of the West Antarctic ice sheet in January 2005, using NASA's QuikScat satellite. The total area of the melting was about the size of the state of California, portions were as close as 310 miles to the south pole and at altitudes of more than 6,000 feet, and temperatures reached more than five degrees Celsius (forty-one degrees Fahrenheit) for about a week.

Meanwhile, according to Drew Shindell and Gavin Schmidt, as well as the new GISS modeling study, Antarctica as a whole is expected to reverse course and start warming over the next few decades; and even a moderate sea level rise stands to lift the buttressing ice shelves and, as Jim puts it, "unhinge the ice from pinning points."

Waleed Abdalati says, "Those are dynamics that are only going to work one way. I don't see that getting better." And Jim writes in the Royal Society paper, "We find it implausible that business-as-usual scenarios . . . would permit a West Antarctic ice sheet of present size to survive even for a century."

With this as a backdrop, it is no surprise that the forty-seven authors of the new modeling study found Earth's climate to be "close to critical tipping points, with potentially dangerous consequences for the planet"—this from the lead of the accompanying press release, which, according to Jim, "sailed through NASA public affairs, who, indeed, were very helpful."

The authors also took the unprecedented step, utterly avoided by the IPCC, of putting the marker down. They concluded "that a CO_2 level exceeding about 450 parts per million is 'dangerous,' but reduction of non-CO_2 forcings can provide modest relief on the CO_2 constraint." The dangerous limit was determined with the aid of their global circulation model, of course, which also shows that the GISS alternative scenario keeps the level below this limit, while *every* business-as-usual scenario envisioned by the IPCC does not. Of course, this also means that the business-as-usual scenarios exceed the temperature limit that the alternative scenario was designed to meet: no more than 1°C in additional warming after the year 2000. In fact, the most pessimistic IPCC scenario attains almost three degrees by the end of this century, and they all keep temperatures rising in the twenty-second century.

It is relevant to remind ourselves of some paleoclimate evidence here. As Jim showed me in the paper we reviewed at his breakfast table in early 2006, the last time temperatures were three degrees warmer than today was in the mid-Pliocene, more than 3 million years ago. Seabed records yield evidence that the level of atmospheric carbon dioxide was not more than 425 parts per million in those ancient times—"it seems unlikely that the mid-Pliocene warm period was a doubled CO_2 world," the study's authors noted. Yet sea level was about twenty-five meters or eighty feet higher in the mid-Pliocene than it is today.

More than a billion people presently live within twenty-five meters of sea level.

In his out-of-the-box way, Jim argues that the low ceiling presented by the tipping point of sea level actually has a bright side: "It implies an imperative: we must find a way to keep the CO_2 amount so low that it will also avert other detrimental effects that had begun to seem inevitable, e.g., ocean acidification, loss of most alpine glaciers and thus the water supply for millions of people, and shifting of climatic zones with consequent extermination of species." Other incidentals include the preservation of the Arctic, the ways of life of its indigenous peoples and the habitat of the polar bear, and a great reduction in air pollution, thus "restoring a more pristine, healthy planet."

It's great that the press release for the modeling paper "sailed" through public affairs, but one can't help but wonder at the timing of the remarks Michael Griffin made to a reporter from National Public Radio as the release was working its way through his public affairs department, a few days before it would go public. This was near the end of May 2007.

"I can't say" whether global warming "is a long-term concern," the administrator told the reporter. "I have no doubt that global—that a trend of global warming exists. I am not sure that it is fair to say that it is a problem we must wrestle with. To assume that it is a problem is to assume that the state of Earth's climate today is the optimal climate, the best climate that we could have or ever have had, and that we need to take steps to make sure that it doesn't change. First of all, I don't think it's within the power of human beings to assure that the climate does not change, as millions of years of history have shown, and second of all, I guess I would ask which human beings—where and when—are to be accorded the privilege of deciding that this particular climate that we have right here today, right now, is the best climate for all other human beings. I think that's a rather arrogant position for people to take."

This from the man who, despite the cuts he had made to his Earth science budget, led the organization that did more climate-related research than any other single organization in the world. As Jerry Mahlman, the former director of the Geophysical Fluid Dynamics Laboratory, told *The New York Times,* these remarks demonstrated that Mr. Griffin was either "totally clueless" or "a deep anti–global warming ideologue." A few days earlier, Griffin had written a carefully worded letter to *The Washington Post* that would indicate to the unaware that he had actually increased NASA's support for Earth science in his tenure.

There is uncertainty about the danger level, and it is not reassuring. The mid-Pliocene seabed record seems to set the dangerous limit somewhere below 425 parts per million, while Jim's Royal Society paper states, "We have presented evidence [in the modeling paper] that the dangerous level of CO_2 can be no more than approximately 450 parts per million. Our present discussion, including the conclusion that slow feedbacks (ice, vegetation and greenhouse gases) can come into play on century time-scales or sooner, makes it probable that the dangerous level is even lower."

The forty-seven authors of the modeling paper use estimates by the U.S. Energy Information Administration of future growth in oil and gas reserves to show that "full exploitation" of these two fuels would take atmospheric carbon dioxide to 450 parts per million all by themselves. Therefore, they write, it is absolutely essential that coal be "phased out over the next several decades except for uses where the CO_2 produced can be captured and sequestered" and that "the massive amounts of unconventional fossil fuels"—tar sands, shale oil, gasified coal, and the like—be subject to the same constraint.

The remarkable thing about these two recommendations is that Jim first voiced them, tentatively, in the 1981 *Science* paper that kicked off his long string of accurate predictions. His present understanding is precise enough mathematically that he is no longer tentative.

The likely possibility that global oil production will peak and subsequently decline sometime this century, so-called peak oil, increases the pressure to resort to unconventional fuels. For this reason, Jim and a GISS postdoc, Pushker Kharecha, explored the climatic implications of peak oil in one of the six papers that were simultaneously released. They fed a number of different fuel use scenarios into their global circulation model, subject to a sensible peak oil constraint. This demonstrated that if Jim's alternative scenario is to be met, it will be necessary to stretch the supplies of conveniently mobile oil and natural gas, both through efficiency and through the judicious use of a carbon tax, a notion that will be explored in a moment. The stretching of mobile fuel sources makes sense irrespective of its climatic implications. Indeed peak oil enthusiasts have been pointing this out for years.

Unfortunately, the modeling paper presents evidence that things have been going the wrong way, recently. Since the A-team looked at emissions growth rates in 2001, they have increased from 1.3 percent to about 2 percent per year, and there has been an uptick in coal use. Coal seems "poised to retake from oil the role of the largest current CO_2 source." One of the main reasons is the incredible rate of coal-fired power plant construction in China right now. That country has recently passed the United States as the leading emitter of carbon dioxide, though on a per capita basis the citizens of China still produce less than a fifth the emissions of their U.S. counterparts. And if you look at cumulative emissions since the beginning of the industrial era, the United States is way out in front and will remain so for the next several decades—in other words, the United States will continue to bear the greatest overall responsibility for the changes that are already under way. Furthermore, a significant fraction of China's emissions should rightfully be attributed to the United States, since they arise from the manufacturing of consumer products for American markets.

The introduction to the modeling paper contains a warning that the last section "goes one step beyond the usual scientific paper":

> These stark conclusions about the threat posed by global climate change and implications for fossil fuel use are not yet appreciated

by essential governing bodies, as evidenced by ongoing plans to build coal-fired power plants without CO_2 capture and sequestration. In our view, there is an acute need for science to inform society about the costs of failure to address global warming, because of a fundamental difference between the threat posed by climate change and most prior global threats.

In the nuclear standoff between the Soviet Union and United States, a crisis could be precipitated only by action of one of the parties. In contrast, the present threat to the planet and civilization, with the United States and China now the principal players (though . . . Europe also has a large responsibility), requires only inaction in the face of clear scientific evidence of the danger.

Thus scientists are faced with difficult choices between communication of scientific information to the public and focus on basic research, as there are inherent compromises in any specific balance. Former American Vice President Al Gore, at a plenary session of the December 2006 meeting of the American Geophysical Union, challenged earth scientists to become involved in informing the public about global climate change. The overwhelmingly positive audience reaction to his remarks provides hope that the large gap between scientific understanding and public knowledge about climate change may yet be closed.

At Jim's invitation, Gore had spoken at the AGU meeting in December 2006, one year after the Keeling talk. More than 6,000 scientists—almost half the attendees of the conference—had packed themselves into the largest ballroom at the San Francisco Marriott, as well as an adjacent room connected by video, to hear Mr. Gore speak.

Jim is doing his best to close the gap. In his testimony to Ed Markey's committee, he presented clear recommendations:

First, we must phase out the use of coal and unconventional fossil fuels except where the CO_2 is captured and sequestered.

There should be a moratorium on construction of old-technology coal-fired power plants.

Second, there must be a rising price (tax) on carbon emissions, as well as effective energy efficiency standards, and removal of barriers to efficiency. These actions are needed to spur innovation in energy efficiency and renewable energies, and thus to stretch oil and gas supplies to cover the need for mobile fuels during the transition to the next phase of the industrial revolution "beyond petroleum."

Third, there should be focused efforts to reduce non-CO_2 human-made climate forcings, especially methane, ozone and black carbon.

Fourth, steps must be taken to "draw down" atmospheric CO_2 via improved farming and forestry practices, including burning of biofuels in power plants with CO_2 sequestration.

As Jim sees it, the most important barrier in the second recommendation is the incentive on the part of utility companies to sell more electricity, rather than promote efficiency. It seems obvious that it will take some sort of government regulation to achieve such a major transformation in the habits of so powerful an industry—and that, given the stranglehold this industry has exercised over the federal government lately, it will take a vibrant grassroots democratic movement to spark the government to action.

Many economists, including Alan Greenspan, former chairman of the Federal Reserve, see the sense in imposing a tax on carbon emissions. Jim clarifies his recommendation about a "rising price (tax)" by pointing out that it could be "composed of one or more of a carbon tax, industry 'cap and trade,' or individual 'ration and trade,' chosen for economic effectiveness and fairness." But he and most economists agree that the most straightforward and effective mechanism would be a simple tax applied to all emissions, be they from cars, electrical plants, heating systems, or whatever. Most suggest that it be "revenue neutral," that it be offset by a cut in payroll taxes, for example.

No elected officials of any consequence showed the nerve to propose such an idea until Democrat John Dingell of Michigan brought it up in the summer of 2007. Many doubted the sincerity of Dingell's proposal, since he had consistently backed the automobile industry in his fifty-two years in Congress and he had recently voted yet again against increased mileage standards. Indeed, when he first mentioned the carbon tax proposal, he told C-SPAN that he doubted "the American people are willing to pay what this is really going to cost them"; he just wanted "to sort of see how people really feel about this." But Mr. Dingell professes to a recent change of heart about global warming. We'll see.

Jim's fourth recommendation is new, and it springs from his dawning realization that we may already have passed a tipping point. The idea is to employ the burning of biomass to *extract* carbon dioxide from the air. For various reasons, corn is a bad idea. Sugarcane may be better; but both hold out the danger of increasing the cost of food, which would hit the poor especially hard. There is more promise in the use of agricultural waste; natural grasses, such as switchgrass; and in new bioengineered cellulosic fibers.

Simple biomass burning can be renewable in the sense that as you burn it and then grow more, you first send carbon into the air and then remove it. If you were to combine this with carbon sequestration as the biomass was burned, you would actually draw down the amount of carbon dioxide in the air. The scale would have to be massive: huge biomass-burning power plants in the interiors of continents with pipelines carrying the captured carbon dioxide to the coasts for sequestration in the deep ocean below the bed—the best place to put it, according to the latest thinking. "The potential of these 'amber waves of grain' and coastal facilities for permanent underground storage 'from sea to shining sea' to help restore America's technical prowess, moral authority and prestige, for the sake of our children and grandchildren, in the course of helping to solve the climate problem, has not escaped our attention," reads the final footnote in the Royal Society paper.

*　*　*

As of September 2007, Jim Hansen remains deeply engaged in his life's work. For more than twenty years now, he has been trying to wake the world to the dangers of global warming. He has improved the science; he has proposed solutions; he has constantly spoken truth to power. He continues to work his eighty-hour weeks. He strives to maintain his equanimity as he watches us move closer and closer to the cliff's edge. Jim is acutely aware that no real progress is being made. The bottom line is that emissions continue to grow every year and look as though they will grow for the foreseeable future. This is the only measure that counts. The battle has just begun.

He saw how quickly fossil fuel interests moved in and quashed all movement toward change when he first "shifted global warming from science to the policy realm" in 1988, so he knows how furiously they will tighten their grip if the status quo seems truly threatened again.

He realizes that the censors and deniers (or contrarians) and leaders of government agencies who have taken up a significant fraction of the present story are only bit players. Not only that, they have succeeded yet again simply by taking up so much of this story: so much of his and so many other people's time and energy over the last twenty months. Anything that distracts and delays constructive action serves their purpose.

"Make no doubt," he writes, "if tipping points are passed, if we, in effect, destroy Creation, passing on to our children, grandchildren, and the unborn a situation out of their control, the contrarians who work to deny and confuse will not be the principal culprits. The contrarians will be remembered as court jesters. There is no point to joust with court jesters. They will always be present. They will continue to entertain even if the *Titanic* begins to take on water. Their role and consequence is only as a diversion from what is important.

"The real deal is this: the 'royalty' controlling the court, the ones with the power, the ones with the ability to make a difference, with the ability to change our course, the ones who will live in infamy if we pass the tipping points, are the captains of industry, CEOs in fossil fuel companies such as ExxonMobil, automobile manufacturers, utilities, all of the leaders who have placed short-term profit above the fate of the planet and the well-being of our children. The court jesters are their jesters, occasionally paid for services, and more substantively supported by the captains' disinformation campaigns. . . . The captains of industry are smarter than their jesters. They cannot pretend that they are unaware of climate change dangers and consequences for future generations."

It is now more than a year since Jim helped shift the discussion from science to the policy realm for a second time. There has been much talk, but little action. Bills that won't do much anyway plod through a divided Congress in which neither party takes an undivided stand. None have been signed into law. In April, the Supreme Court ruled in favor of Massachusetts and the scientists who supported it, agreeing that the federal government has the authority to regulate greenhouse emissions from cars and trucks; but there is little expectation that the government will exercise that authority under the present administration. As one expert told *The New York Times,* "This flips the debate from an environment in which Congress must act if there is to be federal action to one in which the EPA can act as soon as an administration friendly to the concept is in power."

Jim knows that this battle is fundamentally about democracy. He has been quoting the Constitution and the Founding Fathers a lot lately. He believes that while American democracy may be crippled by the influence of special interests, it is not yet dead. He knows the American people still hold the power. This is why he has worked energetically for the past year and a half on education and spreading the word.

This past spring, he gave the commencement talk at his high school in Denison, Iowa. He tells the story of driving from Denison to Dunlap, the town where his parents are buried. "For most of twenty miles," he writes, "there were trains parked, engine to caboose, half of the cars being filled with coal.

"If we cannot stop the building of more coal-fired power plants, those coal trains will be death trains—no less gruesome than if they were boxcars headed to crematoria, loaded with uncountable irreplaceable species."

He returned to his home state in early August, to join the final, hot day of a march to "ReEnergize Iowa." He spoke to his fellow marchers at the rally in Des Moines at the march's end. Stepping up to the microphone after a pastor who had mentioned stewardship, he opened by noting that the pastor's words "fit very well" with those he was about to deliver. He then introduced a Declaration of Stewardship for the Earth and All Creation to be presented to every candidate in the 2008 elections, in order to make her or his position clear on each of the following points:

> Declaration 1. Moratorium on Dirty Coal. I will support a moratorium on construction of coal-fired power plants that do not capture and store CO_2.

> Declaration 2. A Price on Carbon Emissions. I will support a gradually rising price on carbon emissions, reflecting costs to the environment, with mechanisms to adjust the price that are economically sound. A first step will be to eliminate subsidies of fossil fuels.

> Declaration 3. Increased Energy Efficiency and No-Carbon Energy Sources. I will support effective actions to increase energy efficiency and conservation, remove barriers to efficiency, and increase use of low-carbon and no-carbon energy sources.

He is trying to rally young people especially around the crucial need for a moratorium on traditional coal-fired power plants, for he believes the livability of the planet in their lifetimes is very much at stake.

It was his consideration of the obligation that every generation should feel for those who follow that led to this story in the first place. And it wasn't theoretical. Jim was at home with his children and grandchildren over the Christmas holidays in December 2005, still unsure how, or if, he should respond to the particular set of jesters who were hounding him at the moment. As he told Tom Ashbrook a few weeks later, during the NPR interview that headquarters had hoped to prevent, "In thinking about whether I was going to speak up or not, what really brought me to this conclusion was, I don't want, in the future, my grandchildren to say,

'Opa understood what was going to happen, but he didn't make it clear.' And so I'm trying to make it clear." (Actually, the plan was for the two grandchildren, Sophie and Connor, to call Jim and Anniek "Opa" and "Oma" in the Dutch way; but Sophie, the oldest, began calling Jim "Bopa" and the name has stuck.)

In July 2007, Jim was invited to participate in Al Gore's Live Earth, a benefit to raise awareness of global warming, the largest "concert for a cause" ever held. There were performances on all seven continents, including Antarctica. Jim agreed, on the condition that he could take Sophie and Connor along. There was a small communications problem. He had thought that he, his grandchildren, and Mr. Gore would appear together on the stage and have an impromptu chat. But when Jim and his extended family arrived at Giants Stadium in New Jersey, he learned that he and the two kids would be going onstage in front of tens of thousands of people alone. Also—no problem for Jim—he had to prepare some words for the teleprompter right away. The previous day, he had told eight-year-old Sophie that he might ask her about saving animals from global warming, but it was too loud to talk to her backstage.

They went on between Jon Bon Jovi and Smashing Pumpkins. As for the animals, Sophie said we should try to save "all of them." Three-year-old Connor agreed:

"Me, too."

Sources and Suggested Reading

The best source of information about Jim Hansen's work would be Jim himself. He posts his most important talks and general interest papers on his personal Web page at Columbia University (www.columbia.edu/ ~jeh1). He also posts periodic notices to an e-mail list, and it is possible to sign on to this list on the Columbia page. I particularly recommend Jim's April 2007 testimony to the House Select Committee on Energy Independence and Global Warming, since it synthesizes his current thinking. His NASA institute, the Goddard Institute for Space Studies, maintains a Web site at www.giss.nasa.gov, where one can download Jim's scientific papers and those of his GISS colleagues and find other useful and educational information about climate science and climate research.

It was beyond the scope of this book to tell all the gory details of the possibly criminal and certainly immoral campaign that special interests have waged to obscure the true science and prevent any effective action against devastating climate change. Much of that story has been told by Ross Gelbspan in two books, *The Heat Is On* (Addison-Wesley, 1997) and *Boiling Point* (Basic Books, 2004), as well as an article in the June 1998 issue of *The Atlantic*. The last is the source for the quote about the ICE public relations campaign that appears on page 237. More has been revealed recently in *Redacting the Science of Climate Change* by Tarek Maassarani of the Government Accountability Project and *Smoke, Mirrors & Hot Air* by the Union of Concerned Scientists. These reports, which can be downloaded from the GAP (www.whistleblower.org) and UCS (www .ucsusa.org) Web sites, inform sections of chapters 5, 6, and 7. The UCS report is particularly informative. For insights into the first critical days of the Bush-Cheney administration, I highly recommend *The Price of Loyalty* by Ron Suskind (Simon & Schuster, 2004), which is mentioned in Chapter 5.

If certain passages in chapters 8 and 9 seem familiar, that is because they are based on passages from my first book, *Thin Ice* (Henry Holt, 2005). These chapters also benefited from two interviews that Erik Conway of the Jet Propulsion Laboratory conducted with Jim in January 2006, and which Jim shared with me.

We decided early on to forgo footnotes and endnotes in this book. Therefore, I have made some effort in the text to reveal the sources for the pieces of information that I did not uncover on my own. The creative use of a Web-based search engine will turn up most of the relevant news articles, and most of the scientific papers mentioned in the book will be found on the Web sites of the scientists who wrote them. I am intending to post more sources on my own Web site, www.mark-bowen.com.

Acknowledgments

You might be surprised to learn that the experience of writing this book has left me with a sense of admiration for the vast majority of the public servants who work in our federal government. With the exception of a few political appointees, I found virtually everyone I met at NASA and in the House of Representatives to be honest, intelligent, dedicated, professional, and good at what they do. It was inspiring for me to be able to share in their dedication and courage as each, in his or her own way, went through a human struggle to tell the truth in the face of very real dangers. Most had been waiting for the opportunity.

It is inappropriate to rank people on the basis of the courage they seem to have shown, because everyone's circumstances and vulnerability are unique. I would like to single out Gretchen Cook-Anderson, however, first for telling me her story and then for allowing me to include it. Her struggle probably *was* the most difficult. It went through stages and took about three months—not counting the suffering she endured in order to have a story in the first place. She finally allowed me to tell it, she said, "because it's the right thing to do." Gretchen still has a young family to raise and to support. She has already experienced the sort of abuse that can be meted out even on a supposedly protected civil servant, and in her present position she does not have civil servant protection.

I would also like to recognize Leslie McCarthy for her courage, her honesty, her professionalism, and her help. It was her willingness to talk to *The New York Times* that made this particular round of censorship visible, after all. Leslie and her notes (which she never showed to me, by the way) were the key to unraveling the other parts of the story. She was not necessarily aware of everything—Gretchen's travails, for instance—but she recorded and shared central details that provided the ground for further investigation. Thanks to both Leslie and Gretchen for reviewing the sections of the manuscript in which their stories were involved.

Special thanks go to Waleed Abdalati for coming forth with his own censorship stories, for sharing his scientific insight, and for reviewing relevant parts of the manuscript. Jay Zwally shared his insights, stories, unpublished data, and sense of humor, and also reviewed portions of the manuscript.

David Goldston and Johannes Loschnigg helped me work through the confusion of contradictory stories about the events of December 2005 through February 2006. I was impressed by their openness and integrity. Not only did they agree to be interviewed, they engaged in a lot of back-and-forth, and they eventually decided to let me use everything they said. Johannes also educated me about NASA budgets.

Bill Blakemore provided me with his recollections and with transcripts of his broadcasts. More importantly, though, he shared his insights into the practice and philosophy of journalism, the philosophy of science, the thuggery of the deniers, and Jim Hansen's "radical innocence." I shall remember my interactions with Bill as high points of this experience.

Andy Revkin was generous in sharing his insights as well, along with as much of the backstory as he could, given the professional and ethical constraints of investigative journalism. In fact, Andy taught me a lot about those constraints—and, within them, managed to point me in fruitful directions.

Paul Thacker freely shared the FOIA documents he had obtained from NOAA.

Makiko Sato designed the graphs in the final chapter.

Returning to NASA again, very special thanks to Dolores Beasley and Dwayne Brown. My nearly three-hour conversation with Dwayne, late on a Thursday night, also ranks as one of the high points of this experience. It is clear that he loves the agency.

Deep thanks, finally, to the handful of NASA employees who chose to remain anonymous, and to the Clinton-era "political on the Ninth Floor, behind the glass doors at NASA."

In addition to those mentioned above, the following individuals gave of their time and energy for interviews: Dean Acosta, Ghassem Asrar, Chuck Atkins, Brian Berger, Darnell Cain, Ralph Cicerone, Mary Cleave, Franco Einaudi, Michael Griffin, Mark Hess, J. T. Jezierski, Andy Lacis, Laurie Leshin, David Mould, Paul O'Neill, David Rind, Clayton Sandell, Don Savage, David Steitz, Larry Travis, Ed Weiler, and a few anonymous others.

Mark Cane and Michael Oppenheimer might be surprised to see their words in these pages, since the interviews I did with them were aimed at my last book. Thanks also to Cecilia Boras, David Dobbs, Kerry Emanuel, Jim Giles, James D. Hayes, David Kestenbaum, Marc Morano, and Drew Shindell.

I am grateful to the team that has helped make this book possible. Brian Tart and Mitch Hoffman were its first champions at Dutton and got it off the ground. Stephen Morrow had the difficult task of stepping in as editor partway through. He met that challenge gracefully, and I thank him for his patience, gentle support, and editorial sense. Mike Tennican, friend, reader, and editor extraordinaire, made important contributions to the rigor of the thinking and the telling of the story. Wendy Stein's wisdom informs a number of important passages. My parents provided me with a retreat-like setting when we spent time together in Maine this summer. And I am especially grateful to Anniek Hansen for her warmth, openness, and hospitality. She has a certain radical innocence herself.

The two people who have helped the most have been Amy Hughes, my agent, and, of course, Jim Hansen. Amy has been involved since about a week after Jim and I first decided we'd like to write a book together on February 28, 2005, the Tibetan New Year. She has been tough with me, she has managed me, and she has supported me through the ups and downs. I can't thank her enough.

As for Jim, it has been an inspiration. I consider myself lucky to have had an opportunity to catch a glimpse of the way he lives his life and to tell a part of his astonishing story. I hope I have done it some justice, and I wish him and the rest of us the best of luck in the continuing struggle.

Index

Note: Page numbers in *italics* refer to graphs.

About the Author

MARK BOWEN, Ph.D. (physics), is the author of the highly acclaimed book *Thin Ice,* which was praised as "one of the best books yet published on climate change" (*New York Review of Books*) and named the best science book of 2005 by NPR's *Living on Earth.* He lives in the Boston area.